The Wadsworth College Success™ Series

Living and Learning, by Gerald Corey, Cindy Corey, and Heidi Jo Corey (1997), ISBN: 0-534-50500-7

Orientation to College Learning, by Diana L. Van Blerkom (1995), ISBN: 0-534-24528-5

Learning Success: Being Your Best at College and Life, by Carl Wahlstrom and Brian K. Williams (1996), ISBN: 0-534-51346-8

The 'Net, the Web, and You: All You Really Need to Know About the Internet… and a Little Bit More, by Daniel J. Kurland (1996), ISBN: 0-534-51281-X

Learning Your Way Through College, by Robert N. Leamson (1995), ISBN: 0-534-24505-8

I Know What It Says…What Does It Mean? Critical Skills for Critical Reading, by Daniel J. Kurland (1995), ISBN: 0-534-24486-6

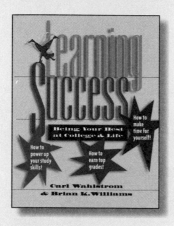

College Study Skills: Becoming a Strategic Learner, Second Edition, by Dianna L. Van Blerkhom (1997), ISBN: 0-534-51681-5

Integrating College Study Skills: Reasoning in Reading, Listening, and Writing, Fourth Edition, by Peter Elias Sotirou (1996), ISBN: 0-534-25686-4

Right From the Start: Managing Your Way to College Success, Second Edition, by Robert Holkeboer (1996), ISBN: 0-534-21570-X

Orientation to College: A Reader on Becoming an Educated Person, by Elizabeth Steltenpohl, Jane Shipton, and Sharon Villines (1996), ISBN: 0-534-26484-0

Foundations: A Reader for New College Students, by Virginia N. Gordon and Thomas L. Minnick (1996), ISBN: 0-534-25422-5

The Freshman Year Experience™ Series

Your College Experience: Strategies for Success, Third Edition, by John N. Gardner and A. Jerome Jewler (1997), ISBN: 0-534-51894-X

Your College Experience: Expanded Reader Edition, by John N. Gardner and A. Jerome Jewler (1997), ISBN: 0-534-51898-2

Your College Experience: Expanded Workbook Edition, by John N. Gardner and A. Jerome Jewler (1997), ISBN 0-534-51897-4

Success, Your Style! Left and Right Brain Techniques for Learners, By Nancy L. Matte and Susan Green Henderson (1995), ISBN: 0-534-24468-8

The Power to Learn: Helping Yourself to College Success, Second Edition, by William E. Campbell (1997), ISBN: 0-534-26354-2

The Senior Year Experience™ Series

Ready for the Real World, by William C. Hartel, Stephen W. Schwartz, Steven D. Blume, and John N. Gardner (1994), ISBN: 0-534-17712-3

Professional Development: The Dynamics of Success, Fifth Edition, by Mary Wilkes-Hull and C. Bruce Crosswait (1996), ISBN: 0-534-51160-0.

For more information or to purchase any of these Wadsworth texts, please contact your local bookseller.

Your College Experience

STRATEGIES FOR SUCCESS

Third Concise Edition

John N. Gardner
Executive Director, University 101 and The National Resource Center
  for The Freshman Year Experience and Students in Transition
Professor, Library and Information Science
University of South Carolina, Columbia

A. Jerome Jewler
Professor, Journalism and Mass Communications
University of South Carolina, Columbia

Wadsworth Publishing Company
I(T)P® An International Thomson Publishing Company

Belmont, CA • Albany, NY • Bonn • Boston • Cincinnati • Detroit • Johannesburg • London • Madrid
Melbourne • Mexico City • New York • Paris • San Francisco • Singapore • Tokyo • Toronto • Washington

Publisher: *Karen Allanson*
Editorial Assistant: *Godwin Chu*
Development Editor: *Heather Dutton*
Marketing Manager: *Chaun Hightower*
Senior Project Manager: *Debby Kramer*
Production: *Cecile Joyner, The Cooper Company*
Designers: *Ann Butler, Carolyn Deacy, 17th Street Studios*
Print Buyer: *Barbara Britton*
Permissions Editor: *Robert Kauser*
Cover Design: *Stephen Rapley*
Compositor: *Monotype Composition Co.*
Printer: *Banta Company*
Cover Printer: *Phoenix Color Corp.*

Illustration Credits
John Nelson: Exercise, Journal, Box icons; chapter opening illustrations; and the illustrations on the following pages: 54, 75, 110, 117, 120, 164, 173, 185, 190, 211, 224, 275.
Mary Ross: Illustrations on pages 122, 123, 176.
Monotype Composition Co.: Illustrations and graphs on pages 50, 52, 83, 102, 183, 198, 243.
Alexander Teshin Associates: Illustrations on pages 130, 227.

Printed in the United States of America
2 3 4 5 6 7 8 9 10

For more information, contact Wadsworth Publishing Company, 10 Davis Drive, Belmont, CA 94002, or electronically at http://www.thomson.com/wadsworth.html

International Thomson Publishing Europe
Berkshire House 168-173
High Holborn
London, WC1V 7AA, England

International Thomson Publishing GmbH
Königswinterer Strasse 418
53227 Bonn, Germany

Thomas Nelson Australia
102 Dodds Street
South Melbourne 3205
Victoria, Australia

International Thomson Publishing Asia
221 Henderson Road
#05-10 Henderson Building
Singapore 0315

Nelson Canada
1120 Birchmount Road
Scarborough, Ontario
Canada M1K 5G4

International Thomson Publishing Japan
Hirakawacho Kyowa Building, 3F
2-2-1 Hirakawacho
Chiyoda-ku, Tokyo 102, Japan

International Thomson Editores
Campos Eliseos 385, Piso 7
Col. Polanco
11560 México D.F. México

International Thomson Publishing Southern Africa
Building 18, Constantia Park
240 Old Pretoria Road
Halfway House, 1685 South Africa

Library of Congress Cataloging-in-Publication Data
Your college experience : strategies for success / edited by John N. Gardner, A. Jerome Jewler—3rd concise ed.
   p. cm.
   Includes bibliographical references and index.
   ISBN 0-534-53748-0
   1. College student orientation—United States.   2. Study skills—United States.   3. Critical thinking—United States.   4. Success—United States.   I. Gardner, John N.   II. Jewler, A. Jerome.
   LB2343.32.Y68   1998
   378.1'98—dc21
                                                                97-29940

We thank our wonderful families and colleagues for their patience over the past several years as we watched the newest edition of this book take shape. We thank our students for proving to us that the basic assumptions in this book really do work. We thank faculty, staff, and administrators at colleges and universities for believing in those same basic assumptions. Most important of all, we welcome all new students to their college experience and urge them, in the words of Tennyson, to be "strong in will, to strive, to seek, to find, and not to yield."

Brief Contents

Contents

Contents   ix

In a World of Differences

■ A FLEXIBLE APPROACH TO MEET THE NEEDS OF ALL NEW STUDENTS

In this third edition of *Your College Experience, Concise Edition,* we specifically address the concerns of many different types of students: commuting and residential, urban and suburban, "minority" and "majority," traditional and returning. At the same time we bear in mind that regardless of how an individual student may be categorized, he or she also shares many continuing and emerging needs with virtually all new college students:

- building friendships, support groups, and contact with teachers
- self-awareness and growth in terms of personal resources, goals, and commitment
- an analytic frame of mind that integrates individual study skills with focused critical thinking and an appreciation of the liberal arts
- awareness of the new technology of computers and of the Internet, the World Wide Web, and e-mail as tools for learning and communicating
- ways to make each dollar count and to avoid money management problems such as over-reliance on credit cards
- a clear idea of how diversity touches and enriches each of our lives

In view of these needs, this book supports a dynamic, holistic, timely program of study and an interactive, constructive classroom experience for each and every student.

■ NEW INTEGRATED FEATURES

In addition to making many changes in existing chapters (such as an expanded approach in "Diversity on Campus," now including issues of sexual orientation), we have also made several other pervasive changes: the inclusion of Internet activities in each chapter, resources for success pages in every chapter, and a new emphasis on collaborative learning.

Internet Activities

Written by Daniel J. Kurland, author of *The 'Net, the Web, and You,* Internet Activities now appear in every chapter of the book, helping students to explore Web resources on issues such as learning styles, time management, e-mail, health, and academic resources.

Resources for Success Pages and Keys to Success

Resource pages can be found at the end of every chapter, where students can create a notebook of key personal resources including phone numbers, addresses, and e-mail numbers of their classmates, instructors, and study-group members as well as information on their own motivations, goals, and skills. The resource pages draw on the "21 Keys to Success" from Chapter 1, which are also now linked to each chapter.

A New Focus on Collaborative Learning

Research increasingly indicates the importance of collaborative learning for both student learning and student retention. It has been linked to higher levels of student comprehension and success in math, science, and technology. It helps students to develop their speaking and writing skills. It encourages independent, self-directed learning. And it prepares students for the teamwork and persistence required in today's workplace. In this edition, Joe Cuseo (Marymount College, Palos Verdes, CA), whose research specialty is collaborative learning and its application to learning and teaching, has added special text and boxes on students working in teams, collaborative learning suggestions for exercises in all of the chapters, and special annotations for all chapters of the Annotated Instructor's Edition focused on collaborative activities that instructors can do with their students. They are identified by the collaborative learning icon .

■NEW CHAPTERS

We have brought new approaches to several topics. By combining the speaking and test taking chapters and the library and technology chapters, as well as integrating collaborative learning throughout, we have managed to add new coverage without increasing the overall length of the book. The following chapters have been rewritten: Time Management by Johanna Dvorak, Listening and Learning in the Classroom by Donald W. Jugenheimer, Reading Textbooks for Clarity and Understanding by Mary Walz-Chojnacki and Johanna Dvorak, and the Taking Exams portion of Making the Grade by Mary Walz-Chojnacki and Johanna Dvorak.

New chapters include the following:

MANAGING MONEY   In response to overwhelming demand, a new chapter on money matters, written by Ray Edwards, includes close attention to "the perils of plastic" (credit card abuses) especially for new college students.

RELATIONSHIPS AND CAMPUS INVOLVEMENT   Tom Carskadon and Nancy McCarley bring wisdom and humor to a new chapter on relationships. The chapter speaks to a broad range of student concerns and includes activities for traditional and nontraditional students.

■TEACHING AIDS FOR THE INSTRUCTOR

Teaching Your College Experience, Concise Edition (ISBN 0-534-53750-2)

This is a major revision of the instructor's manual for this edition! In addition to containing additional exercises, suggestions on how to approach each chapter, quiz master sheets' and numerous transparency masters, this new edition of the instructor's manual features the following: An extensive new section on YCE's major *learning/teaching* themes, written by collaborative learning specialist Joe Cuseo, which support the themes with scholarship and research on effective learning/teaching; a new comprehensive section of *practical instruction strategies* organized around course planning, classroom, and assignments/tests/grading; and new suggestions on how to conduct classroom research and assessment.

Annotated Instructor's Edition (ISBN 0-534-53749-9)

No other text offers this resource for the Freshman Seminar that is designed to make teaching the course so much easier! The AIE contains the complete text, plus helpful and research-based annotations, many specifically focused on collaborative learning, in the margins for teachers on how to use the text and exercises most effectively in different classroom configurations.

The Wadsworth College Success Course Guide (ISBN 0-534-22991-3)

This general resource for instructors and administrators covers topics such as building campus support for a first-year course, creating and administering the course, and refining it in the future.

The Wadsworth Video Series

The Wadsworth Film and Video Policy will include videos on AIDS, stress management, improving grades, healthful eating and nutrition, substance abuse prevention, and maximizing mental performance. Also available is the Matsumoto Video set, *World of Diversity,* and the USC/SCETV Video Series, *Your College Experience: Strategies for Success,* produced by the University of South Carolina and South Carolina Educational Television and specifically based on the text by John Gardner and Jerome Jewler. There are twelve 5-to-7 minute videos, which can be obtained through The National Resource Center for the Freshman Year Experience: (803) 777-6029. Please see your ITP sales representative for the complete video list.

■ LEARNING AIDS FOR THE STUDENT

AT&T WorldNet Service

Through an alliance with AT&T WorldNet℠ Service, ITP can now offer you one of the most reliable Internet service providers around. When you purchase selected ITP products you will receive a CD-ROM that provides one free month* of unlimited access to AT&T WorldNet Service and the Internet. At the end of the free month, you may choose to continue the service for a low hourly or monthly fee. And to add even more value, ITP has customized AT&T WorldNet Service to include links specific to selected subjects and courses. This customization grants you immediate access to course-related Internet sites and resources that expedite your search for helpful, interesting, and relevant information for learning and research.

InfoTrac College Edition

There's no better reason to use the Internet than with Wadsworth's exclusive offer of InfoTrac College Edition. Give your students access to the over 600 scholarly and popular publications available on InfoTrac. Ask your Wadsworth/ITP representative how to get the four month "Account I.D." for your students.

College Edition Franklin Quest Planner

This valuable resource—a professional daily planner that students can use through college and career—is available when shrink-wrapped with any Wadsworth College Success text. Franklin Quest will also feature specific

---

* Telephone access and other charges and taxes may apply. Other terms and conditions apply.

suggestions and exercises related to time management on the Wadsworth "Success Online" service, which can be used to build and reinforce your students' time-management skills. For more information contact your local ITP sales representative.

College Success Guide to the Internet
by Daniel J. Kurland (ISBN 0-534-54369-3)

This guide is designed for both students and professors who are unfamiliar with, or would like to learn more about, working on the Internet. This brief reference guide and handbook is specifically tailored to students and instructors of College Success courses on campus. In addition, this helpful guide contains a substantial collection of sites and activities grouped by key topics discussed in College Success courses, like health issues, study skills, time management, test-taking skills, and so on. This exciting new resource will ensure that technology and the "Information Highway" become pathways to success, not barriers.

College Success Internet-at-a-Glance
by Daniel J. Kurland (ISBN 0-534-54370-7)

This handy little pocket guide contains URL sites related to topics such as health, finance management, career choice, and much more. This Trifold can be shrink-wrapped with any Wadsworth College Success text at very little cost. Please see your ITP sales representative for more information.

■ TEACHING AIDS FOR THE INSTRUCTOR AND STUDENT

Success Online at http://success.wadsworth.com

Wadsworth is proud to announce Success Online, an Internet service combining professional resources, opportunities for online discussion and participation, valuable online library offerings and services, tutorials for students, and online education and virtual conference center opportunities.

This service is available to anyone for a minimal fee. However, qualified adopters of Wadsworth texts can access Success Online without cost. Success Online is designed to provide the most current and innovative material for your classroom needs. It will provide guidance on starting orientation courses, sample syllabi, an online library of ITP/Wadsworth texts, e-mail access to Wadsworth authors, and electronic access to the Keystone newsletter. The site provides students access to a complete online library of magazines, journal articles, and other ideal research resources contained in InfoTrac College Edition, plus helpful material on learning styles, study skills, choosing careers, and virtual community discussion opportunities.

Additional Supplements

To enhance the book's integrated approach to critical thinking, we recommend William T. Daly's *Beyond Critical Thinking: Teaching the Thinking Skills Necessary to Academic and Professional Success*. It is available from The National Resource Center for the Freshman Year Experience and Students in Transition: Phone 803-777-6029, fax 803-777-4699, or e-mail ninal@gwm.sc.edu. Please request Monograph #17.

■ RESOURCES FOR BUILDING YOUR OWN COURSE MATERIALS

Three-Hole Punched Nonbound Version

Instructors who want to add their own campus specific materials and have students work from a notebook format can order the nonbound three-hole punched version of the text by requesting ISBN 0-534-53751-0.

Building Your Own Customized Book

It is possible for you to build your own campus-specific custom book by selecting chapters from this and/or other Wadsworth College Success books, and combining them with your own campus materials. For immediate assistance and information regarding content, quantities, binding options, and prices of customized texts or bundled products, contact the ITP Custom Solutions Center at 1-800-245-6724.

Additional Optional Chapters

In a customized book you may also include additional chapters not contained in this text. Optional chapters deal with leadership, women in college, returning students, living on campus, assertiveness, wellness, and critical thinking. To inspect the complete set of optional Gardner/Jewler custom chapters or other Wadsworth College Success materials, contact your local Wadsworth/ITP sales representative.

The Reader/Workbook Option

Your College Experience is now also available in a new alternative format, splitting the book into a separate Reader and Workbook. The Reader contains articles written by experts on topics such as assertiveness, career planning, managing stress, and much more. The Workbook contains all the exercises found in Gardner and Jewler's best-selling text *Your College Experience*, Third Edition, plus chapter quizzes, chapter review questions, and chapter journal questions. Designed to be used in tandem, these texts will allow students to both learn and practice the skills necessary to achieve a lifetime of success. A three-hole punched version is also offered for instructors who want their students to use a "notebook" format or who want to incorporate their own material. Contact your local Wadsworth/ITP sales representative for sample copies.

■ VIDEO SUPPLEMENTS

Wadsworth's Film and Video Policy and New Video Series

The Wadsworth Film and Video policy is one way to enhance your course presentations. In addition, Wadsworth is developing a new series of short videos on key topics such as time management, stress, and general study skills. Ask your local Wadsworth/ITP sales representative for more details.

The USC/SCETV Video Series

The video series *Your College Experience: Strategies for Success* is produced by the University of South Carolina and South Carolina Educational Television. Twelve 5- to 7-minute video programs, based on the text, are designed to teach, inform, motivate, and stimulate lively group discussion. The series is highly adaptable to many educational settings. To order or to request information, write The National Resource Center for The Freshman Year Experience and Students in Transition at 1728 College St., University of South Carolina, Columbia, SC 29208. Or call 803-777-6029 or fax 803-777-4699.

■INSTRUCTOR TRAINING

Teacher Training Seminars with Wadsworth Authors

Held several times a year in various regions, these workshops allow you to interact with the author and develop your teaching skills in general.

Additional Training and Seminar Information

Additional training is available through The National Resource Center for The Freshman Year Experience and Students in Transition at the University of South Carolina at 803-777-6029 or by calling Jerry Jewler at 803-787-7174 (e-mail:jewler-a.jerome@sc.edu).

■ACKNOWLEDGMENTS

First thanks must go to the many continuing adopters of the text who have kept in touch with us about their evolving needs by direct communication or by responding to our occasional surveys.

Thanks also to the following astute reviewers for this new concise edition:

Peter Biegel, Purdue Statewide Technology

Vicki Van Steenhouse, Delta Community College

Kristen Anderson, Augsburg College

Benita Durban, New York Institute of Technology

Alice Lanning, University of Oklahoma

Mary O'Neill, Lock Haven University

Barbara Wade, Penn State—Main Campus

Michael Stone, Texas Tech

Peter Dorman, Central Virginia Community College

Molly McGuine, Radford University

John Anthony, Eastern Wyoming College

We are grateful for new major contributions to the book from Johanna Dvorak, Donald Jugenheimer, Tom Carskadon, Nancy McCarley, Daniel J. Kurland, Mary Walz-Chojnacki, and Joseph Cuseo.

For us, *Your College Experience* continues to be an exhilarating collaboration with colleagues, students, and friends across the country.

John N. Gardner

A. Jerome Jewler

CHAPTER ➔

Keys to Success

John N. Gardner
University of South Carolina

I just stood in line for an hour and spent over a hundred dollars on two books. Now I'm broke and have three exams scheduled for the same week in October. First week of college and I'm already stressing out.

At least I've met a few interesting people. Wish I had the time to talk to them!

This chapter will help you turn the following keys to success:

2. Learn what helping resources your campus offers and where they are located.

3. Understand why you are in college.

9. Develop critical thinking skills.

Chapter Goals *This chapter has been designed to help you*

- *understand more fully why you chose to attend college.*

- *learn about the diversity in today's student body.*

- *deal with your newfound freedom in positive ways.*

- *learn the 21 keys to success in college, which future chapters will explore.*

- *develop a clear sense of the value of college and how it can change your life.*

- *learn where to go for help when you need it.*

- *learn to set meaningful goals for success in college.*

- *improve your critical thinking powers.*

You've just taken another major step in life: You've decided to invest in a college education. Will the results be worth the investment? That depends on one thing more than any other: the goals you set as you begin. Before you read on, take a few moments now to consider what you hope to accomplish.

EXERCISE 1.1 **Your Reasons for Attending College**

Note: Many of the exercises in this book are marked by one or more of the following icons to help you and your instructor choose those best suited for you and others in your class.

 writing

 collaborative learning

 critical thinking

 computer technology

 self-assessment: a chance to think systematically about your abilities and concerns

 presentation: a chance to practice speaking skills or lead group discussion

 goal setting

group discussion

Less Todd/photo courtesy of Duke University

List three reasons you've entered college.

1. _____

2. _____

3. _____

Which one of these three is the most important? Why?

_____

_____

_____

_____

We'll come back to this soon.

■WHO ARE YOU, ANYWAY?

People attend college for different reasons. Which of the following sound *most* like you?

- You did just fine in high school and are ready for everything college can throw at you. You're also ready for a lot more personal freedom.
- You're not really sure what you're after. You just want to test the waters, find what's out there, try a few courses, and see what happens.

- You know exactly what you want to study. You have a career in mind, and you can see yourself making your mark on the world.
- You started a few other things before you got around to college—job, marriage, kids. Your attention feels a bit divided.
- You know why you're in college but wonder how well you'll fit in.
- You're wondering how you're going to raise the money you need and still keep up with a full college course load.
- You like attending college locally, but you wonder how you're going to deal with commuting and living at home.
- You're proud to be the first in your family to get this far academically. You don't plan to stop until you graduate.
- You've just had a major life change: You've lost your job, your marriage has ended, or your last child has "left the nest."
- You tried college a long time ago but weren't motivated. Now you've finally decided to return.
- Your parents expected you to go to college. Everyone else in your high school group did.

EXERCISE 1.2   Why You Decided on College

In a small group discuss the list of reasons on pages 3–4 for attending college. Which ones seem most relevant to you personally? Would you need to write a different statement to accurately describe your own situation? What would it be?

Do any of your goals in Exercise 1.1 relate to the statement that best describes you? How? Discuss this with the group as well.

Today's Student Body

For most of us college is a necessity, not an option. New technologies and the information explosion are changing the workplace so drastically that few people will be able to support themselves and their families well without at least some education beyond high school. That may not have been true for earlier generations, but it's true for yours.

In 1900 fewer than 2 percent of Americans of traditional college age attended college. Today more than 50 percent attend, with over 3,500 colleges serving more than 14 million students. Over 55 percent of college entrants start in two-year colleges, and more often than not these students combine studies at a local college with work or family commitments. At the same time, four-year schools are admitting increasing numbers of increasingly diverse students. Adult students also are enrolling in college in record-breaking numbers, and by the end of the 1990s, over one-third of college students will be over 25.

Although a higher percentage of high school graduates in the United States (or people with equivalent education) choose college than in any other country in the world, 40 percent of students who start in four-year programs never earn their degrees. Of those who do, about one-third will take up to ten years to do so. In two-year colleges, up to half of the entering class will drop out by the end of the first year.

Internet

Activity 1.1
Using the *Digest of Education Statistics* On-line

The Internet is particularly useful as a source of statistical information. The *1995 Digest of Education Statistics* provides data on post-secondary education. Figure 15 in Chapter Three of the *Digest* (http://www.ed.gov/NCES/pubs/D95/dfig015.gif) presents a graph of changes in enrollment in institutions of higher education, by age, from the Fall of 1970 to the Fall of 2000.

Which age group has the highest percentage of individuals enrolled? _____

Which age group has the smallest percentage of individuals enrolled? _____

For the years 1975 to 1993, which age group increased the most? _____

For the years 1975 to 1993, which age group increased the least? _____

What do these trends say about how the face of college students will change by the year 2000?

_____

What explanation can you offer for these changes? _____

_____

Dealing with Freedom

Of those who quit, about three-fourths are in good academic standing. Clearly, a lot besides academic talent will affect your success in college.

One problem is simply choosing the courses you will need to complete in order to graduate. Today's students often face a staggering number of course and program options, and most need an advisor to help them choose and coordinate courses.

The editors of this book strongly believe that the overriding problems traditional college students (those fresh out of high school) have is what to do with their newfound freedom. If you are a new student, no one tells you it's time to do your homework. Or get up on time to make class. Or eat breakfast, attend classes, allow sufficient time to complete an assignment, choose friends who will support you, exercise, get enough sleep, choose a major, or choose what to do with the rest of your life.

For returning students, the lack of freedom may be a deterrent. If you're working, taking care of a family, or both, adding college courses to your timetable may leave you with little freedom for yourself. Throughout this textbook, we will be addressing these concerns and suggesting ways to make the choices that are best for you.

This book won't take the place of a living, breathing advisor or counselor, but it will help you avoid some common pitfalls and support your academic goals and enjoyment of college in the broadest sense.

Eliminate the Negatives

A self-fulfilling prophecy is something you predict is going to happen, and by thinking that's how things will turn out, you greatly increase the chances

Commuter Power

About how many of America's 14.5 million college students would you guess are commuters? (The answer appears at the bottom of page 17.)

a. 2.83 million (20 percent)

b. 5.66 million (40 percent)

c. 8.49 million (60 percent)

d. 11.32 million (80 percent)

1. **The fact that you commute may work to your advantage in some ways.** In others you will need to work harder than the campus resident. Look over the twenty-one "persistence factors" on pages 7–11. Do you think any of these will be harder for you to achieve because you commute?

2. **Interact fully with your campus.** Use the goal-setting process to ensure that you do *get involved* in a campus activity, do *explore* campus resources, and do *find* someone on campus who knows and cares about you.

3. **If you are living at home with your parents, negotiate home responsibilities up front.** Your parents may need to understand that your college work will take more time than high school. You may not have as much time to devote to family errands and chores as before.

that they will. For instance, if you decide that today just isn't going to be your day, chances are it won't be. You'll look for ways that things can go wrong—and you'll find them. Do any of these apply to you?

- Fear of too much freedom or not being able to manage your time
- Anxiety over adjusting to a new environment
- Fear that college will be too difficult
- Homesickness
- Lack of good study habits
- Difficulty in understanding instructors
- Fear of competition from brighter, younger, or older students
- Fear of disappointing people or not getting their support
- Problems with new living arrangements
- Worry over choosing the wrong major
- Shyness
- The feeling that you may have to cheat to survive
- Fear of being perceived by other students as a klutz
- Problems in juggling work, family, and studies
- Inability to pay for college

If some of these concerns sound familiar, take comfort: Most other entering students share the same fears. Each of the worries is attached to a negative self-fulfilling prophecy that you can exchange for a positive one. That's basically what setting goals is all about.

The New Majority

American women were at one time barred from higher education. In 1833 Oberlin College became the first to admit women, as well as African Americans. It was only when publicly funded, land grant universities were founded under the Morrill Act of 1862 that "coeducation" became at all common. And only in the last twenty-five years have most men's colleges become schools for men and women, with fully integrated degree programs, residences, and curricula. Facing social and financial pressures, many formerly all-women's colleges have also opened their admissions to men. Women now make up the majority of college students—about 54 percent.

Photo by David Gonzales

EXERCISE 1.3 Solving a Problem

What has been your biggest unresolved problem to date in college? What steps have you attempted to solve this? Write a letter or memo to your instructor about these two questions.

■KEYS TO SUCCESS IN COLLEGE

Researchers have identified certain things students can do to ensure success. Ironically, students are often unaware of what these "persistence factors"— or keys to success—are and how much they really matter. Here are twenty-one basic things you can do to thrive in college. This book is built on these suggestions and will show you how to implement them. With a pencil, checkmark (✔) every item that you think will be particularly important or difficult for you. Later, after you've accomplished them, come back and turn the checkmark into an ✘.

1. **Find and get to know one individual on campus who cares about your survival.** It takes only one. It might be the leader of your orientation seminar or some other instructor, an academic advisor, someone at the career or counseling center, an advisor to a student organization or group, or someone where you have an on-campus job. You may have to take the initiative to establish this relationship—but it will be well worth it.

Tips for "Minority" Students

The "minority" population of the United States is growing so fast that the common use of the term to denote Americans of non-European ancestry is rapidly becoming outdated. For the present, however, students of non-European ancestry still often find themselves in a distinct minority on campus.

Some of the twenty-one keys to success are particularly important for most students of color, especially the keys related to establishing contact with faculty and other students. Focus on those keys. Don't let yourself become isolated. Form or join study groups. Visit your instructors outside class. Take advantage of support services. Join activities outside class.

1. **Keep that "I can do it" attitude and stay in college.** A positive attitude matters.

2. **Shoot for an A. Grades matter.** If you're not already thinking about getting a master's degree or doctorate now, you probably will in the future. Your undergraduate GPA will be an important part of your application to graduate school and jobs.

3. **Attend college full-time if you can.** If you work, look for a campus job and try to work no more than 20 hours a week. Ask at your financial aid office for information about work–study programs, grants, and scholarships.

4. **Take advantage of minority support services.** Your campus may have centers for minority students. Visit these places and introduce yourself. Ask for help with problems. Take advantage of mentoring programs.

5. **Don't be afraid to take math and science courses or to go into math- and science-based fields.** Scholarships for minority students may be available for math and science careers.

6. **Practice for standardized tests.** Anyone can improve his or her performance on tests such as the ACT, SAT, or GRE. Enroll in test preparation sessions, especially if you're heading for graduate school.

7. **Choose a career with long-term payoffs.** Shoot for being a teacher, not a teacher's aide; a lawyer, not a paralegal; a doctor or registered nurse, not a doctor's or nurse's assistant. Be sure that your course work matches your goal.

2. **Learn what helping resources your campus offers and where they are located.** Most campuses have academic and personal support services that are free and confidential. Successful people use them.

3. **Understand why you are in college.** Identify specific goals. This chapter introduces you to a useful goal-setting process.

4. **Set up a daily schedule and stick to it.** If you can't do it alone, find someone in your academic skills or personal counseling center. Get a day-timer or "week-at-a-glance" calendar from your bookstore. Chapter 3 will get you started at assigning sufficient time for study, work, sleep, and recreation. If you have family or work obligations, find ways to balance them with academic demands.

5. **If you're attending classes full time, try not to work more than 20 hours a week.** Most people begin a downhill slide beyond 20 hours. If you need more money, talk to a financial aid officer. Also, students who work on campus tend to do better in classes and are more likely to stay enrolled than those working off campus. Visit your college placement office.

8. **Explore alternative learning activities and environments.** Find out about co-op opportunities, internships, and exchange programs. Consider spending a semester at a historically black college. Studying at another school through a campus exchange program may not cost any more than being at your present school.

9. **Maintain connections with your "home base."** But be aware of the changes you may be going through and the impact of those changes on family and friends. They may put pressure on you to stay the same or accuse you of "selling out" for being a successful student. Use campus e-mail or a commercial on-line service to stay in touch with parents and friends at other schools.

10. **Be proud of your heritage and culture.** In college you may hear racist remarks and witness or be the target of behaviors rooted in ignorance, bigotry, fear,

Photo courtesy of Bill Denison

and hatred. Stand tall. Be proud. Refuse to tolerate such behaviors.

Take courses in African American, Hispanic, and other cultural studies. Help other minority students. Make friends with students from different racial and ethnic backgrounds. Get to know minority faculty and administrators. Get involved in sensitizing others to cultural diversity.

6. **Assess and improve your study habits.** Find out about your own learning style. This will help you learn how to take better notes in class, read more efficiently, and do better on tests. If your campus has an academic skills center, pay a visit.

7. **Join at least one study group.** Studies have shown that students who study in groups often get the highest grades and survive college better.

8. **See your instructors outside class.** It's okay to go for help. Students who interact with instructors outside class tend to stay in college longer.

9. **Develop critical thinking skills.** Challenge. Ask why. Look for unusual solutions to ordinary problems and ordinary solutions to unusual problems. (See "Four Aspects of Critical Thinking" on pages 18–19.)

10. **Choose instructors who involve you in the learning process.** Take classes in which you can actively participate and develop your critical thinking skills. Unfortunately, most students choose their classes based on what will fit best in their schedule. Ask upper-class students who the best instructors are.

11. **Know how to find information in your campus library, on the Internet, and through other sources.** You should be able to

"Am I Smart Enough?"— Tips for Returning Students

1. **Don't doubt your abilities.** Recent studies have shown learning ability does not decline with age. In fact, verbal ability actually increases as one grows older.

2. **Expect teachers to be glad to see you.** Most will welcome you because your practical life experiences will enrich the class. Your experiences will also be good material for written assignments.

3. **If school seems stressful, enroll part-time.** Adjust the number of courses you're taking to control the amount of strain.

4. **Enlist the support of your spouse, partner, or family.** Seek adjustments in household routines and duties. Let family members know when you'll need extra time for exams. An actively supportive partner is a great ally. A nonsupportive partner who interferes with study time can reduce your success in college. If your partner feels threatened and seems to undermine what you are doing, sit down and discuss the problem. Or seek counseling. Changes in relationships between partners often go hand in hand with enormous growth.

5. **Find faculty and staff support on campus. Find out about child care.** If your school has special advisors for adult students, they will know the most about weekend and evening courses. Look for adult advocates in student affairs or continuing education programs.

6. **Develop peer support.** Find out about classes and organizations where you can meet other adult learners. Or put an ad in the campus paper and form your own group. Find a classmate to meet for coffee, study with, or exchange notes with if one of you has to miss a lecture.

7. **Take review courses or a course in how to study.** Most adults have let their study habits become rusty. After learning the study skills tools in this book, consider taking a longer study skills course. You may need to review basic math or languages. Fortunately, relearning something is much easier than learning new material. Look for review courses on campus or in adult programs at local high schools.

8. **Embrace new technologies.** Ask how to use word processors at the campus computing center, computerized library search or journal access programs, or e-mail. The computer skills you develop on campus will be valuable in later employment.

9. **Be realistic.** Weigh your expectations about grades against your other important commitments.

Photo by Angela Mann

access the Internet, the World Wide Web, and CD-ROM data, in addition to books, journals, and magazines at your college library. Electronic data and library searches may be accessible in computer labs across campus or even in your own room!

12. **Improve your writing and speaking skills.** Employers want graduates who can speak before groups and write. Write every day. Speak up in class. The more you do so, the more you will develop these skills. Do the journal and other writing assignments in this book, as well as the presentation and discussion assignments.

13. **Find a great academic advisor or counselor.** The right advisor will support and guide you.

14. **Visit the career center early in your first term.** See a career counselor before you get too far along in college, even if you have chosen your academic major.

15. **Make at least one or two close friends among your peers.** Choose your friends for their own merits, not for what they can do for you. In college, as in life, you become like those with whom you associate.

16. **If you're not assertive enough, take assertiveness training.** Check at your counseling center for workshops on assertiveness training. Learn how to stand up for your rights in a way that respects the rights of others.

17. **Get involved in campus activities.** Visit the campus (or student) activities office—usually found in the student union. Work for the campus newspaper or radio station. Join a club or support group. Play intramural sports. Most campus organizations welcome newcomers—you're their lifeblood. Students who join even one group are more likely to graduate.

18. **Take your health seriously.** How much sleep you get, what you eat, whether you exercise, and what decisions you make about drugs, alcohol, and sex all contribute to your well-being. Be good to yourself and you'll be happier and more successful. Find healthy ways to deal with stress. Your counseling center can help.

19. **Polish your computer skills.** At the very least, you should be comfortable with basic file manipulation, the use of a standard word processing program, e-mail, and the Internet.

20. **Show up for class.** When asked what they would do differently if they could do it all over again, most seniors say, "go to class." Instructors tend to test on what they discuss in class, as well as grade in part on the basis of class attendance and participation. Be there.

21. **Try to have realistic expectations.** At first you may not make the grades you could be making or made in high school. If you were a star athlete in high school, you might not be in college. This book can help you develop more realistic goals.

Do most of these suggestions sound simple? They are.

EXERCISE 1.4 **Focusing on Your Concerns**

Go back and browse the table of contents of this book. Find one or more chapters that address your most important concerns. Why have you chosen them? How can you get help for them?

■THE VALUE OF COLLEGE

Few decisions will have as great an impact on your life as your decision to go to college. In addition to increasing your knowledge and self-understanding, college will expand your career horizons and can help you make the right career decisions. It will probably also affect your views on family matters, social issues, community service, politics, health, recreation, and consumer issues.

Education, Careers, and Income

Will your college education lead to greater income? Facing a job market that places a higher premium on education and technical knowledge, young men with only a high school education have found that they are making less than their counterparts did from 1974 to the present. High school-educated women have held their own on salaries since the 1970s. Although college-educated females' wages have increased more quickly than those of their male counterparts, much of that overall gain has come from working more hours.

According to a report by the Carnegie Commission on Higher Education, as a college graduate you will have a more continuous, less erratic job history; will be promoted more often; and are much less likely to become unemployed than nongraduates. You are also likely to be happier with your work than those who didn't attend college.

Critics of higher education occasionally point out that some people with college degrees are unemployed or underemployed (particularly due to the recession of the early 1990s), but you have only to look at the employment figures of high school graduates and high school dropouts to see that the better educated you are, the better your opportunities. As the saying goes, "If you think education is expensive, try ignorance."

The Broader Benefits of a College Education

Of course college will affect you in many ways besides financially. How will you change in ways that differ from those of people who decided to go directly to work, join the military, or do something else rather than go to college? The evidence from many studies suggests:

- College has a strong positive impact on how effectively people think. Expect to increase significantly your knowledge, intellect, tolerance, and interest in lifelong learning.

- College educates the *whole* person. It gives students the opportunity to clarify and improve their sense of possibility and self-worth. This self-esteem is one of the principal benefits of college and may help you realize how you might make a difference in the world.

- You will tend to be more adaptable, more future-oriented, more liberal in your outlook, more interested in political and public affairs, and less prone to criminal activity.

- College has an important influence on family life. You will tend to delay getting married and having children, to have fewer children, and to share child-care and household responsibilities. You will also tend to devote more energy to child rearing. You will have a slightly lower divorce rate than non-college-educated people, and your children generally will have greater abilities and achieve more than children of non-college-educated parents.

- In addition to making more money, you will be a more efficient consumer. Chances are you will save more money, make better investments, and spend more money on home, intellectual, and cultural interests and on your children. You will also be more able to deal with bureaucracies, the legal system, tax laws and requirements, and advertising claims.

- For leisure you will spend less time and money on television and movies and more time on continuing education, hobbies, community and civic affairs, and vacations.

- You are likely to be more concerned with wellness and preventive health care. Through diet, exercise, stress management, a positive attitude, and other factors, you will live longer and suffer fewer disabilities.

EXERCISE 1.5 Goals: Your Own and Others'

Look back at the reasons for attending college you listed in Exercise 1.1. Did your list include any long-term goals—say, something you want to achieve five or ten years from now? Compare your goals to the benefits of higher education just listed. Add a long-term goal to your list, or make other changes that now seem appropriate.

In small groups, compare your goals with the goals of others in the group. Do you share the same goals? How do you differ? Compare your findings with those of other groups in the class.

■SKILLS AND RESOURCES

Whatever your goals, you'll get off to the best start if you know your own strengths and also know where to look for help when you need it. In later chapters we'll focus on specific study skills. For now, let's take an informal preliminary look at your basic study skills.

EXERCISE 1.6 Assessing Your Basic Skills

Think about your strengths and weaknesses in areas such as reading, writing, and math. Have you ever consciously thought about exactly how you approach listening in class, taking notes, writing papers, reading textbooks, and studying for tests?

For each item below, rank yourself either 1 (very strong); 2 (okay); or 3 (not strong).

_____ Taking notes in class   _____ Time management

_____ Learning facts and concepts   _____ Oral presentation skills
from textbooks   _____ Studying for tests

_____ Understanding readings   _____ Writing

_____ Computer literacy   _____ Math and science skills

If you found yourself writing some 3's, you'll want to look for help on campus. Keep this in mind as you do the next exercise.

Most college campuses offer a multitude of support and recreational resources. The box on page 15 lists typical support services on a college campus, along with the types of services they offer. If a vital support service is not offered on your campus, ask that it be made available. Many colleges will welcome petitions to extend support services.

EXERCISE 1.7

Finding Out About Campus Resources

Make a list of types of campus support services or resources you might be interested in. Include not only "serious" support needs but also things that will help you relax and enjoy campus life to the fullest.

1. _____

2. _____

3. _____

4. _____

5. _____

Pool your list with others in your class. Use a campus map, student handbook, or other tools to find out which are available on your campus.

■SETTING GOALS

College is an ideal time to begin fulfilling short- and long-term goals. Begin to test some of your short-term goals. It's okay if you don't yet know what you want to do with the rest of your life or what you should be majoring in. Be patient. Practice setting and achieving some short-term goals by means of the following process:*

*Adapted from *Human Potential Seminars* by James D. McHolland and Roy W. Trueblood, Evanston, Illinois, 1972. Used by permission of the authors.

Where to Go for Help

College support services are not always located where you might think or named what you might expect. If you're not certain where to look for a particular service, there are several ways to begin. You might ask your academic advisor or counselor; consult your college catalog, phone directory, and home page on the World Wide Web; or call or visit the office of student services (called student affairs at some schools) for assistance. The majority of these services are free.

- **Academic Advisement Center**
  Guidance about choosing classes
  Information on degree requirements

- **Academic Skills Center**
  Improve study skills and memory skills
  Help on how to study for exams
  Individual tutoring

- **Academic Computing Center**
  Minicourses and handouts on campus and other computer resources

- **Adult Re-Entry Center**
  Programs for returning students
  Supportive contacts with other adult students
  Information about services such as child care

- **Career Planning and Placement**
  Career materials library
  Career interest assessments
  Career goal counseling
  Computerized guidance programs
  Assistance finding a major
  Full-time, part-time, co-op, internship, and campus job listings
  Opportunities for graduating students to interview with employers
  Help with resumes and job interview skills

- **Chaplains**
  Worship services and fellowship
  Personal counseling

- **Commuter and Off-Campus Services**
  Listings of nearby available housing
  Roommate listings

Orientation to the community
Maps, information on public transportation, babysitting lists, and so forth

- **Counseling Center**
  Confidential counseling on personal and interpersonal concerns ranging from roommate problems to prolonged states of depression
  Programs on managing stress

- **Financial Aid and Scholarship Center**
  Information about financial aid programs, scholarships, and grants

- **Health Center and Enrichment Services**
  Tips on personal nutrition, weight control, exercise, and sexuality
  Information on substance abuse programs, adult children of alcoholics, and general health care, often including a pharmacy

- **Housing Center**
  Assistance in locating on- or off-campus housing

- **Legal Services**
  Legal services for students (If your school is affiliated with a law school, check to see whether senior students in the law school are available for counseling.)

- **Math Center**
  Help with math courses

- **Physical Education Center**
  Free or inexpensive facilities for exercise
  Recreational sports facilities and equipment for swimming, racket sports, basketball, archery, weight training, dance, and so on

- **Services for Students with Disabilities**
  Support in overcoming physical barriers or learning disabilities

- **Writing Center**
  Help with writing papers and reports

Don't put off making contact until everyone seems too busy. Get to know as many people as you can before you and they slide into isolated routines.

Photo by Angela Mann

1. **Select a goal. State it in measurable terms.** Be specific about what you want to achieve and when (not "improve my study skills" but "master the double-entry system of note-taking by the end of October").

2. **Determine whether the goal is achievable.** Do you have enough time to pursue it, and more important, do you have the necessary skills, strengths, and resources? Modify the goal as needed to make it achievable.

3. **Be certain you genuinely want to achieve this goal.** Don't set out to work toward something only because you feel you should or because others tell you it's the thing to do. Be sure that your goal will not have a negative impact on yourself or others and that it is consistent with your most important basic values.

4. **Identify why this goal is worthwhile.** Be sure that it has the potential to give you a sense of accomplishment.

5. **Anticipate and identify difficulties you might encounter.** Plan ways to overcome these problems.

6. **Devise strategies and steps for achieving the goal.** What will you need to do to begin? What comes next? What may you need to avoid? Set a timeline for the steps.

EXERCISE 1.8 Set a Short-Term Goal

Review your responses to the previous exercises in this chapter. Pick one problem that you can resolve as a short-term goal.

Start by discussing this goal with your group. Identify how this short-term goal relates to your long-term goal of doing well in college.

In group discussion and writing, complete the six steps for achieving a short-term goal. Establish a date (perhaps a week or a month from now) when you will determine whether the goal has been achieved. At that time set at least one new goal.

Be sure your goal is:

● Something you genuinely want to achieve

● Written down in measurable terms

● Achievable

A First-Year Journal

At the end of each chapter in this book, a journal assignment reminds you to ask questions as you read the chapter and keep track of your thoughts in writing. Periodically, you should be jotting down your thoughts to questions such as these:

1. What do I think of what I just read?
2. What did I learn? What was left out that I still need to know?
3. How am I reacting to what I learned?
4. How can I apply this learning to my own life?

Photo by David Gonzales

Although each journal assignment is designed to help you focus your thoughts, you may wish to address other related issues that concern you. You may also wish to share events in your life with your instructor if you need advice on how to solve them.

Your instructor may ask you to write these entries strictly for your own reflection, or he or she may collect and read them, make appropri-

ate comments, and return them to you. This provides you with a way to communicate with your instructor privately and develop a more meaningful relationship.

Be sure to save your returned journal entries with your instructor's comments so that you can periodically review them and take pride in the progress you are making.

Also be certain to:

- Identify and explore potential problems
- Create a specific set of steps for achieving the goal
- Set a schedule for the steps
- Set a date for completion

In completing this exercise, you are learning a goal-setting process that with practice can become a lifelong skill. Apply this process at least three times this term and you will have mastered a technique that will help you all your life.

This book will ask you to use this goal-setting process in later chapters. Look for other chances to use it. Point these out to your instructor and other members of the class.

ANSWER (to question in box on page 6): **d.** commuters account for 11.32 million of America's 14.5 million college students. That number is more than the combined populations of Norway and Israel. There are more commuter students than there are people in the greater Boston and Philadelphia areas combined. If all commuter students parked in the same parking lot, the lot would have to be larger than the city of Boston. No wonder parking is often cited by commuters as one of their major problems!

Four Aspects of Critical Thinking: Improving Your Powers

The single most important goal of higher education is to help you learn to think more critically and creatively. This involves training yourself to go beyond common sense and personal opinion when you try to analyze a problem or to communicate ideas to others. It means freeing yourself of your emotional attachments to certain ideas and relying on factual information and conscious, systematic reasoning. It means basing what you think and say on knowledge gained through careful reading and ordered study.

Higher education goes beyond memorizing facts. This is not to say that facts are unimportant. Nothing substitutes for thorough, truthful information. But equally important are your abilities to judge the truth of supposed facts and to think logically from the facts. Such thinking is often referred to as *critical thinking*.

For you to develop critical thinking skills, your teachers will ask more open-ended questions—Why? How? and What if? Rather than expecting you to absorb knowledge like a sponge, teachers will encourage you to think problems through, analyze, conceptualize, ask questions, be questioned, and reflect on how certain beliefs might compare to others. In addition to memorizing facts and figures for a final examination, you will be challenged to apply what you have learned to the real world. College instructors will reward you more quickly and more handsomely for higher-level thinking skills than for anything else you do in class.

FOUR ASPECTS OF CRITICAL THINKING*

Critical thinking involves skills that take effort to learn and practice. Although there is no easy formula, the process may be simplified if we break it down into four general stages or abilities:

- abstract thinking
- creative thinking
- systematic thinking
- precise communication of thought

Each of these abilities corresponds roughly to a step in an overall process. Throughout this book we will be asking you to practice and improve your abilities in each of these steps, largely through exercises that require you to think about an issue and then write or speak about it. To a great extent, critical thinking results from first carefully reading what others have written about a topic and then writing or speaking in response. Think about how far along you are in each of the following areas:

1. **Making abstractions out of details.** From large amounts of facts or information learn to find the big ideas, the patterns and abstractions behind the facts. What are the general and recurring truths or arguments reflected in the details? What are the key ideas? Even fields like medicine, which involve countless facts of biology, culminate in general ideas: the principle of circulation; the basic patterns of cell biology; the principles of genetics. In essence, what larger concepts do the details suggest? What is the speaker or writer really saying?

2. **Finding new possibilities.** Practice creative thinking to discover the meaning and implications of abstractions. What questions do the large ideas suggest? Avoid making immediate decisions. Put off closure. Reject nothing at first. If the facts of economic history seem to show that free markets (the free exchange of goods and services among free people) lead to economic growth, what new questions can you ask about how to create more free markets? Can you apply this idea to the country as a whole? To your city? To your campus? Brainstorm questions. Brainstorm answers. Is the universe round? Astronomers entertain what may seem to others to be wild ideas. But so did the early geographers who proposed that the earth was round. Look for many possible answers rather than the elusive (and probably nonexistent) "one correct solution."

3. **Organizing new ideas and possibilities in a logical order.** Love is blind. The ideas you are most in love with may be wrong. In the long run you must weigh ideas more carefully than your emotions may at first accept. What do the facts really suggest? What is the logic of your thinking? In what ways do small conclusions or newly discovered facts lead to new abstractions, new broad ideas? Two hundred years ago someone thought about the fact that milkmaids rarely contracted smallpox. That observation led to the first inoculations against a devastating disease. It's not enough to dream up a new idea. It must be tested against the facts. Ideas that don't stand up under scrutiny must be discarded or modified so that they are consistent with the broader truth. Here dedicated research makes the difference. Is there some important additional information that needs to be gathered and evaluated before it is possible to reach a conclusion? Ultimately, what new abstractions and new conclusions have resulted from your thinking?

4. **Precisely communicating your ideas to others.** Organize your ideas to show others how your conclusions follow from your assumptions and the facts. Are your conclusions well supported? If you seem to be relying mainly on your personal opinions, experiences, or emotions to convince others, how can you broaden your support with reliable sources? Consider what your audience will need to know to follow your line of reasoning and to be persuaded through speech and writing.

WILL COLLEGE DEVELOP YOUR CRITICAL THINKING SKILLS?

None of us ever completely masters the four basic steps. Great scientists make great mistakes. (Consider the famous nineteenth-century French physician Paul Broca who thought he could judge the relative intelligence of different races simply by comparing the sizes of people's brains, as measured by cranial capacity of the skull. He was embarrassed to find that Europeans' brains *weren't* the largest!) But colleges and universities are communities of people who are committed to trying. Be confident that effort pays off.

The more you associate with others who practice critical thinking skills, the more opportunity you will have to practice them yourself. The more you read, the better you will write. The more you write, the more you will be able to both think and speak. No miracle, no luck, no gift is involved. Begin by recognizing that some ideas have more logical and empirical validity than others, and that one of your obligations as an educated citizen is to be able to distinguish the valid from the invalid.

CAN THIS BOOK IMPROVE YOUR THINKING?

This book suggests ways to improve your thinking, both on your own and in the company of others. Certain exercises are marked with the icon 🔲 to let you know that they specifically target one or more of the four basic steps. Each time you complete one of these critical thinking exercises, turn back to this section and reconsider how what you have done has helped you to become a better thinker.

*For many of the ideas in this section we are indebted to William T. Daly, professor of political science at The Richard Stockton College of New Jersey. We recommend his article "Thinking as an Unnatural Act" in the *Journal of Developmental Education*, 18(2), Winter 1994. For his complete monograph, see *Teaching Independent Thinking*. Columbia, SC: National Resource Center for the Freshman Year Experience and Students in Transition, 1995.

Internet

Activity 1.2
Critical Thinking Resources on the Internet

The first step in looking for information on the Internet is to use a broad search program. You might also visit the World Wide Web homepages of relevant professional societies, associations, or academic research centers, as well as those of commercial sites.

The Center for Critical Thinking offers extensive resources and discussion of the fundamentals of critical thinking. Their Web site includes discussion of "Three Categories of Questions," with examples (http://www.sonoma.edu/cthink/university/univlibrary/3catquest.nclk).

What are the three categories?

1. _____

2. _____

3. _____

Offer two examples of each type of question that might be asked in one of your current courses.

_____

_____

EXERCISE 1.9   Critical Thinking—"Unnatural Acts"?

William T. Daly, a professor at The Richard Stockton College of New Jersey, proposes that the critical thinking skills discussed in the box on pages 18–19 ("Improving Your Powers") are "unnatural acts"—not things that people do easily or without training. Do you agree? In what ways has your previous education or other experiences prepared you to form abstractions? To generate new ideas or foresee new possibilities? To question the facts or logic of what other people write and say? To examine the logic or evidence behind your own written or spoken arguments?

SUGGESTIONS FOR FURTHER READING

Astin, A. W., Linda J. Sax, Kathryn M. Mahoney, and William S. Korn. *The American Freshman: National Norms for Fall 1995.* Los Angeles: Higher Education Research Institute, University of California.

Bird, Caroline. *The Case Against College.* New York: McKay, 1975.

Boyer, E. L. *College: The Undergraduate Experience in America.* New York: Harper & Row, 1987.

Erikson, Erik. *Identity: Youth and Crisis.* New York: Norton, 1968.

Friedan, Betty. *The Feminine Mystique.* New York: Dell, 1962.

Hartel, William C., et al. *Ready for the Real World.* Belmont, Calif.: Wadsworth, 1994.

Parks, Sharon. *The Critical Years: Young Adults and the Search for Meaning, Faith and Commitment.* New York: HarperCollins, 1991.

Sheehy, Gail. *Passages: Predictable Crises of Adult Life.* New York: Dutton, 1974.

Upcraft, L., and J. N. Gardner. *The Freshman Year Experience.* San Francisco: Jossey-Bass, 1989.

RESOURCES

One purpose of this book is to be a continuing resource for you throughout your college career. Many of the activities and topics covered in this book will be important throughout your life (particularly the management of time, stress, and money). The resource pages at the end of each chapter are for you to fill out with names, phone numbers, addresses, e-mail addresses, and other relevant information. Filling out these pages will help you to create your own personal resource book for college success.

YOUR PERSONAL INFORMATION

Your name:

School name:

School address:

   this year:

   second year:

   third year:

   fourth year:

   additional years:

(Job and financial aid applications often ask for several addresses.)

Permanent address:

Social security number: School ID number:

Driver's license, state and number:

(Marking or engraving your belongings with your social security and driver's license numbers can help you recover them if they are ever stolen.)

KEY PERSONAL RESOURCES

List several names, phone numbers, and addressess for the following categories. Choose people who are supportive of your college goals, good listeners when you need to talk, and fun people to hang out with.

Family	Friends	Extracurricular Groups	Faculty

JOURNAL

NAME _____

DATE _____

Which of the "keys to success" listed in this chapter have you already begun to incorporate into your college life?

....

....

....

....

....

Which others will you start working on soon? Why?

....

....

....

....

....

....

If you are a returning student, what advice would you give the younger students in your class?

....

....

....

....

....

If you are a younger student, what advice would you give returning students about studying effectively? Taking part in college life?

....

....

....

....

....

Consider sharing these thoughts in class.

Exploring the Student–Teacher Connection

A. Jerome Jewler
University of South Carolina

She's so smart; how can I talk to her? Walks in and starts talking about her passion for geology; then asks us questions about things I've never even thought about. We have to have a conference with her during office hours to talk about how we're doing. Alone. And mine is today. I'm doing all right in the course, I think. But what in the world am I going to say to her?

This chapter will help you turn the following keys to success:

1. Find and get to know one individual on campus who cares about your survival.

8. See your instructors outside class.

10. Choose instructors who involve you in the learning process.

Chapter Goals   *This chapter has been designed to help you*

- *take a serious approach to learning.*
- *understand what your instructors expect of you.*
- *understand the many responsibilities of a college teacher.*
- *make the most of the teacher–student relationship.*
- *accept that teachers who challenge you do so because they want you to participate in class and succeed in college and in life.*
- *understand the meaning of academic freedom in the classroom.*
- *find the teachers that best suit your needs.*

Quite often, theater can be more revealing than real life, or so it seemed as I walked along a New York City street after being blown away by a performance of David Mamet's play *Oleanna*.

This brief two-character drama gives us John, a college professor who does not really believe in teaching but relishes the opportunity to lay down the law. John has never forgotten how he hated his own pompous, unfeeling college instructors. Yet somehow, in a sort of twisted form of revenge, he has become one of them.

The other character, Carol, is a student. Although earnest in her quest for education, she appears to be confused about its purpose. Her belief is that teachers ought to teach, that they owe it to students; but she seems to resent the fact that they know things she does not.

As one drama critic explains, John teaches not in order to lead, but to hear himself talk; he listens admiringly as his brain disposes of the problems and uncertainties of others. When he explains something, however, it only sounds more confusing.

He has the power; the pupil has the responsibility. "I'm not here to teach you," he explains to Carol, "I'm here to tell you what I think." He describes higher education as a game in which those who hold the power (the teachers) test the powerless (the students) by asking idiotic questions that only measure one's ability to "retain and spout back information." Pure nonsense, John tells Carol.

Yet when she fails to understand anything he says, Carol revolts. She reports him, alleging incompetence, sexual harassment, and a number of other violations that threaten his career as a professor. She reprimands him for forgetting just how hard she has worked to get to college and how he is depriving her of her natural right to learning by "one low grade that keeps us out of graduate school . . . one capricious or inventive answer on our parts, which, perhaps, you don't find amusing." Now he understands what it is to be subject to that power, she concludes.

In a scene from David Mamet's Oleanna, *Carol tries to get a clear message from her professor about how he is reacting to her work. The play probes the complexities of the college teacher–student relationship.*

Ken Friedman/photo courtesy of American Conservatory Theater of San Francisco

EXERCISE 2.1 Is the Power Struggle for Real?

Mamet's *Oleanna* makes some bold assertions about the relationship between college instructor and student. Do you agree that instructors hold absolute power over students, that whether a student passes or fails is sometimes subject to the whims of the instructor? Another related question: Do you believe that higher education is a game of memorizing and regurgitating information? Write your thoughts about this issue, and be prepared to share them in class.

■ YOUR TEACHER'S RESPONSIBILITIES

Although some teachers may be involved in power trips, the majority of us look on teaching as a challenge to help students develop themselves as more literate individuals and as critical thinkers by presenting them with challenges of their own.

I experienced this challenge from a different perspective when I signed up for an undergraduate acting course, a subject not related to my discipline of mass communications, but rather to an avocation—theater—that I have pursued seriously for the last ten years.

I called the instructor ahead of time to ask how she would feel about having a middle-aged professor in the class. I had been fortunate to have been cast in a local show under her direction and I respected her talent greatly. Her first words were, quite frankly, a surprise to me.

"Are you going to be serious about this?" she asked.

"Of course I'm going to be serious!" I told her. "Matter of fact, it's going to be a real pleasure to be a student again, to have a chance to learn more about a field I find exciting, personally rewarding, and mind broadening."

Later, as I pondered her question, I found it to be quite appropriate. As teachers, we want every student to be "serious" about what takes place in our classroom. So the very next term, I gave my class a new assignment to turn in. It was this:

EXERCISE 2.2 How Serious Are You Going to Be?

Using this course or another you are currently taking, write a paper that answers this question:

Just how serious are you planning to be about this course?

> Consult the syllabus. List topics or aspects of the course you believe you will find particularly challenging, as well as topics or aspects you believe will be easy for you. Note any foreseeable problems that the syllabus suggests (deadlines, reading assignments, work load, and so on), and suggest how they might be solved. Also state, in detail, just what you believe you will gain from the successful completion of this course and how you might apply that knowledge in future endeavors.

Internet

Activity 2.1
Your Teachers'—and
Your Own—Responsibilities

Like everyone else, teachers must juggle many responsibilities. Indicate what percentage of their working time you think faculty spend in each of the following activities.

teaching _____

research _____

administration _____

outside consulting _____

advising students, conducting workshops, and other non-teaching activities _____

Check your answers against the data in the *1995 Digest of Education* (http://www.ed.gov/NCES/pubs/D95/dtab220.html). Remember that these percentages are averages for all faculty at all schools surveyed. The particular percentages at any school or for any particular faculty member may vary considerably.

Compare this breakdown of professional activity to your day as a student. What percentage of your working time do you spend in each of the following activities?

in class _____

reading and studying _____

library research and writing _____

doing exercises and other homework _____

extracurricular activities _____

What Your Instructors Expect

If you have just completed high school, you may be in for an awakening as you begin your first term in college. For example, in high school you may have been conditioned to believe that things are either right or wrong, black or white. If your instructor asked, "What is the purpose of advertising?" you may have simply answered, "To sell things." Such "lower level" questions will rarely be asked by your college instructors. Instead, they may ask, "What effect does advertising have on society, and what should be done about it?"

What's the answer? There is no single answer, so your instructor may engage you in a critical thinking process to discuss what the most logical answer might be. He or she might have you do research on advertising and society. Your instructor might even say, "Here are a few things off the top of my head, but I'm sure you can find many more possible answers from other sources."

In college, your instructor wants you to develop a new way of thinking about things, to see the middle ground between two polarities, to question existing data, and to take prudent risks in class. Asking sensible questions or suggesting possible answers are first steps toward higher-level thinking skills.

This new attitude toward learning is not the only difference you'll be aware of during your first term in college. Generally, college teachers:

- will supplement textbook assignments with related information from other sources.
- will give quizzes and exams covering both assigned readings and lectures.
- will insist there is more than one way to interpret information, may question conclusions of other scholars, and may accept several different opinions from students regarding some question of the day.
- may never check to see if you are taking adequate notes.
- may or may not take attendance—or count it in determining grades.

What's more, college teachers are likely to expect much more of you than your high school teachers did. They may

- be more demanding in how much they ask you to read, how many quizzes they give, and how much participation they expect in class.
- expect you to be aware of topics related to their field and the particular course as well as the material for the course itself.
- be sympathetic to excuses you may have for missing class or assigned work, but hold firm to high standards for grading. You may be on good terms with your instructor and find you have failed the course because you did not complete some part of the assigned work!

EXERCISE 2.3 What Do College Teachers Expect of Students?

Look back over the differences between high school and college teachers. Then list five to ten qualities and behaviors you believe college teachers want in their students. Compare your response with that of several classmates. Consider asking one of your teachers to comment as well.

What Your Instructors Do

To understand why college teachers approach learning in this manner, it helps to know more about their lives beyond the classroom and the financial constraints they have been under in recent years.

Faced with the reality of shrinking budgets, colleges and universities have been demanding more of their faculty: more teaching, more committee assignments, more publications, and more service to the college and community. Yet, despite other demands on their time, effective teachers know that teaching takes time and patience, that it goes beyond the classroom, spilling over into student conferences, academic advising, and career counseling. Thus, while the average teacher may spend 9–15 hours in the classroom each week, he or she probably works another 60 or more hours between Monday and Monday.

To stay current in their fields, college teachers are constantly reading books, journals, and magazines. They update lecture notes, which takes more time than delivering the lecture. They may conduct experiments in their fields, review manuscripts for journals, or write articles and books. They may address community and professional groups, as well as consult with private corporations or government agencies. They advise students on academic courses, career paths, personal problems, or specific class assignments. In the time left, they'll work as administrators on campus, serve on committees, grade papers, and still find time to be responsible parents and providers to their own families.

EXERCISE 2.4 **A New Look at What College Teachers Do**

The last few paragraphs describe how college teachers spend their time and should dispel the popular misconception that college teachers don't work very hard. What have you learned about the duties of a college teacher that you didn't know before? How much does this knowledge help you understand the actions of your current college teachers? Discuss in class.

■ MAKING THE MOST OF THE LEARNING RELATIONSHIP

Just as most college teachers work faithfully to succeed at their roles as teachers, so should you feel an obligation to gain the most from your hours in class, if for no other reason than that you've probably paid dearly for the right to an education. Here are some ways to accomplish your goals and to show your teachers that you are serious about learning.

1. **Make it a point to attend class regularly and on time.** If you must miss a class, you'll need to ask another student for notes. That's okay as long as the student agrees and you don't make a habit of it. But remember, learning is easier when you are there every day. Save your cuts for emergencies; you will have them. When you know you will be absent, let your instructor know in advance. Depending on the size of the class, you may choose to do so by a written note delivered to the instructor's office, a phone message, an e-mail, or in person at the end of a class period.

2. **Sit near the front.** Studies indicate that students who do so tend to earn better grades. That should be no surprise; sitting up front forces you to focus, to listen, and to participate.

3. **Speak up!** Although you may be nervous about challenging instructors when you don't agree with them or about asking questions when you want clarification, you'll find that most of your comments will be appreciated.

4. **See a teacher outside of class when you need help.** Instructors are required to keep office hours for you. If possible, make an appointment by phone or at the end of class. Doing so will make the conference more convenient for both parties.

■ TEACHING AND LEARNING: A TWO-WAY CHALLENGE

What other effects did that undergraduate acting course have on my teaching? At first I felt awkward and isolated sitting on a bare stage with twenty or so people who were much younger than I. But things improved rapidly. I became a player in the chatter that goes on during lulls in instruction. I became part of their group. In addition, I was able to watch a teacher who came to class prepared, who set reasonable deadlines for assignments and made it clear how failure to meet those deadlines would throw the entire class schedule out of whack, who went out of her way to be certain students were developing the skills appropriate for this course, and who used her knowledge of plays and playwrights to instill in us a new way of thinking about those works. I learned not only how you students feel sitting "out there" but also how much energy and preparation it takes to keep a class interesting day after day after day.

What's more, seeing another teacher in action, I became aware of how motivating teachers can be when they take the time to bring out the best in each student. As in any group, ability levels ran the gamut, yet I never felt a single individual was slighted because he or she didn't perform as well as someone else. Like any good teacher, this one believed in the importance of establishing a comfortable, positive relationship with each student in the class. If put into words, this relationship might be summed up as follows: "As long as you make an effort to do the assigned work to the best of your ability, as long as you listen to my advice and attempt to improve your understanding of this work, and as long as you demonstrate persistence to learn throughout this class, you're worth the time it's taking me to help you."

Effective teachers constantly attempt to challenge their students. They make an effort to connect with you and to establish a relationship that will support both their goals and yours. Many of your instructors may encourage relationships with their students through active teaching techniques that stress class participation (discussions, presentations). Some may write extensive comments on your written assignments and quizzes. Others may even ask you to write your feelings, anonymously, about the class and drop them off at the end of the hour. During a major study of teaching at Harvard University, one of the many suggestions for fostering relationships that could improve learning in the classroom was a simple feedback exercise called "The One-Minute Paper." At the end of each class, students were asked to write what they felt was the main issue of that class and what the unanswered questions were for the next class. Remarkably, as students became aware they would be asked to do this daily, they found themselves beginning to listen more deliberately for "the main issue" each day! Even though the responses were unsigned, most students wanted to let the professor know they were listening.

EXERCISE 2.5 **The One-Minute Paper**

Whether or not your teacher asks for it, choose one of your classes and consider writing at the end of each class what you thought was the main issue of the day and what the unanswered questions are for the next class. During the next class, see if those questions are answered. If not, consider raising your hand to ask them. Try this for a week. Did this help you master the information in the class? In what way?

■ COMMUNICATION AND ACADEMIC FREEDOM

Although academic freedom has its origins in the Middle Ages, it continues to be a burning issue. You may have college teachers who don't give a hoot if the basketball team has a winning season, who criticize the college administration for its lenient admissions policies, or who argue that you're wasting your time watching TV sitcoms and soaps. As college instructors, we believe in the freedom to speak our thoughts, whether it be in a classroom discussion about economic policy or at a public rally on abortion or gay rights. What matters more than what we believe is our right to proclaim that belief to others without fear. Think of where education would be if we were governed by more stringent rules regarding free speech! On the other hand, no one says you must think as we do.

Colleges and universities have promoted the advancement of knowledge by granting scholars virtually unlimited freedom of inquiry, as long as human lives, rights, and privacy are not violated. Such freedom is not usually possible in other professions.

Some teachers may insult a politician you admire or speak sarcastically about the president. In college, as in life, you must tolerate opinions vastly different from your own. You need not accept such ideas, but you must learn to evaluate them for yourself, instead of basing your judgments on what others have always told you is right.

■ FINDING THE RIGHT TEACHER

When students were asked in a survey to rank the characteristics of good teaching, they listed clarity and organization at the top. Close in importance were those things that help "humanize" the teacher: high levels of interaction with students outside the classroom, a genuine effort to make courses interesting, frequent examples and analogies in teaching, references to contemporary issues as appropriate, and relating the course to other fields of study.

In fact, studies of teaching confirm that the best learning takes place when the teacher involves students in the learning, through class discussion, library research, oral presentations, and small discussion groups that report their findings to the rest of the class. Add enthusiasm and clear, well-organized presentations, and the fact that students appreciate teachers who assign more work and more difficult work, and you have a complete picture of the effective teacher:

one who is actively involved with students, who comes to class prepared, who gives students a voice in the classroom, and who is academically demanding but highly nurturing. One teaching expert likens teaching to coaching, explaining that a good teacher challenges students and works them hard, but somehow students know that this same teacher cares about their success.

EXERCISE 2.6 Describing Your Ideal Teacher

Jot down some adjectives that describe the best teachers you have ever had. Now jot down some adjectives that describe the worst teachers you have ever had. Be prepared to explain why you chose these words to describe good teachers and poor teachers.

Best Teacher   **Worst Teacher**

_____   _____

_____   _____

_____   _____

_____   _____

_____   _____

How do you find great teachers? Ask. Ask other students, especially juniors and seniors in your major. Ask your academic advisor. If you enroll in a class and your "gut feeling" tells you on the first day that there is going to be a

Most college teachers are busy people who enjoy contact with their students. That's one reason they chose to become teachers.

Photo © Charles Gupton/Stock Boston

Finding a Mentor

In his study of the aging process in men, Yale psychiatrist Daniel J. Levinson discovered several things about those who tended to be successful in life:

- They had developed a dream in adolescence, an idealized conception of what they wanted to become.

- They went on to find a mentor—an older successful individual—who personified that dream.

- They also enjoyed relationships with a few other people who encouraged, nurtured, and supported them in their pursuit of that dream.[*]

A mentor is a person who, in some respect, is now what you hope to be in the future. What mentors have you had previously? What specific qualities have you tried to emulate? Do you have a mentor right now? If you do, what might you do to make more use of him or her? What are you looking for in a college mentor?

[*]D. J. Levinson et al., *The Seasons of a Man's Life* (New York: Ballantine Books, 1978).

Photo © David Weintraub/Photo Researchers, Inc.

conflict with your style of learning and this teacher's approach to the topic, consider changing sections immediately. Visit a teacher before you register for class; by asking about the class, you'll learn more about the person, too.

You can often discover what fellow students think of a course or a professor from student evaluations. Student groups at many schools make these evaluations available at the library, on-line, or as handouts at registration. However, use these evaluations with caution. They may not represent the views of all students taking a course or of students sharing your own special concerns and standards.

What if you get a bad instructor? See if you are beyond the point in the term when you can drop the course without being penalized. Arrange a meeting to see if you can work things out. Getting to know the teacher as a person may help you cope with the way the course is taught.

If things are really bad, you might consider sharing your concerns with higher levels of authority, in keeping with the prescribed chain of command (department head, dean, and so on). Keep in mind, however, that a teacher's freedom to grade is a sacrosanct right, and no one can make teachers change their grades against their will. Don't let a bad instructor sour you on the rest of college. Even a bad course will be over and done with by the end of the term.

EXERCISE 2.7 | ## Describing Your Ideal Mentor

Think about the kind of person who would make an ideal mentor for you. Focus on the characteristics, interests, knowledge, and personality of this person. If you already know such a person, who might be or already is your mentor, reflect on the reasons for your choice and write a short paper about them. If you don't believe you have found a mentor yet, describe your ideal mentor in terms of what that person might offer as a model for succeeding in college. A mentor may be your academic advisor, a teacher, a counselor, another student your age, or an older student. Or it may be someone else entirely. Don't narrow your choices; broaden them. This process may help you discover who your mentor should be, and you might suddenly realize you already know such a person!

EXERCISE 2.8 | ## Interviewing a Teacher

Choose a teacher to interview—perhaps your favorite instructor or one you'd like to know more about. You may even wish to choose an instructor whose course is giving you problems, in hopes that you can find out how to resolve those problems in the course of the interview. Make an appointment for the interview and prepare your questions before you go, but also be ready to "go with the flow" of your conversation. Then write a paper about what you learned and what surprised you the most.

Suggested Questions

1. What was your first year of college like?
2. At what point in your life did you decide to teach? Why?
3. What steps did you take to become a teacher in your field?
4. What do you like most about teaching? Least?
5. What are some of the things that keep you busiest outside the classroom?
6. What do you expect from your students? What should they expect from you?
7. Where did you go to college? Why did you go there?
8. What is your advice to first-year students?

Handling Uncomfortable Situations Between Teacher and Student

So far, we've described teachers who want you to succeed, who grade fairly, who invite you to chat with them about the course, and who generally seem to make you comfortable as they challenge you to learn. Even with teachers such as these, you may experience some conflict over assessment of your work. What should you do?

First, make an appointment to see the instructor and discuss the assignment. Although the grade is ultimately up to your teacher, he or she may give you a second chance because you took the time to ask for help, especially if the assignment is a paper as opposed to an exam.

Exploring the Student–Teacher Connection   **33**

If you get a low grade on an exam, you may want to question how your instructor grades the exam items. Make an appointment. Don't be defensive. Simply ask if he or she will review certain answers with you. Sometimes teachers do make errors in calculating your points and will quickly correct them, but only if you point them out. Perhaps in rereading an essay answer, your instructor will reevaluate your thoughts and add a few points. Don't expect this to happen every time, but use your right to confer with your instructor. It can't hurt and it may help.

WHAT IF A TEACHER ISN'T STUDENT-FRIENDLY?
It can happen on any campus. Usually you have about a week to drop one section of a class and sign up for another. Check your campus calendar for the "drop/add" date and change classes if you know right away that things may not work out. You may have to drop the course altogether and pick up a different course. See your academic advisor or counselor to help you with this decision.

If it's too late to add or change classes, you may still want to drop the course before the "drop date," which occurs later in the term. Again, get advice from your advisor or counselor before you act. If it's past the drop date, do your best to succeed, remembering the term is about half over and your life will go on after the term ends.

DEALING WITH SEXUAL HARASSMENT AND SEXISM
Sexual harassment of a student is highly serious and a cause for grievance. See your department chair if an instructor makes inappropriate or threatening remarks of a sexual nature to you or to others. No instructor should ask to date a student or otherwise pressure students to become involved in a personal relationship, since the implied threat is that, if you refuse, you may not pass the course. Sexism, which implies that the instructor has a bias for the abilities of males or females and denigrates the other gender, also deserves to be reported. Such comments as "I don't know why women just can't understand chemistry," are not only false but may cause students to lose confidence in their abilities and to fail to establish a meaningful relationship with the instructor.

In summary, if you feel you are not being treated fairly, see the instructor first. If you don't get satisfaction or if you feel the situation is too touchy to discuss with the instructor, see the department chair. If you still don't feel satisfied, see the dean of the college.

EXERCISE 2.9 Patching a Less-Than-Perfect Student–Teacher Relationship

When you approach one of your teachers to explain that you missed class because you were stressed out by the breakup of a long-term relationship, which resulted in pounding headaches, stomach upsets, and extreme fatigue, your teacher tells you that's no excuse. He adds that stress is natural, that people end relationships all the time, and that you should be ashamed for acting like a baby about it.

Although he grudgingly agrees to let you off the hook, you come away feeling angry, embarrassed, and insecure about your behavior. You're determined to write him a note about it, but you need some expert information on stress so that you won't sound like you're begging for sympathy. For starters, check out the information on stress in Chapter 13. Using critical thinking strategies, read the relevant portions of Chapter 13 and then do the following:

1. Abstract the main ideas and write them down.

2. Brainstorm ways to defend your position that stress is sometimes unavoidable, but that you are learning to get it under control.

3. Organize your defense in a logical manner. Consider what you would agree with, what you would disagree with, and how to support what you believe is right. Don't be too apologetic, but at the same time don't argue about everything. Use your newfound knowledge to assert your beliefs in a way that shows respect for your teacher.

4. Look at what you have written. Put it away for a few days. Then get it out, revise it, and turn it in.

Dr. Eliot Engel of North Carolina State University believes teaching is very much like farming. We cultivate our crops in the fall and harvest them in the spring, he explains. We boast of the sprouts that burst into vibrant bloom and sigh over those that withered on the vine, believing like a farmer that luck had much to do with the blooms, and our own failure with the blights. Engel warns that a society blighted by a dearth of great teachers soon finds itself in danger of growing nothing but a bunch of blooming idiots. He continues:

> Great teachers know their subjects well. But they also know their students well. In fact, great teaching fundamentally consists of constructing a bridge from the subject taught to the student learning it. Both sides of that bridge must be surveyed with equal care if the subject matter of the teacher is to connect with the gray matter of the student. But great teachers transcend simply knowing their subjects and students well. They also admire both deeply.*

That's a far cry from the relationship of the instructor and student in Mamet's *Oleanna*, discussed at the beginning of the chapter. Mamet's professor seems to instill fear in his student. He might have listened to Albert Einstein, who said, "The worst thing seems to be for schools to work with methods of fear, force and artificial authority. Such treatment destroys the healthy feelings, the integrity, and the self-confidence of pupils."

Finally, if you doubt the value of a well-taught class, one in which you know the instructor is working hard to make learning enjoyable, heed the words of Alfred North Whitehead, noted American philosopher, mathematician, and logician, writing in the *Atlantic Monthly* in 1928: "The university imparts information, but it imparts it imaginatively. . . . A university which fails in this respect has no reason for existence. . . . A university is imaginative or it is nothing—at least nothing useful."

Perhaps it is this imaginative imparting of information that distinguishes the best teachers from all the rest. What do you think?

*From a column in the *Dickens Dispatch,* the newsletter of the North Carolina Dickens Club, January 1989.

EXERCISE 2.10 A Teaching Experience

Chapters 11 and 12 include some useful information on relationships and diversity. Choose either topic, and read the chapter carefully to prepare a 5-minute presentation to your class on some aspect of either topic. Employ note-taking and the critical thinking process to:

1. Abstract the main ideas.

2. Brainstorm various ways to present the material so that students will find it interesting.

3. Organize your best ideas into a logical method of presentation.

4. Write brief notes so that you'll be able to do good, interactive teaching on the topic.

5. Teach.

EXERCISE 2.11 Finding Faculty E-Mail Addresses

More and more, students communicate with their instructors using e-mail. Although e-mail is often a poor substitute for an office visit, it is useful for specific questions or other short communications.

To send e-mail, just as with regular mail, you have to know someone's address. Find the e-mail addresses of your instructors on the campus network, or ask them for their e-mail addresses on the first day of class.

SUGGESTIONS FOR FURTHER READING

Distinguished Teachers on Effective Teaching. New Directions for Teaching and Learning, #28. San Francisco: Jossey-Bass, 1986.

Freedman, Samuel G. *Small Victories. The Real World of a Teacher, Her Students, and Their High School.* New York: Harper Perennial, 1991.

Guide to Effective Teaching. A national report on eighty-one outstanding college teachers and how they teach: lectures, computer, case studies, peer teaching, simulations, self-pacing, multimedia, field study, problem solving, and research. New Rochelle, N.Y.: Change Magazine Press, 1978.

Mamet, David. *Oleanna.* New York: Pantheon Books, 1992.

Pirsig, Robert. *Zen and the Art of Motorcycle Maintenance: An Inquiry into Values.* New York: Morrow, 1974.

RESOURCES

Who are your instructors for this semester?
You can learn a lot about your instructors both from the information they give you and from the information the school can give you. Connecting with your instructors inside and outside of class can make your college experience much more meaningful and successful. Fill in the following information about your instructors this semester. *(Copy this page before you fill it out if you have more than five instructors.)*

Instructor's name: .... Course name: ....

Other courses he or she teaches: ....

(You may want to take another class with him or her. Hint—look in your course catalogue.)

Office hours: .... Office location: .... Phone: ....

Home phone number: .... E-mail address: ....

Is it ok to call this instructor at home? .... To send e-mail? ....

Instructor's name: .... Course name: ....

Other courses he or she teaches: ....

Office hours: .... Office location: .... Phone: ....

Home phone number: .... E-mail address: ....

Is it ok to call this instructor at home? .... To send e-mail? ....

Instructor's name: .... Course name: ....

Other courses he or she teaches: ....

Office hours: .... Office location: .... Phone: ....

Home phone number: .... E-mail address: ....

Is it ok to call this instructor at home? .... To send e-mail? ....

Instructor's name: .... Course name: ....

Other courses he or she teaches: ....

Office hours: .... Office location: .... Phone: ....

Home phone number: .... E-mail address: ....

Is it ok to call this instructor at home? .... To send e-mail? ....

Instructor's name: .... Course name: ....

Other courses he or she teaches: ....

Office hours: .... Office location: .... Phone: ....

Home phone number: .... E-mail address: ....

Is it ok to call this instructor at home? .... To send e-mail? ....

JOURNAL

NAME _____

DATE _____

Obviously your college teachers are different from your high school teachers. What differences have you observed?

....

....

....

....

How are you reacting to those differences?

....

....

....

....

....

Describe one of your greatest instructors and one of your worst instructors.

....

....

....

....

....

What do you like most about your best instructor? Why?

....

....

....

....

What do you like least about your worst instructor? Why?

....

....

....

....

Time Management: The Foundation of Academic Success

Johanna Dvorak
University of Wisconsin—Milwaukee

Big test tomorrow! It's gonna be a late night tonight. I was going to study with Jack, but then we started talking and the time just sort of disappeared. Now I have to pull it all together. Let's see, now. Did I read all those chapters? Did I read any of them? Do I remember what I read if I did?

This chapter will help you turn the following keys to success:

4. Set up a daily schedule and stick to it.

5. If you're attending classes full time, try not to work more than 20 hours a week.

6. Assess and improve your study habits.

17. Get involved in campus activities.

18. Take your health seriously.

20. Show up for class.

21. Try to have realistic expectations.

Chapter Goals *After reading this chapter, you should be able to*

- *use a time management system effectively.*
- *assess your use of time.*
- *adjust to college demands on your time.*
- *identify your priorities.*
- *set long-term goals.*
- *develop a master plan.*
- *make a timetable and a daily plan.*

How do you approach time? People have different personalities, come from different cultures, and view time in different ways. People's perspectives on time can differ depending on their age, their gender, and their culture.

Some people like to get things done in an organized way; others are more spontaneous. Some like to keep to a time schedule; others prefer to be more flexible. Learning theorists have studied people's views of time and come up with some very interesting findings. For example, the Myers-Briggs Type Indicator, a widely used personality instrument similar to the one in Chapter 4 of this text, suggests that people approach time in different ways and that people who learn more through their senses rather than their intuition are better at time management.

EXERCISE 3.1 Self-Assessment: The First Step

A Take a few minutes to reflect on your personality and your cultural background, and then write a few paragraphs on how you view time. Use these questions as guidelines:

1. What are my personal views on time? How conscious am I of time passing? Do I wear a watch? How important is time in my life?

2. How do I think my views on time have been influenced by my parents, my culture, my friends, my lifestyle, my gender, my age, or other factors?

3. What are my behaviors related to time? Am I punctual or a procrastinator? Can I concentrate or am I easily distracted? Do I try to control time or does it seem to control me?

B What do you think of the idea of time management? How much do you try to control your time? Answer the following questions on your use of time.

1. Am I early, prompt, or late to class, appointments, or meetings? Do I often skip class or miss appointments?

2. Do I complete my assignments and papers early, on time, or late?

3. How much time do I generally spend on social time, such as talking on the phone, watching TV, web browsing, or enjoying the company of friends? How important are each of these uses of time to me?

4. How is my use of time affecting my level of stress? Am I good at estimating the amount of time it will take me to do a task? Do I tend to worry that I am not getting things done that need to be done? How does my anxiety level affect my performance?

5. How has being in college affected or changed how I use my time?

6. What are some specific things I do to manage my time? How do I balance work and social activities?

C Share your thoughts in a small group. Appoint someone in your group to share the group's views with the class. As a class, discuss all perspectives of time management.

■ADJUSTING TO COLLEGE DEMANDS ON YOUR TIME

One thing you can be sure of as a student is that there will be many different demands on your time and that you will be pulled in many different directions. If you are a traditional student, just out of high school and on a college campus away from home, you may be experiencing your first taste of freedom. There are new friends to meet, and many social activities to choose from. Your parents aren't around to ask you if you got your studying done. It's up to you!

If you are an adult student, you'll find extra demands on your time to attend classes, commute, and study. You may have to go to class in the evening after work and make trips back to campus to conduct library research. Families, meals, and chores still need your attention. How will you fit in everything?

EXERCISE 3.2   Assessing Your Use of Time: Identifying Priorities

A Make a daily log of how you spend your time for one week. Copy the grid on page 42. Each evening jot down the amount of time you spend on different activities during the day. At the end of the week, add up the time you spent and enter it in the different categories in the table below. Next, record the amount of time you would like to spend on each category. Remember, there are only 168 hours in a week!

Your time management plan should reflect your personal philosophy and help you to reach both your personal and your professional goals. Use this chapter to tailor a plan that works for you.

Photo by Angela Mann

Categories	Actual Hours per Day	Targeted Hours per Day
Class time	_____	_____
Studying	_____	_____
Work	_____	_____
Travel		
Home to college	_____	_____
Between classes	_____	_____
College to work	_____	_____
Work to home	_____	_____
Other	_____	_____
Total travel	_____	Total travel _____
Home responsibilities		
Shopping	_____	_____
Meals	_____	_____
Housecleaning	_____	_____
Laundry	_____	_____
Other	_____	_____
Total home	_____	Total home _____
Family responsibilities		
General time	_____	_____
Child care	_____	_____
Care for elderly or disabled	_____	_____
Other		
Total family	_____	Total family _____
Civic responsibilities		
Volunteer work	_____	_____
Other	_____	_____
Total civic	_____	Total civic _____
Personal		
Grooming/dressing	_____	_____
Reading for pleasure	_____	_____
Hobbies, games, entertainment	_____	_____
Watching TV, listening to music	_____	_____
Talking with or e-mail with friends	_____	_____
Exercise	_____	_____
Rest	_____	_____
Other	_____	_____
Total personal	_____	Total personal _____
Other	_____	_____
Total time for all responsibilities	======	======

Maximizing Your Time On-line

No matter how fast your connection to the Internet, your access can be slowed by excessive traffic on the network or by limits on the capability of the site you are accessing.

You can optimize your time accessing the World Wide Web in a number of ways:

- Turn off graphics.
  With Netscape Navigator 3.0, click on Options / Auto Load Images
  With Internet Explorer 3.0, click on View / Options / General / Show Pictures

- Use more than one browser window at a time.
  With Netscape Navigator 3.0, click on File / New Web Browser

With Internet Explorer 3.0, click on File / New Window

- Use appropriate search programs and techniques.
  Use Internet Navigation (http://riceinfo.rice.edu/Internet/) and Sink or Swim: Internet Search Tools & Techniques (http://www.sci.ouc.bc.ca/libr/connect96/search.htm#top)

Use off-line browsers that can download many pages at a time and off-line search programs that can search while you are sleeping. See the listing of Off-line Web Page Readers at http://www.slaughterhouse.com/offline.html.

B The following shows how typical *residential* first-year students allocate their time on a weekday.*

Activity	Hours per Day
Class time	3
Studying	3
Employment	$\frac{1}{4}$
Idle leisure	3
Social	$2\frac{1}{4}$
Travel (between classes)	1
Eating	$1\frac{1}{2}$
Grooming	1
Resting	$6\frac{1}{2}$
Recreation	$1\frac{1}{2}$
Other	1

Notice that new students who live on campus devote almost 7 hours each day to socializing, recreation, and leisure pursuits, while a commuter must spend much of this time on travel, work, and responsibilities.

C Discuss with a partner your use of time. How do your actual hours differ from your ideal time allotments for each category? Discuss some ways to deal with too much or too little time. Write down ideas to deal with your specific concerns. Decide what changes you could make now. List two or three time management goals for this term.

_____

_____

_____

*Data adapted from David W. Desmond and David S. Glenwick, "Time-Budgeting Practices of College Students: A Developmental Analysis of Activity Patterns," *Journal of College Student Personnel* 28, no. 4 (1987): 318–23.

Internet

Activity 3.1
Limiting Your Time On-line

Anyone who has surfed the World Wide Web has realized its addictive nature. The Web can be a veritable black hole as far as your time goes. It is thus essential that you limit your on-line time.

As with any addiction, the first step is to realize that you have a problem. Make a log of how you spend your time at each of the following activities over a week's time. Then, create a target time for each area.

	Actual Time	Target Time
Reading and writing academic e-mail	____	____
Reading and writing personal e-mail	____	____
Surfing casually for academic topics	____	____
Surfing casually for personal interest	____	____
Searching rigorously for academic materials	____	____
Searching rigorously for personal information	____	____

How many times a day do you check your e-mail? _____

How might you limit the time you spend in each activity? _____

_____

_____

■ SETTING GOALS AND PRIORITIES

Time management involves planning, judgment, anticipation, flexibility, and commitment. First, you must know what your goals are for college and for your future career. Look at the big picture and ask yourself some serious questions.

Where am I going?

_____

_____

_____

Where do I want to be after college?

_____

_____

_____

What major can help me to reach this goal? (Once you've chosen a major your academic advisor can help you plan each term's courses.)

_____

_____

_____

What are my goals for this semester?

_____

_____

_____

Goal Setting for Courses

A List each course you are taking this term. List the grade you hope to earn. Finally, estimate the time you think you will need each week to achieve your goal. When deciding how much time to study for a course, take into consideration this rule of thumb: one hour of study for every hour in class for a "C," two hours of study for every hour in class for a "B," and three hours for every hour in class for an "A." Then consider the difficulty of the course as you complete the following chart.

Course	Grade	Estimated time per week
_____	_____	_____
_____	_____	_____
_____	_____	_____
_____	_____	_____
_____	_____	_____

Total study time _____

B Now list additional steps you will need to take to achieve your goal. Some examples follow: Attend tutoring sessions each week; join a study group or work with a study buddy; learn a computer program used for the course; learn to access a database for your paper in the library.

_____

_____

_____

_____

_____

_____

▮DEVELOPING A MASTER PLAN

After deciding where your priorities lie and setting your semester goals, make a master plan of your long-term assignments, a timetable of your weekly schedule, and a daily plan. Allow for flexibility in scheduling so that you can adapt to changes that occur without losing valuable time. Time management helps you control your time so that you can have more freedom to balance required and optional activities. Finally, make a commitment to yourself to control your time and carry out your time management plan.

Time management is a life-long skill. The better the job you have after college, the more likely that you'll be managing your own and possibly other people's time.

Photo by David Gonzales

A good way to start the semester is to look at the "big picture" in your master plan. You should complete your term assignment preview by the beginning of the second week of class so that you can continue to plan, anticipate, judge, and use your time effectively. Gather your syllabi and use Exercise 3.4 to look closely at your long-term projects, papers, midterms, and final exams for this semester.

EXERCISE 3.4

Planning for the Semester: The Term Assignment Preview ✏

To see the big picture of your workload this term, fill in the assignment preview sheet in Figure 3.1, listing all tests, reports, compositions or term papers, and other long-term projects.

■ORGANIZING YOUR WEEK

Guidelines for Scheduling

1. Examine your toughest weeks. Can you finish some of these assignments early in order to free up some time to study for tests?

2. Break large assignments like term papers down into smaller steps (choosing a topic, doing research, writing an outline, writing a first draft, and so on). Add deadlines in your schedule for each of these smaller portions of the project.

Figure 3.1 Term Assignment Preview

	Sunday	Monday	Tuesday	Wednesday	Thursday	Friday	Saturday
Week 1							
Week 2							
Week 3							
Week 4							

	Sunday	Monday	Tuesday	Wednesday	Thursday	Friday	Saturday
Week 5							
Week 6							
Week 7							
Week 8							

Figure 3.1 *(continued)*

	Sunday	Monday	Tuesday	Wednesday	Thursday	Friday	Saturday
Week 9							
Week 10							
Week 11							
Week 12							

	Sunday	Monday	Tuesday	Wednesday	Thursday	Friday	Saturday
Week 13							
Week 14							
Week 15							
Week 16							

3. Start working on assignments days before they are due. Good student time managers frequently finish assignments before actual due dates to allow for emergencies.

4. Allocate specific times for potentially repetitive tasks. You might, for instance, check your e-mail at the beginning and end of the day, not every hour.

5. Allow time to learn to do your assignments productively. Instructors may expect you to be computer literate, and they usually don't have time to explain how to use a word processor, spreadsheet, or statistical computer program. Seek out the academic support center on your campus for assistance. Most campuses offer tutoring, walk-in assistance, or workshops to assist students with computer programs, e-mail, or the World Wide Web and the Internet. Your library may have short sessions to show you how to search for information using computer databases. These services will save you time and usually are free to students.

EXERCISE 3.5 Your Weekly Plan/Timetable

Using your term assignment preview, develop a weekly plan for one week of the semester. Look at Figure 3.2 as an example of a well-developed weekly plan.

A Using the timetable provided in Figure 3.3, block out your time commitments. Start by filling in all of your classes and any other regularly scheduled activities (refer to Exercise 3.2). Then look up that week on your term assignment preview and reread the syllabi for your courses. Most instructors use a syllabus to map out the entire semester for you. What are your tests, assignments, and readings for that week? What long-term assignments should you start this week? When should you plan your weekly reviews for each course?

B Fill in your total study time for the week in one-hour blocks at appropriate times. Refer to Exercise 3.4 for your ideal study hours for each course. Remember that the best times to review course material are directly before and after that class. It is best to schedule your hardest subjects earliest in the day when you are fresher.

C Share and discuss your timetable with a partner. Make sure you are spending an adequate amount of time studying. Discuss where you placed your study hours on the timetable and why. If you are an adult student, ask yourself if your work schedule or family responsibilities are too demanding and might prevent you from putting in the study hours you need.

D Try to follow your timetable for a week. Keep a record of the major obstacles you encounter during the week. Brainstorm strategies to overcome these obstacles in a small group to share with the class.

■ORGANIZING YOUR DAY

A well-known time management consultant, Alan Lakein, advises us to "work smarter, not harder." Lakein's words ring true, particularly for college students, who have to juggle many deadline pressures. Once the framework of the semester and weekly schedules are set, use a daily plan to help you set priorities, stay flexible, and balance your work and leisure.

Figure 3.2 Sample Timetable

	Sunday	Monday	Tuesday	Wednesday	Thursday	Friday	Saturday
6:00							
7:00							
8:00		*History*		*History*		*History*	
9:00		*College 101*	*Read/ Study Psych.*	*College 101*	*Read/ Study Psych.*	*College 101*	
10:00		*Review Hist. & College 101*	↓	*Review Hist. & College 101*	↓		
11:00		*Geology*	*Psych.*	*Geology*	*Psych.*		
12:00		LUNCH	↓ LUNCH	LUNCH	↓ LUNCH	LUNCH	
1:00		*Study Geology*		*Study Geology, etc.*		*Read/ Study History,*	
2:00		*Geology Lab*	*on Writing* ↑ *Work*	↓		*College 101, etc.*	
3:00						↓	
4:00		↓	↓	*Work on Writing*			
5:00				↓			
6:00	*Library Job*		*Expository Writing*			*Library Job*	
7:00			*Workshop*				
8:00			↓	*Library Job*			
9:00	↓			↓		↓	
10:00							

Total class hours: 16
Total study hours needed: 16 x 2 = 32

Total study hours allotted: 17
Additional study hours needed: 15

Figure 3.3 Weekly Timetable

(1) List all class meeting times and other fixed obligations (work, scheduled family responsibilities, and so forth).
(2) Try to reserve about 1 hour of daytime study for each class hour. Reserve time for meals, exercise, and free time.
(3) Try to plan a minimum of 1 hour additional study in evenings or on weekends for each class.

	Sunday	Monday	Tuesday	Wednesday	Thursday	Friday	Saturday
6:00							
7:00							
8:00							
9:00							
10:00							
11:00							
12:00							
1:00							
2:00							
3:00							
4:00							
5:00							
6:00							
7:00							
8:00							
9:00							
10:00							
11:00							
12:00							

DAILY PLANNER

DATE   MON TUE WED THU FRI SAT SUN

APPOINTMENTS

TIME

8 —————————————

9 —————————————

10 ————————————

11 ————————————

12 ————————————

1 —————————————

2 —————————————

3 —————————————

4 —————————————

5 —————————————

6 —————————————

7 —————————————

8 —————————————

—————————————————

—————————————————

DAILY PLANNER

DATE   MON TUE WED THU FRI SAT SUN

☑ **TO DO**

PRIORITY   ESTIMATED TIME

☐ ————————————

☐ ————————————

☐ ————————————

☐ ————————————

☐ ————————————

☐ ————————————

☐ ————————————

☐ ————————————

☐ ————————————

☐ ————————————

☐ ————————————

☐ ————————————

EXERCISE 3.6 Your Daily Plan

Using one day from this week's schedule, make a daily plan by filling in the Daily Planner above. Fill in the "To Do" list of the day's activities. Using Lakein's ABC Priority System, label them with an A, B, or C, with A's deserving the most attention. By tackling the A's first, you may not complete your list but you will probably be more satisfied with your accomplishments.

Check out the different calendar formats at your bookstore and get one that works for you. Make a commitment to use it. You may want to put your schedule on your computer using Personal Information Management (PIM) software or a spreadsheet program. Writing and revising the schedule, however, should not become a goal in itself. The real concern is that you make and keep a schedule, not how you write it.

All Work and No Play?

Being a good student does not necessarily mean grinding away at studies and doing little else. Keep the following points in mind as you write out your daily schedule.

- Reading and reviewing notes will help prepare you for class.
- To prevent forgetting it's very important to review as soon after class as possible.
- Right after lunch is a good time for miscellaneous activity. It's hard to study on a full stomach.

- Always take a short break in the middle of a study session to maintain alertness.
- Regular exercise is important. It actually aids studying by promoting alertness.
- Schedule free time. It keeps you balanced emotionally.
- In extended study sessions schedule a variety of activities, each with a specific objective.

■ MAKING YOUR TIME MANAGEMENT PLAN WORK

Can you make your time management plan work? Many college students get overcommitted. Be realistic! Is there really enough time to carry your course load and meet your commitments? If not, be sure to drop any courses before the "drop date," so you won't have a low grade on your permanent record. If you are on financial aid, keep in mind that you must be registered for a certain number of hours (usually 12) to be considered a full-time student.

Some commuters prefer block scheduling, which runs classes together without breaks. Block scheduling allows students to cut down on travel time or attend school one or two days a week. Although this may seem to be an attractive alternative, there are some pitfalls. You'll have little time to process information between classes. If you become ill on a class day, you could fall behind in all of your classes. You may become fatigued sitting in class after class for a long period of time. Finally, you would become stressed when exams are held in several classes on the same day. Block scheduling may work better if you can attend lectures at an alternative time in case you are absent, if you alternate classes with free periods, and if you seek out instructors who allow you flexibility to complete assignments.

Reduce Distractions and Procrastination

Two things to avoid when you need to study are distractions and procrastination. Where should you study? Places associated with leisure, such as the kitchen table, the living room, or in front of the TV set, lend themselves to interruptions by others. And your association with social activities in these locations can distract you even when others aren't there. The solution is to find quiet places, both on campus and at home, where you can concentrate. You can then develop a study "mindset" when you sit down to do your work.

Find a routine that helps you work toward your goals. Biking can be both good exercise and efficient transportation.

Photo by Angela Mann

How to Beat Procrastination

Procrastination may be your single greatest enemy. Getting started when it's time to start takes self-discipline and self-control. Here are some ways to beat procrastination:

1. Say to yourself, "A mature person is capable and responsible and is a self-starter. I'm that kind of person if I start now." Then start!

2. On a 3 × 5 notecard write out a list of everything you need to do. Check off things as you get them done. Use the list to focus on the things that aren't getting done. Move them to the top of your next day's list and make up your mind to do them. Working from a list will give you a feeling of accomplishment and lead you to do more.

3. Break big jobs down into smaller steps. Tackle short, easy-to-accomplish tasks first.

4. Apply the goal-setting technique described in Chapter 1 to whatever you are putting off.

5. Promise yourself a suitable reward (an apple, a phone call, a walk) whenever you finish something that was hard to undertake.

6. Take control of your study environment. Eliminate distractions—including the ones you love! Say no to friends who want your attention at *their* convenience. Agree to meet them at a specific time later. Let them be your reward for doing what you must do now. Don't make phone calls during planned study sessions. Close your door.

Follow a Routine

Try to stick to a routine as you study. The more firmly you have established a specific time and a quiet place to study, the more effective you will be in keeping up with your schedule. Try to take advantage of large blocks of time that may be available on the weekend to review or catch up on major projects. If you break large tasks down and take one thing at a time, you'll make more progress toward your ultimate goal—an A!

EXERCISE 3.7 Study Time Without Distractions

Whether you live on campus or at home, there will be distractions that interfere with your ability to study. List the things that tend to distract you the most. Then, using the goal-setting process in Chapter 1, work in small groups to brainstorm ways to avoid distractions and send signals to distractors that you are not to be disturbed.

Internet

Activity 3.2
Procrastination Resources

The Internet offers access to a wide variety of academic, governmental, and association resources. The Procrastination Research Group at Carleton University in Ottawa (http://superior.carleton.ca/~tpychyl/) offers access to information and research on procrastination from all over the world.

What is the earliest reference they cite for the use of the term *procrastination*?

_____

What strategies do they offer for reducing procrastination?

_____

List three organizations for which links are offered for further study.

_____

_____

_____

ON CAMPUS

Study location: _____ Time: _____ to _____

Potential distractors (human and physical).

_____

_____

Actions against physical distractions:

_____

_____

Signals to human distractors:

_____

_____

AT HOME (OFF-CAMPUS OR ON-CAMPUS RESIDENCE)

Study location: _____ Time: _____ to _____

Potential distractors (human and physical):

_____

_____

Actions against physical distractions:

_____

_____

Signals to human distractors:

_____

_____

■TIME AND CRITICAL THINKING

You may be tempted to think that most college assignments can and should be done quickly and that, once they are done, instructors simply have to mark them right or wrong. However, most questions worthy of study in college do not have clear and immediate yes or no answers; if they did, no one would be paying scholars to spend years doing careful research. Good critical thinkers have a high tolerance for uncertainty. Confronted by a difficult question they begin by saying, "I don't know." They suspend judgment until they can gather information and take the time it requires to find and verify an answer.

Thus, effective time management doesn't always mean making decisions or finishing projects quickly. Effective critical thinkers resist finalizing their thoughts on important questions until they feel they have developed the best answer possible. This is not an argument in favor of ignoring deadlines. But it does suggest the value of beginning the research, reading, and even the writing phases of a project early, so that you will have time to change direction if necessary as you gather new insights.

Give your thoughts time to "incubate." Allow time to visit the library more than once. Sometimes insights come unexpectedly, when you're not consciously thinking about a problem. So, begin reviewing as early as you can, take a break from your studies, and then return to the topic. If you're successful, you'll be well ahead of the game when it's time for class, for quizzes, or for that final exam.

SUGGESTIONS FOR FURTHER READING

Burka, Jane B., and Lenora M. Yuen. _Procrastination: Why You Do It, What to Do About It_. Reading, MA: Addison-Wesley, 1983.

Fanning, Tony, and Robbie Fanning. _Get It All Done and Still Be Human: A Personal Time Management Workshop_. Menlo Park, Calif.: Open Chain, 1990.

Hunt, Diane, and Pam Hait. _The Tao of Time_. New York: Henry Holt, 1989.

Lakein, Alan. _How to Get Control of Your Time and Your Life_. New York: New American Library, 1973.

MacKenzie, Alec. _The Time Trap: The New Version of the 20-Year Classic on Time Management_. New York: AMACOM (Div. of American Management Association), 1990.

Smith, Laurence N., and Timothy L. Walter. "Five Strategies for Time Management," _The Adult Learner's Guide to College Success_ (Chapter 3), Rev. ed. Belmont, CA: Wadsworth, 1995.

Sotiriou, Peter Elias. _Integrating College Study Skills: Reasoning in Reading, Listening, and Writing_, 4th ed. Belmont, Calif.: Wadsworth, 1996. See Chapter 2, "Your Learning Inventory: Your Learning Style, Study Time, and Study Area."

RESOURCES

*One very helpful time saver is your own **personal phone directory** of important numbers and addresses. Keeping it handy (tacked up near the phone) can save you the struggle of trying to find that scrap of paper with so-and-so's number on it. Continue the list you began in the Resources page for Chapter 1 by filling in the following:*

FRIENDS		
Name	Phone number/address	e-mail

FAMILY		
Name	Phone number/address	e-mail

INSTRUCTORS		
Name	Phone number/address	e-mail

Academic advisor:

Campus security/local police:

Campus lost and found:

Campus health center/hospital:

Doctor/dentist:

Campus counseling center:

Dean of students:

Campus legal services:

Child-care centers:

Emergency road service/mechanic:

Landlord (home and work):

Employer (home and work):

Campus tutorial or learning center:

Campus commuter student service center:

Neighbors:

Local taxi service:

Campus library:

Public library:

Campus FAX numbers:

JOURNAL

NAME _____

DATE _____

Look back to Exercise 3.1 when you first assessed your time management skills. How would you evaluate yourself as a time manager now?

....

....

....

How much did you have to change in your approach to time management?

....

....

....

How did you apply the term assignment plan, weekly plan, and daily plan?

....

....

....

Which worked best for you? Why?

....

....

....

How can you modify the ideas in this chapter to fit your own biological clock?

....

....

....

What successes have you seen as a result of your work in this chapter?

....

....

....

CHAPTER →

Learning Styles

4

Steven Blume
Marietta College

My friend Janet always sleeps through U.S. history. That is totally weird because I could listen to Dr. Moroney lecture on Grant and Lee all day. Janet says she likes discussion classes. Those freak me out. I guess there's more than one way to learn. I hope so.

This chapter will help you turn the following keys to success:

6. **Assess and improve your study habits.**

7. **Join at least one study group.**

10. **Choose instructors who involve you in the learning process.**

Chapter Goals

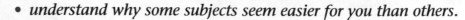

This chapter has been designed to help you

- *understand why some subjects seem easier for you than others.*
- *determine how you learn best and why.*
- *assess your learning style by completing an inventory.*
- *learn possible strengths and weaknesses of various learning styles.*
- *organize study groups that make the most of differing learning styles.*
- *learn how to develop your less-dominant learning style.*
- *deal with your teachers' learning/teaching styles.*
- *further develop your critical thinking skills using your preferred learning style.*

In high school, certain subjects appealed to you more than others. For one thing, some came easier than others. Perhaps you found history easier than mathematics, or biology easier than English. Part of the explanation for that has to do with what is called your *learning style*—that is, the way you acquire knowledge.

Learning style affects not only how you process material as you study but how you absorb it. Some students learn more effectively through visual means, others through listening to lectures, and still others through class discussion, hands-on experience, memorization, or various combinations of these.

Your particular learning style may make you much more comfortable and successful in some areas than in others. Consider Mark, whose favorite subject is history. Mark generally receives B's on his history exams, and he is satisfied with his performance. One of the things he likes best about history is the study of historical movements—the development of ideas as they inform historical events. When he studies for his exams, he analyzes those events, trying to determine what is responsible for the various social, political, and historical changes he has been reading about. Although he recognizes the importance of names and dates, they are less significant and interesting to him than the analysis of why certain events occurred and what effects have resulted from such occurrences. For example, he studies to understand *why* the pilgrims came to America and *how* they created the Plymouth Plantation rather than to discover who the leaders of the emigration were, who the first settlers were, when they arrived in America, what crops they grew, and what treaties they signed with the Indians. What he is interested in and how he studies are integral parts of his learning style.

Mark is also taking Introductory Biology, and as is natural for him, he studied for his biology exam in the same way he studied for his history test. Unfortunately, he was able to use very little of the knowledge gained from his studying and thus received an F on his biology exam. Instead of studying facts, committing important terminology to memory, and learning definitions, Mark had stressed concepts when he studied, and this *analytical learning style* turned out to be inappropriate for this course, or at least for the way his instructor taught the course.

One student's analytical style may thrive on the complexities of history. Another's satisfaction at mastering facts and understanding how they are related may lead her into science.

Walter Calahan/Earlham College

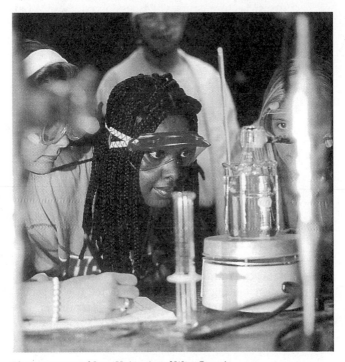

Photo courtesy of State University of West Georgia

The reverse can also be true. Another student, Anne, has a *factual learning style* that makes her comfortable with memorizing facts. Anne would do very well on that same biology test and yet find the history exam that stressed concepts and analysis of material very difficult. Just as we all have different skills, so we have different learning styles. Although no one learning style is inherently better than another, it is important to be able to work comfortably no matter what style is required in a given course. An awareness of your learning style can be helpful in emphasizing your strengths and helping you compensate for your weaknesses.

In this chapter, we'll examine learning styles of students both in and out of the classroom, as well as discuss the teaching styles of professors.

■ AN INFORMAL MEASURE OF LEARNING STYLE

To begin to define your own learning style and to understand how it affects your responses in class, do the following exercise.

Your Learning Style: A Quick Indication

A List three or four of your favorite courses from high school or college:

1. _____

2. _____

3. _____

4. _____

What did these courses have in common? Did they tend to be hands-on courses? Lecture courses? Discussion courses? What were the exams like? Do you see a pattern from one course to the next? For example, did your favorite courses tend to use information-oriented tests such as multiple-choice or true-false? Or did they often include broader essay exams? Did the tests cover small units of material or facts, or did they draw on larger chunks of material?

Now list three or four of your least favorite courses from high school or college:

1. _____

2. _____

3. _____

4. _____

What did these courses and their exams have in common? How did they tend to differ from the courses you liked?

What conclusions can you draw about your preferences for learning based on these common elements in course presentation or exams? Do you prefer to make lists and memorize facts or to analyze the material, searching for concepts and considering broader implications? If you prefer the former, your learning style is more factual, like Anne's; if you prefer the latter, your learning style is more analytical, like Mark's. Can you understand why Anne prefers biology and Mark prefers history?

B After doing part A, form a small group with two or three other members of the class. Brainstorm about what courses you are taking that seem to require factual learning styles, analytical learning styles, or a combination of both. Prepare an oral group presentation to the class about your conclusions and the reasons for them. What is the best way to prepare for an exam in these classes, and why? (Read the rest of this chapter before you give your presentation.)

If you prefer listening to lectures, taking notes, and reading your notes aloud to yourself, you have a more *auditory learning style.* You might even read your notes into a tape recorder and play them back when you study for an exam. If you prefer instructors who outline their lectures on the blackboard or who make liberal use of the board by illustrating the important

Internet

Activity 4.1
Learning Style Inventory

Students process information differently. Which of the following best describes your most efficient learning style?

Visual learner—rely on visual cues, on things you see

Auditory learner—rely on auditory stimuli, on things you hear

Tactile learner—rely on touch, on working with your hands

Your learning style: _____

Go to http://www.hcc.hawaii.edu/hccinfo/facdev/lsi.html and take the twenty-four question Learning Style Inventory. Which type of learner are you?

Visual Preference Score _____

Auditory Preference Score _____

Tactile Preference Score _____

What do your scores suggest about how you might adjust your study habits to optimize your learning?

_____

_____

_____

_____

_____

_____

points they are trying to make, you have a more *visual learning style*. You probably find that copying and recopying your notes helps you learn the material better. If you learn best by a "hands-on" approach, you may prefer a *kinesthetic, or physical, learning style*.

Being more aware of your learning style preferences can help you exploit your strengths in preparing for classes and also help you better understand why you may be having difficulty with some of your courses and what you might do to improve.

■MORE FORMAL MEASURES OF LEARNING STYLE

A number of instruments can help you determine more effectively just what your preferred learning style is and better understand other learning styles as well.

Classroom Behavior

One approach is based on the ways in which students behave in the classroom. For instance, psychologists Tony Grasha and Sheryl Riechmann have put together the *Grasha-Riechmann* instrument. This tool assesses six learning styles based on classroom behavior: (1) *competitive,* (2) *collaborative,* (3) *participant,* (4) *avoidant,* (5) *dependent,* and (6) *independent.*

To understand which classroom learning style you are most comfortable with, you need to answer certain questions. For example, do you find the study questions or review questions passed out by your instructor helpful? Do you enjoy and find helpful studying with and learning from other students in your class? Do you like it when the instructor engages the class in discussion? If so, then you probably have a more collaborative, participant, and dependent learning style and will work best with an instructor who has a corresponding teaching style. On the other hand, you may prefer an instructor who lectures in class with minimal class participation. You may feel that straightforward study of your lecture notes and textbook is the most effective means of study. If so, your learning style is more competitive, independent, and avoidant.

Personality Preferences

Another approach explores basic personality preferences that make people interested in different things and draw them to different fields and lifestyles. The *Myers-Briggs Type Indicator,* based on Carl Jung's theory of psychological types, uses four scales:

- **E/I (Extroversion/Introversion).** This scale describes two opposite preferences depending on whether you like to focus your attention on the outer or the inner world.
- **S/N (Sensing/Intuition).** This scale describes opposite ways you acquire information—that is, whether you find out about things through facts or through intuition.
- **T/F (Thinking/Feeling).** This scale describes how you make decisions, whether by analysis and weighing of evidence or by analysis and weighing of feelings.
- **J/P (Judging/Perceiving).** This scale describes the way you relate to the outer world, whether in a planned, orderly way or in a flexible, spontaneous way.

You will often feel most comfortable around people who share your preferences, and you will probably be most comfortable in a classroom where the instructor's preferences for perceiving and processing information are most like yours. But the Myers-Briggs instrument also emphasizes our ability to cultivate in ourselves all processes on each scale.

EXERCISE 4.2 Assessing Your Learning Style

PERSONAL STYLE INVENTORY

Just as every person has differently shaped feet and toes from every other person, so we all have differently "shaped" personalities. Just as no person's foot shape is "right" or "wrong," so no person's personality shape is right or wrong. The purpose of this inventory is to give you a picture of the shape of your preferences, but that shape, while different from the shapes of other persons' per-sonalities, has nothing to do with mental health or mental problems.

The following items are arranged in pairs (*a* and *b*), and each member of the pair represents a preference you may or may not hold. Rate your preference for each item by giving it a score of 0 to 5 (0 meaning you *really* feel negative about it or strongly about the other member of the pair, 5 meaning you *strongly* prefer it or do not prefer the other member of the pair). The scores for *a* and *b must* add up to 5 (0 and 5, 1 and 4, or 2 and 3). Do not use fractions such as 2½.

I prefer:

_____ 1a. making decisions after finding out what others think

_____ 1b. making decisions without consult-ing others

_____ 2a. being called imaginative or intuitive

_____ 2b. being called factual and accurate

_____ 3a. making decisions about people in organizations based on available data and systematic analysis of situations

_____ 3b. making decisions about people in organizations based on empathy, feelings, and understanding of their needs and values

_____ 4a. allowing commitments to occur if others want to make them

_____ 4b. pushing for definite commitments to ensure that they are made

_____ 5a. quiet, thoughtful time alone

_____ 5b. active, energetic time with people

_____ 6a. using methods I know well that are effective to get the job done

_____ 6b. trying to think of new methods of doing tasks when confronted with them

_____ 7a. drawing conclusions based on logic and careful step-by-step analysis

_____ 7b. drawing conclusions based on what I feel and believe about life and peo-ple from past experiences

_____ 8a. avoiding making deadlines

_____ 8b. setting a schedule and sticking to it

_____ 9a. inner thoughts and feelings others cannot see

_____ 9b. activities and occurrences in which others join

_____ 10a. the abstract or theoretical

_____ 10b. the concrete or real

_____ 11a. helping others explore their feelings

_____ 11b. helping others make logical decisions

_____ 12a. communicating little of my inner thinking and feelings

_____ 12b. communicating freely my inner thinking and feelings

_____ 13a. planning ahead based on projections

_____ 13b. planning as necessities arise, just before carrying out the plans

_____ 14a. meeting new people

_____ 14b. being alone or with one person I know well

_____ 15a. ideas

_____ 15b. facts

_____ 16a. convictions

_____ 16b. verifiable conclusions

_____ 17a. keeping appointments and notes about commitments in notebooks or in ap-pointment books as much as possible

_____ 17b. using appointment books and note-books as minimally as possible (although I may use them)

_____ 18a. carrying out carefully laid, detailed plans with precision

_____ 18b. designing plans and structures with-out necessarily carrying them out

_____ 19a. being free to do things on the spur of the moment

_____ 19b. knowing well in advance what I am expected to do

_____ 20a. experiencing emotional situations, discussions, movies

_____ 20b. using my ability to analyze situations

PERSONAL STYLE INVENTORY SCORING

Instructions: Transfer your scores for each item of each pair to the appropriate blanks. Be careful to check the *a* and *b* letters to be sure you are recording scores in the right blank spaces. Then total the scores for each dimension.

	Dimension			Dimension	
	I	**E**	**N**	**S**	
	1b. _____	1a. _____	2a. _____	2b. _____
	5a. _____	5b. _____	6b. _____	6a. _____
	9a. _____	9b. _____	10a. _____	10b. _____
	12a. _____	12b. _____	15a. _____	15b. _____
	14b. _____	14a. _____	18b. _____	18a. _____
TOTALS:	I _____	E _____	N _____	S _____

	Dimension			Dimension	
	T	**F**	**P**	**J**	
	3a. _____	3b. _____	4a. _____	4b. _____
	7a. _____	7b. _____	8a. _____	8b. _____
	11b. _____	11a. _____	13b. _____	13a. _____
	16b. _____	16a. _____	17b. _____	17a. _____
	20b. _____	20a. _____	19a. _____	19b. _____
TOTALS:	T _____	F _____	P _____	J _____

PERSONAL STYLE INVENTORY INTERPRETATION

Letters on the score sheet stand for:

I — *Introversion* **E** — *Extroversion*
N — *iNtuition* **S** — *Sensing*
T — *Thinking* **F** — *Feeling*
P — *Perceiving* **J** — *Judging*

If your score is:	*The likely interpretation is:*
12–13	balance in the strengths of the dimensions
14–15	some strength in the dimension; some weakness in the other member of the pair
16–19	definite strength in the dimension; definite weakness in the other member of the pair
20–25	considerable strength in the dimension; considerable weakness in the other member of the pair

Your typology is those four dimensions for which you had scores of 14 or more, although the relative strengths of all the dimensions actually constitute your typology. Scores of 12 or 13 show relative balance in a pair so that either member could be part of the typology.

DIMENSIONS OF THE TYPOLOGY

The following four pairs of dimensions are present to some degree in all people. It is the extremes that are described here. The strength of a dimension is indicated by the score for that dimension and will determine how closely the strengths and weaknesses described fit the participant's personality.

INTROVERSION/EXTROVERSION

Persons more introverted than extroverted tend to make decisions somewhat independently of culture, people, or things around them. They are quiet, diligent at working alone, and socially reserved. They may dislike being interrupted while working and may tend to forget names and faces.

Extroverted persons are attuned to the culture, people, and things around them. The extrovert is outgoing, socially free, interested in variety and in working with people. The extrovert may become impatient with long, slow tasks and does not mind being interrupted by people.

INTUITION/SENSING

The intuitive person prefers possibilities, theories, invention, and the new and becomes bored with nitty-gritty details and facts unrelated to concepts. The intuitive person thinks and discusses in spontaneous leaps of intuition that may neglect details. Problem solving comes easily for this individual, although there may be a tendency to make errors of fact.

The sensing type prefers the concrete, factual, tangible here-and-now, becoming impatient with theory and the abstract, mistrusting intuition. The sensing type thinks in detail, remembering real facts, but possibly missing a conception of the overall.

THINKING/FEELING

The thinker makes judgments based on logic, analysis, and evidence, avoiding decisions based on feelings and values. As a result, the thinker is more interested in logic, analysis, and verifiable conclusions than in empathy, values, and personal warmth. The thinker may step on others' feelings and needs without realizing it, neglecting to take into consideration the values of others.

The feeler makes judgments based on empathy, warmth, and personal values. As a consequence, feelers are more interested in people and feelings than in impersonal logic, analysis, and things, and in harmony more than in being on top or achieving impersonal goals. The feeler gets along well with people in general.

PERCEIVING/JUDGING

The perceiver is a gatherer, always wanting to know more before deciding, holding off decisions and judgments. As a consequence, the perceiver is open, flexible, adaptive, nonjudgmental, able to see and appreciate all sides of issues, always welcoming new perspectives. However, perceivers are also difficult to pin down and may become involved in many tasks that do not reach closure, so that they may become frustrated at times. Even when they finish tasks, perceivers will tend to look back at them and wonder whether they could have been done another way. The perceiver wishes to roll with life rather than change it.

The judger is decisive, firm, and sure, setting goals and sticking to them. The judger wants to make decisions and get on to the next project. When a project does not yet have closure, judgers will leave it behind and go on to new tasks.

STRENGTHS AND WEAKNESSES OF THE TYPES

Each person has strengths and weaknesses as a result of these dimensions. Committees and organizations with a preponderance of one type will have the same strengths and weaknesses.

	Possible Strengths	**Possible Weaknesses**
Introvert	is independent	avoids others
	works alone	is secretive
	reflects	loses opportunities to act
	works with ideas	is misunderstood by others
	avoids generalizations	dislikes being interrupted
	is careful before acting	
Extrovert	interacts with others	does not work well without people
	is open	needs change, variety
	acts, does	is impulsive
	is well understood	is impatient with routine
Intuitor	sees possibilities	is inattentive to detail, precision
	works out new ideas	is inattentive to the actual and
	works with the complicated	practical
	solves novel problems	is impatient with the tedious
		loses sight of the here-and-now
		jumps to conclusions
Senser	attends to detail	does not see possibilities
	is practical	loses the overall in details
	has memory for detail, fact	mistrusts intuition
	is patient	is frustrated with the complicated
	is systematic	prefers not to imagine future
Feeler	considers others' feelings	is not guided by logic
	understands needs, values	is not objective
	is interested in conciliation	is less organized
	demonstrates feelings	is overly accepting
	persuades, arouses	bases judgments on feelings
Thinker	is logical, analytical	does not notice people's feelings
	is objective	misunderstands others' values
	is organized	is uninterested in conciliation
	has critical ability	does not show feelings
	is just	shows less mercy
	stands firm	is uninterested in persuading
Perceiver	compromises	is indecisive
	sees all sides of issues	does not plan
	is flexible	does not control circumstances
	decides based on all data	is easily distracted from tasks
	is not judgmental	does not finish projects
Judger	decides	is stubborn
	plans	is inflexible
	orders	decides with insufficient data
	makes quick decisions	is controlled by task or plans
	remains with a task	wishes not to interrupt work

NOTE: This exercise is an abridgment of the Personal Style Inventory by Dr. R. Craig Hogan and Dr. David W. Champagne, adapted and reproduced with permission from Organization Design and Development, Inc., 2002 Renaissance Blvd., Suite 100, King of Prussia, Pa., 19406. For information on using the complete instrument, please write to the above address.

As you reflect on your performance on the previous exercise, keep in mind that your score merely suggests your preferences; it does not stereotype or pigeonhole you. Remember, too, that no one learning style is inherently preferable to another and that everyone knows and uses a range of styles. The fact that many of us exhibit behaviors that seem to contradict our preferences shows that we each embrace a wide range of possibilities.

Using Knowledge of Your Learning Style

Discovering your own strengths empowers you to recognize what you already do well. Discovering your weaknesses is also useful, because it is to your advantage to cultivate your less dominant learning styles. While certain disciplines and certain instructors may take approaches that favor certain styles, no course is going to be entirely sensing or entirely intuitive, entirely thinking or entirely feeling, just as you are not entirely one thing or another. You can also use your learning style data to determine how to study more effectively. Diagram? Study aloud? Annotate texts in margins? Focus on details or concepts?

Internet

Activity 4.2
The Keirsey
Temperament Sorter

Go to http://sunsite.unc.edu/jembin/mb.pl and take the seventy-question version of the Keirsey Temperament Sorter.

What is your learning style type? _____

What is your temperament type? _____

Read through the type descriptions linked to the site. How well do they reflect what you know about yourself?

_____

_____

_____

_____

_____

_____

_____

_____

A good study group shares a common goal of success for all its members. It also asks each member to contribute according to his or her own special perspective and style.

Dollarhide/Monkmeyer Press Photo

■STUDY GROUPS AND LEARNING STYLE

Knowing your own learning style preference can help you to study more effectively with other students. When you form a study group, seek out students with some opposite learning preferences, but be sure, too, that you have some preferences in common. The best teamwork seems to come from people who differ on one or two preferences. If you prefer intuitive fact gathering, you might benefit from the details brought forth by a sensing type.

The Many Uses of Learning Teams

In the box on page 71, we note that learning teams may be used for many tasks in addition to studying for exams. Here are a few of those tasks:

1. **Note-Taking Teams.** Team up with other students immediately after class to share and compare notes. One of your teammates may have picked up something you missed or vice versa. By meeting immediately after class, your group may still have the opportunity to consult with the instructor about any missing or confusing information before he or she leaves the classroom.

2. **Reading Teams.** After completing reading assignments, team up with other students to compare your highlighting and margin notes. See if you all agree on what the author's major points were and what information in the chapter you should study for exams.

3. **Library Research Teams.** Studies show that many first-year students are unfamiliar with library research and sometimes experience "library anxiety." Forming library research teams is an effective way to develop a social support group for reducing this fear and for locating and sharing

Student Learning Teams: Collaborating with Your Peers Can Improve Your Academic Performance!

Research has shown that college students can learn as much, or more, from peers as they do from instructors and textbooks. When students work effectively in a supportive group, the experience can be a very powerful way to improve academic achievement and satisfaction with the learning experience.

Recent interviews with college students at Harvard University revealed that nearly every senior who had been part of a study group considered this experience to be crucial to his or her academic progress and success.

However, not all learning groups are equally effective. Sometimes group work is unsuccessful or fails to reach its full potential because insufficient thought was given to how groups should be formed or how they should function. The following suggestions are strategies for maximizing the power of peer collaboration.

This course may be the perfect place for you to form learning teams and to start putting principles of good teamwork into practice. The teamwork skills you build in this course can be applied to your future courses, particularly those which you find most difficult. What's more, national surveys of employers of college students consistently show that being able to work effectively in teams is one of the most important and valued skills in today's work world.

1. **In forming teams, seek peers who will contribute quality and diversity.** Look for fellow students who are motivated: who attend class regularly, are attentive and participate actively while in class, and complete class assignments on time.

   Include teammates from different ethnic, racial, or cultural backgrounds, different age groups, and with different personality characteristics. Such variety will bring different life experiences and different styles of thinking and learning strategies to your team, which can increase both its quality and versatility.

   Furthermore, choosing only your friends or classmates who have similar interests and lifestyles can often result in a learning group that is more likely to get "off track" and on to topics that have nothing to do with the learning task.

2. **Keep your group size small (three to six teammates).** Smaller groups allow for more face-to-face interaction and eye contact and less opportunity for any one individual to shirk his or her responsibility. Also, it's much easier for small groups to get together outside of class.

   You might consider choosing an even number of teammates, so you can work in pairs in case the team decides to divide its work into separate parts for different members to work on.

3. **Remember that learning teams are more than study groups.** Effective student learning teams collaborate regularly for other academic tasks in addition to test review sessions. See the list beginning on page 70 for other uses of learning teams.

4. **Hold individual team members personally accountable for their own learning and for contributing to the learning of their teammates.** Research on study groups at Harvard University indicates that they are effective only if each member has done the required course work in advance of the group meeting (for example, completing required readings and other course assignments). One way to ensure proper preparation is to ask each member to come to the group meeting prepared with specific information or answers to share with teammates, as well as with questions or points of confusion for which they would like to receive help from the team.

   Another way to ensure that each teammate prepares properly for the meeting is to have individual members take on different roles or responsibilities. For example, each member could assume special responsibility for mastering a particular topic, section, or skill to be taught to the others.

sources of information. (*Note:* It is ethical for students to share the same information sources or references. This isn't cheating or plagiarizing as long as the final product you turn in represents your own written work.)

4. **Team/Instructor Conferences.** Having your learning team visit the course instructor during office hours to seek additional assistance in preparing for exams and completing assignments is an effective team learning strategy for several reasons. If you are shy or unassertive, it may be easier to see an instructor in the company of other students. In addition, the feedback you receive from the instructor is also received by your teammates, and useful pieces of information are less likely to be missed, misinterpreted, or forgotten. Your team visit also sends a message to the instructor that you are serious about learning because you've taken the time and effort to work with your peers prior to the office visit.

5. **Team Test Results Review.** After receiving test results, the members of a learning team can review their individual tests together to help one another identify the sources of their mistakes and to identify any "model" answers that received maximum credit. This way each team member can get a much clearer idea of what the instructor expects from students. You can use this information as feedback to fine-tune and improve your performance on subsequent tests or assignments.

EXERCISE 4.3 / Working with Other Learning Styles

A Form a group with one or two other students whose learning style preferences are different from yours in one or two dimensions. Review the chart in Exercise 4.2 on strengths and weaknesses and make some notes about yours so that you can find the best "match" with other study group members:

My strengths: _____

_____

_____

_____

My weaknessess: _____

_____

_____

_____

How will your strengths help others? What strengths will you look for in others that will help you?

How I can help others: _____

_____

_____

How others can help me: _____

_____

_____

Improving Your Less Dominant Learning Styles

The key ingredient in developing your less dominant style is awareness. Try to develop one process at a time.

RAISING YOUR SENSING (S) LEARNING STYLE

1. Whenever you walk, try to notice and jot down specific details of the scenery—shapes of leaves; size, color, and types of rocks; and so on.

2. Three or four times a day pay careful attention to, and then describe to a friend, what someone else is wearing.

3. Do a jigsaw puzzle.

4. Break down a physical activity into its component parts.

5. Describe in detail something you just saw, such as a picture, a room, or the like.

RAISING YOUR INTUITIVE (N) LEARNING STYLE

1. Imagine a given situation or circumstance in a new light by considering, "What if . . . ?" For example, what if the pilgrims had landed in California—how would their lifestyle have changed? What if you had gone to a bigger (smaller) school? What if X were your roommate instead of Y?

2. Pretend you saw an article ten years from now about your hometown, your lifestyle, American values, or the like. What would it say?

3. Read a novel and imagine yourself as one of the characters. What would happen to you following the novel's conclusion?

RAISING YOUR FEELING (F) LEARNING STYLE

1. Write down a feeling statement about your class, your day, your job, or your emotions, and make sure you use a simile. For example, "I feel like a puppy that's just been scolded." Note that if you use *think* in a statement, it's not a feeling statement. Write down five feeling statements every day.

2. Write down what matters most in your relationship with someone or something else.

RAISING YOUR THINKING (T) LEARNING STYLE

1. Have someone write down a problem that's bothering him or her or a problem related to the college or your environment. Then answer questions that explain who, what, where, when, and why, and provide the details that back up each response. Doing this every day for 15 or 20 minutes will teach you how to be objective.

In your next session, ask that each person share his or her strengths and weaknesses and talk about how the group might work for everyone's benefit.

B Try working on an assignment with someone who has a preference that is opposite of your own on either the sensing/intuitive or thinking/feeling scale. Discuss how this worked. Did you get more out of the assignment? Did you consider more issues than you might have alone? Did you learn something about how to study? What did you discover about the other person's learning style?

■DEALING WITH YOUR TEACHERS' LEARNING/TEACHING STYLES

Just as your learning style affects how you study, perform, and react to various courses and disciplines, so your instructor's teaching style affects what and how he or she teaches. Some awareness of your instructor's teaching style may also help you study and prepare for exams. The syllabus for the course, the lecture, and the discussion questions, as well as handouts, assignments, and exams, can provide some helpful hints not only about your instructor's teaching style but also about ways you can use the strengths of your own learning style or compensate enough to perform effectively in the class.

Clues to Teachers' Teaching Styles

The best clue to your instructor's teaching style is the language he or she uses. If your learning style is more visual, you can sense those clues more easily from printed material such as the syllabus or course handouts. If your learning style is more auditory, pay attention to the language your instructor uses when lecturing, asking discussion questions, or phrasing oral test questions.

For example, earlier we discussed two ways of receiving and processing information: (1) sensing, that is, factual and informational, and (2) intuitive, that is, analytical and conceptual. An instructor who uses words such as *define, diagram, label, list, outline,* and *summarize* will tend to have a more sensing teaching style. He or she will want you to be extremely specific and provide primarily factual information. Words such as these really ask for very restricted answers. Whereas Anne will be very comfortable with this instructor, Mark will be less so. Recognizing his instructor's teaching style, however, would be to Mark's benefit, since he would have a better idea of what to expect. He could then adjust his approach to the material in order to perform satisfactorily in class and on exams.

On the other hand, an instructor whose syllabus or lecture is sprinkled with words such as *concept, theme, idea, theory,* and *interpretation* will tend to have a much more intuitive and analytical learning style and expect similar kinds of responses from students. On exams or on assignments, he or she may use terms such as *describe, compare, contrast, criticize, discuss, evaluate, explain, interpret, justify,* or *relate.* You may notice that instead of asking you to provide factual data or information, these words ask you to act on that information—that is, to use it in relation to other pieces of information, to evaluate it, or to examine it in terms of your own experience. An instructor who uses these words has a much more intuitive teaching style and will expect more analytical, imaginative, and conceptual responses. He or she will expect you to see that information in a new context rather than simply restate the facts as they have been given to you or as they appear in the textbook.

Mark will, of course, feel far more comfortable with this instructor. Anne will have to recognize when she studies in this course that learning the facts is not enough. She will be expected to see them in other contexts, to think about their relationships to one another. While this may not be easy for her, she can certainly adapt to it if the instructor's teaching style and expectations demand it.

Exam Preparation and Learning/Teaching Style

Understanding learning styles can help you to perceive more clearly the expectations of an instructor whose teaching style is incompatible with your learning style and thus allow you to prepare more effectively for his or her exam. You saw earlier, for example, how Mark's learning style, essentially an intuitive (N) style, was suited to his history course but not to his biology exam. By contrast Anne's more sensing (S) style was suited to the biology course but not the history course. In order to perform better on that biology exam, Mark would need to modify his way of studying.

Let me illustrate further with an experience of my own. When I was learning about the Myers-Briggs Type Indicator, I attended a workshop for college instructors. Those of us attending the workshop were divided into two groups, sensing and intuitive. Each group was given a five-page essay about the effects of divorce on young children and asked to construct a short exam based on the reading. The sensing group was then asked to take the exam constructed by the intuitive group while the intuitive group was asked to take the exam constructed by the sensing group.

In dealing with the questions, we could not believe that both groups had read and discussed the same essay. Those of us in the intuitive group had been asked to construct lists of details and respond to much factual data that we had regarded as less essential than the more analytical and conceptual themes of the essay. And those in the sensing group were quite taken aback by the very broad thematic questions my group had asked about the implications of divorce on the children and the larger questions about the children's future.

It would have been much easier for those who favored sensing to respond to an exam constructed by other sensing people, and vice versa. That same situation has probably been true for you in classes and will continue to be true—you will be most comfortable in a course taught by an instructor with a teaching style similar to your learning style.

EXERCISE 4.4 Exams and Learning Styles

As a class, select some piece of writing such as a newspaper article or short magazine piece. Read the article. Then divide into groups in which people of similar learning styles are together. Within each group create a short test based on the reading. Reconvene as a class and compare the tests from the various groups. Did the different learning styles of the groups have any influence on the kinds of tests they created?

Take some time over the next few days to think about the courses you are taking now. How well does your preferred learning style fit the style reflected in the syllabus, handouts, lectures, and study questions in at least two of your courses? Ask several of your instructors how *they* teach and learn best.

Do any of the key sensing words mentioned previously (*define, diagram,* and so on) or some close approximation of them appear? If so, list them and place a check mark next to each of them each time the word appears. Do any of the key intuition words (*describe, compare,* and so on) or similar words appear? List them also and note their frequency. Listen carefully in class. What key words do you hear? Write these down also. Which type of word do you hear most frequently? That will begin to give you some idea of each instructor's learning/teaching style. You may also wish to assess your academic advisor's preferences.

INSTRUCTOR/COURSE 1: _____

Sensing Words   **Intuition Words**

_____   _____

_____   _____

_____   _____

_____   _____

_____   _____

_____   _____

_____   _____

Instructor's preferred style: Sensing _____   Intuition _____

Other teaching style observations: _____

_____

_____

_____

_____

_____

_____

INSTRUCTOR/COURSE 2: _____

Sensing Words   **Intuition Words**

_____   _____

_____   _____

_____   _____

_____   _____

_____   _____

_____   _____

Instructor's preferred style: Sensing _____   Intuition _____

Other teaching style observations: _____

_____

_____

_____

_____

_____

_____

How does your learning style as measured in Exercise 4.2 fit with the learning/teaching style of each instructor? Which courses will require some adjustment on your part? Discuss these problems with other students in class.

Are there things your instructors could be doing to help you take advantage of your strengths and learn more efficiently? In class discuss what these ideas are and how you might convey them to the appropriate instructor.

If your instructor's teaching style is compatible with your learning style, then you should be able to perform well simply by keeping up with your work. If your instructor's style is incompatible with yours, you might consider either mastering more factual material or interpreting or analyzing that material in order to be better prepared for exams or papers. In any case a greater awareness of both your learning style *and* your instructor's teaching style can be of real benefit.

A variety of additional tests can help you learn more about your learning style. These are generally available through your career planning or learning center. A guidance counselor will both administer the test and help you interpret the results. Ask about the following:

- The Myers-Briggs Type Indicator
- The complete Hogan/Champagne Personal Style Inventory
- The Kolb Learning Style Inventory

EXERCISE 4.6 Learning Styles and Critical Thinking

Can your learning preferences affect the ease or difficulty with which you complete the four stages of critical thinking? It may be easier for intuitive (N) learners to find abstractions amid details and brainstorm possibilities (steps 1 and 2), whereas sensing (S) learners may do well in step 3 where they can list ideas into some logical order. Thinking (T) learners may also find step 3 comes naturally to them, whereas feeling (F) learners may complete step 3 by prioritizing their values, rather than by the logic of the situation. As you complete this exercise, note first how your learning style preferences have made it easy or difficult for you to complete the steps of the critical thinking process and then how your learning style preferences affect your thinking on the following issue.

Imagine that your college newspaper has run a story detailing a new structure for teaching courses. To cut costs and accommodate students who wish to complete their education faster, the administration is considering dividing the year into four equal terms of thirteen weeks each. One term would run January through March, a second term would run April through June, a third July through September, and a fourth October through December. Any holidays—such as Christmas and Thanksgiving—would be shortened to no more than two days to accommodate the schedule. Faculty would teach only three terms a year, on a rotating basis, meaning that some courses might not be available year round. While most students would attend classes only three out of four terms, students would have the option of graduating early if they attended all four terms. Due to a slightly shorter schedule, class length would increase by roughly 10 minutes a period. The average student course load would be four courses per term.

The highly popular president of your student government, who is in favor of the proposal, has asked you to take a stand on this issue at a campuswide meeting. Using the principles of critical thinking, meet with three or four other students (ask your instructor if he or she can group you by opposite N/S and T/F preferences) and complete the first three steps. Then complete the final step.

1. List the broad *abstract* ideas inherent in this proposal to change the school term. What are the truths or arguments here? What are the key ideas? What larger concepts do the details suggest? What is the administration really trying to accomplish?

2. Find new *possibilities*. What questions do the large ideas suggest? What new questions can you ask about the value of adjusting the schedule? What other possibilities might there be besides dividing the year into four equal parts? What are some possible effects of such a change on students? On faculty? Avoid making immediate decisions. Put off closure. Reject nothing at first.

3. *Organize* new ideas and possibilities in a logical order. In what direction do the facts really point? What are the best solutions? To leave the schedule alone? To offer options? Is there some important additional information that needs to be gathered and evaluated before it is possible to reach a conclusion? Ultimately, what new abstractions and new conclusions have resulted from your thinking?

4. Using the results of the group thinking process, write a paper that precisely *communicates* your ideas to others. Are your conclusions well supported? Make certain your conclusions take all parties (the majority of students, faculty, and others) into account. At the end of the paper, state whether you believe your learning style made any of these steps easy or difficult to follow and why.

SUGGESTIONS FOR FURTHER READING

Lawrence, Gordon. *People Types and Tiger Stripes*. Gainesville, Fla.: Center for the Application of Psychological Types, 1982.

Malone, John C., Jr. *Theories of Learning: A Historical Approach*. Belmont, Calif.: Wadsworth, 1991.

Perry, William. *Forms of Intellectual and Ethical Development in the College Years: A Scheme*. New York: Holt, Rinehart & Winston, 1970.

RESOURCES

Read the following descriptions of the sixteen different Myers-Briggs types. Put your name in the box that best describes your type. Where do the other people in your life fit? Put their names in the boxes that best describe their type preferences.

	SENSING TYPES		INTUITIVES	
	WITH THINKING	WITH FEELING	WITH FEELING	WITH THINKING

<table>
<tr>
<td rowspan="2" style="writing-mode:vertical-lr">INTROVERTS</td>
<td style="writing-mode:vertical-lr">JUDGING</td>
<td>

ISTJ

Serious, quiet, earn success by concentration and thoroughness. Practical, orderly, matter-of-fact, logical, realistic and dependable. See to it that everything is well organized. Take responsibility. Make up their own minds as to what should be accomplished and work toward it steadily, regardless of protests or distractions.

</td>
<td>

ISFJ

Quiet, friendly, responsible and conscientious. Work devotedly to meet their obligations and serve their friends and school. Thorough, painstaking, accurate. May need time to master technical subjects, as their interests are not often technical. Patient with detail and routine. Loyal, considerate, concerned with how other people feel.

</td>
<td>

INFJ

Succeed by perseverance, originality and desire to do whatever is needed or wanted. Put their best efforts into the work. Quietly forceful, conscientious, concerned for others. Respected for their firm principles. Likely to be honored and followed for their clear convictions as to how best to serve the common good.

</td>
<td>

INTJ

Have original minds and great drive which they use only for their own purposes. In fields that appeal to them they have a fine power to organize a job and carry it through with or without help. Skeptical, critical, independent, determined, often stubborn. Must learn to yield less important points in order to win the most important.

</td>
<td rowspan="2" style="writing-mode:vertical-lr">JUDGING</td>
<td rowspan="2" style="writing-mode:vertical-lr">INTROVERTS</td>
</tr>
<tr>
<td style="writing-mode:vertical-lr">PERCEPTIVE</td>
<td>

ISTP

Cool onlookers, quiet, reserved, observing and analyzing life with detached curiosity and unexpected flashes of original humor. Usually interested in impersonal principles, cause and effect, or how and why mechanical things work. Exert themselves no more than they think necessary, because any waste of energy would be inefficient.

</td>
<td>

ISFP

Retiring, quietly friendly, sensitive, modest about their abilities. Shun disagreements, do not force their opinions or values on others. Usually do not care to lead but are often loyal followers. May be rather relaxed about assignments or getting things done, because they enjoy the present moment and do not want to spoil it by undue haste or exertion.

</td>
<td>

INFP

Full of enthusiasms and loyalties, but seldom talk of these until they know you well. Care about learning, ideas, language, and independent projects of their own. Apt to be on yearbook staff, perhaps as editor. Tend to undertake too much, then somehow get it done. Friendly, but often too absorbed in what they are doing to be sociable or notice much.

</td>
<td>

INTP

Quiet, reserved, brilliant in exams, especially in theoretical or scientific subjects. Logical to the point of hair-splitting. Interested mainly in ideas, with little liking for parties or small talk. Tend to have very sharply defined interests. Need to choose careers where some strong interest of theirs can be used and useful.

</td>
<td style="writing-mode:vertical-lr">PERCEPTIVE</td>
</tr>
<tr>
<td rowspan="2" style="writing-mode:vertical-lr">EXTRAVERTS</td>
<td style="writing-mode:vertical-lr">PERCEPTIVE</td>
<td>

ESTP

Matter-of-fact, do not worry or hurry, enjoy whatever comes along. Tend to like mechanical things and sports, with friends on the side. May be a bit blunt or insensitive. Can do math or science when they see the need. Dislike long explanations. Are best with real things that can be worked, handled, taken apart or put back together.

</td>
<td>

ESFP

Outgoing, easygoing, accepting, friendly, fond of a good time. Like sports and making things. Know what's going on and join in eagerly. Find remembering facts easier than mastering theories. Are best in situations that need sound common sense and practical ability with people as well as with things.

</td>
<td>

ENFP

Warmly enthusiastic, high-spirited, ingenious, imaginative. Able to do almost anything that interests them. Quick with a solution for any difficulty and ready to help anyone with a problem. Often rely on their ability to improvise instead of preparing in advance. Can always find compelling reasons for whatever they want.

</td>
<td>

ENTP

Quick, ingenious, good at many things. Stimulating company, alert and outspoken, argue for fun on either side of a question. Resourceful in solving new and challenging problems, but may neglect routine assignments. Turn to one new interest after another. Can always find logical reasons for whatever they want.

</td>
<td style="writing-mode:vertical-lr">PERCEPTIVE</td>
<td rowspan="2" style="writing-mode:vertical-lr">EXTRAVERTS</td>
</tr>
<tr>
<td style="writing-mode:vertical-lr">JUDGING</td>
<td>

ESTJ

Practical realists, matter-of-fact, with a natural head for business or mechanics. Not interested in subjects they see no use for, but can apply themselves when necessary. Like to organize and run activities. Tend to run things well, especially if they remember to consider other people's feelings and points of view when making their decisions.

</td>
<td>

ESFJ

Warm-hearted, talkative, popular, conscientious, born cooperators, active committee members. Always doing something nice for someone. Work best with plenty of encouragement and praise. Little interest in abstract thinking or technical subjects. Main interest is in things that directly and visibly affect people's lives.

</td>
<td>

ENFJ

Responsive and responsible. Feel real concern for what others think and want, and try to handle things with due regard for other people's feelings. Can present a proposal or lead a group discussion with ease and tact. Sociable, popular, active in school affairs, but put time enough on their studies to do good work.

</td>
<td>

ENTJ

Hearty, frank, able in studies, leaders in activities. Usually good in anything that requires reasoning and intelligent talk, such as public speaking. Are well-informed and keep adding to their fund of knowledge. May sometimes be more positive and confident than their experience in an area warrants.

</td>
<td style="writing-mode:vertical-lr">JUDGING</td>
</tr>
</table>

"Effects of the Combinations of All Four Preferences in Young People," pp. A-7, A-8, *People Types and Tiger Stripes: A Practical Guide to Learning Styles* by Gordon Lawrence, published by Center for the Application of Psychological Type, Inc. Gainesville, Florida, 1982.

JOURNAL

NAME _____

DATE _____

What are your learning styles? (Auditory, visual, or kinesthetic? Introvert/
Extrovert, Sensing/Intuitive, Thinking/Feeling, Judging/Perceiving?)

....

....

....

....

....

How are you trying to adapt your style to the teaching styles of some of your instructors and academic
advisors?

....

....

....

....

....

Do you tend to associate outside of class with people whose learning styles are different from yours?
What types do they tend to be? (You can use the Resource Page in this chapter to chart the types of your
friends and instructors.) This process may help you uncover some clues about compatibility between
you and some of the significant people in your life, both in short-term and long-term relationships.

....

....

....

....

....

How can you use your understanding of type to deal with differences and tensions you encounter with
friends or other students? Think of a specific situation, and consider how you might use an understanding of learning styles to resolve a problem.

....

....

....

....

....

CHAPTER 5

Listening and Learning in the Classroom

Donald W. Jugenheimer
Southern Illinois University at Carbondale

I was really trying to listen in history class this morning. But then there was this crash of thunder outside, and somehow that broke my train of thought. Now my notes don't make sense, and I really thought I was listening for those main points. Guess I just wasn't listening hard enough.

This chapter will help you turn the following keys to success:

6. **Assess and improve your study habits.**

9. **Develop critical thinking skills.**

10. **Choose instructors who involve you in the learning process.**

Chapter Goals

After reading this chapter, you should be able to

- *understand the importance of listening.*
- *know how to sharpen your listening powers.*
- *realize how to convert good listening into good learning.*
- *improve your note-taking skills in class and while reading and studying.*
- *learn how to use your notes more effectively.*
- *learn what to do before, during, and after class to improve your study habits.*

In virtually every college class you take, you'll need to master two skills to earn high grades: listening and note-taking. What's more, taking an active role in your classes—asking questions, contributing to discussions, or providing answers—will help you listen better and take more meaningful notes, and that in turn will enhance your ability to abstract ideas, find new possibilities, organize those ideas, and recall the material once the class is over.

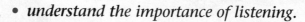

EXERCISE 5.1   **Your Note-Taking IQ**

Mark each of the following statements either T (true) or F (false).

_____ 1. If you can't tell what is really important in a lecture, you should write down everything the instructor says.

_____ 2. If an instructor moves through the material very fast, it is better to tape record the lecture and not worry so much about listening in class.

_____ 3. If the instructor puts an outline on the board or on an overhead projector, you should copy it down immediately.

_____ 4. In a class that is mainly discussion, it is best just to listen and talk rather than to take notes.

_____ 5. The best way to take notes is to use a formal outlining system with Roman numerals, letters, and numbers.

The correct answers are given at the bottom of page 91. Discuss the answers with your instructor or in small groups.

Why are listening and note-taking so critical to your academic success? Why can't you just review the textbook in preparation for quizzes and exams? Because in college, your instructors are likely to introduce new material in class that your texts don't cover, and chances are that much of this material will resurface on quizzes and exams. So, pay attention to the suggestions in this chapter, practice them regularly, and watch your grades improve.

◼LISTENING AND FORGETTING

Ever notice how easy it is to learn the words of a song? Yet you may read a few pages of a book several times or hear a lecture and find it difficult to retain the important ideas and concepts after a few hours. We remember songs and poetry more easily because they are set to a **rhythm and a beat. We remember** prose less easily and, because it is the most unstructured form of communication, we can hardly remember gibberish or nonsense words at all.

As a result, you may sometimes labor over class notes that are only a few weeks old, trying to figure out exactly what they mean and what the central idea is. That's because most forgetting takes place **within the first 24 hours** after you see or hear something. In two weeks, you will have forgotten up to 70 percent of the material!

Forgetting can be a real problem when you are expected to learn and remember a mass of different facts, figures, concepts, and relationships. Once you understand how to improve your ability to remember, you will be able to retain information more easily and completely. At the same time, by learning to listen better and concentrating more on the material in the first place, you can remember facts and concepts longer and relate other information to things you already remember. (See Figure 5.1.)

Because many instructors draw the bulk of their test items from the content of their lectures, remembering what is presented in class is crucial to doing well on exams. A system that diminishes the forgetting curve and organizes information for later recall can greatly improve your chances for success in college.

Figure 5.1 Learning and Forgetting

Psychologists have studied human forgetting in many laboratory experiments. Here are the "forgetting curves" for three kinds of material: poetry, prose, and nonsense syllables. The curves are basically similar. The shallower curves for prose and poetry indicate that meaningful material is forgotten more slowly than nonmeaningful information. Poetry, which contains internal cues such as rhyme and rhythm, is forgotten less quickly than prose.

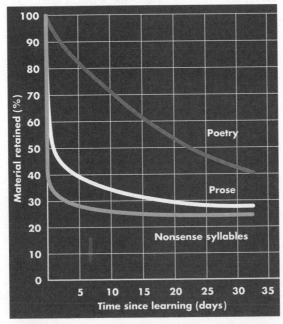

SOURCE: *Used with permission from Wayne Weiten,* Psychology: Themes and Variations *(Pacific Grove, Calif.: Brooks/Cole, 1989, p. 254. Based on data from D. van Guilford, Van Nostrand, 1939).*

The following system will also help you understand concepts and ideas better and relate certain information to other things you already know. It consists of three major parts: preparing to listen before class, listening and taking notes during class, and reviewing and recalling information after class.

■ BEFORE CLASS: PREPARE TO REMEMBER

Even if lectures don't allow for active participation, you can do a number of things to make your listening and note-taking more efficient. Remember that your goals are improved learning in the classroom, a longer attention span, improved retention of information, and clear, well-organized notes to use when it's time to study for exams.

Since many lectures are demanding intellectual encounters, you need to be intellectually prepared before class begins. You would never walk in "cold" to give a speech, interview for a job, plead a case in court, or compete in sports. For each of these situations, you would prepare in some way. For the same reasons, active listening, learning, and remembering begin before the lecture.

1. **Do the assigned reading.** Many students blame lecturers for seeming disorganized and confusing, when in fact the student has not done the assigned reading. Some instructors explicitly assign readings for each class session and refer to them frequently; others may hand out a syllabus and assume you are keeping up with the assigned readings. Either way, completing the assigned readings on time will help you listen better, and active listening in turn promotes good reading.

2. **Warm up for class.** If you have read well and taken good notes, this should be easy. Warm up by referring to the underlined sections in your text as well as the recall columns (see page 88) in your previous classroom notes. This action prepares you to pay attention, understand, and remember.

3. **Keep an open mind.** Don't assume that you already know what is going to be said or that you already know this topic. In almost every situation, you can discover new information and uncover different perspectives.

■ DURING CLASS

Remember that listening in class is not like listening to a TV program, listening to a friend, or even listening to a speaker at a meeting. The difference, of course, is that what is said in class is vital to your success in that class. Knowing how to listen can help you get more out of what you hear, understand better what you have heard, and save you time in the process.

Listen for Information

1. **Be ready for the message.** Prepare yourself to hear, to listen, and to receive the message.

2. **Listen to the main concepts and central ideas,** not just to fragmented facts and figures. Although facts are important, they will be eas-

Photo by David Gonzales

You'll get more out of a lecture if you prepare ahead of time. Stay abreast of the readings. Get your own ideas flowing by reviewing notes from the previous lecture. What questions were left unanswered? Where should today's session begin?

ier to remember and make more sense when you can place them in a context of concepts, themes, and ideas.

3. **Listen for new ideas.** Even if you are an expert on the topic, you can still learn something new. Assuming you have "already heard all this before" means that your mind will be closed to any new information.

4. **Really hear what is said.** Hearing "sounds" is not the same as hearing the intended message. Listening involves hearing what the speaker wants you to receive, to understand, and to learn. Don't give in to distractions, such as daydreaming or looking at other students. And try not to judge what is being said because this will distract you, too.

5. **Repeat mentally.** Words that you hear can go in one ear and out the other unless you make an effort to retain them. Think about what you hear and make an active effort to retain it by repeating it silently to yourself.

6. **Think.** Decide whether what you have heard is important. Reflect on the new information. Think about it intently.

7. **Ask questions.** If you did not hear or understand what was said, raise your hand! Now is the time to clarify things. Typically, one student will ask a question that many students in the room are wondering about. Why not be the one to ask for the rest? If you can't hear another student's question, ask that the question be repeated.

8. **Listen to the entire message.** Try to avoid agreeing or disagreeing with the speaker based only on the opening of the lecture. Then wait to evaluate. Pausing will permit you to consider your reactions and responses rationally and intelligently.

9. **Respect yourself.** You already know a lot of things. Your own thoughts and ideas are valuable, and you need not throw them out just because someone else's views conflict with your own. (At the same time, you should not reject the ideas of others too casually, either.)

10. **Sort, organize, and categorize.** When you listen, try to match what you are hearing with your previous knowledge. Take an active role in deciding how you want to recall what you are learning.

Internet

Activity 5.1
Study Skills Guides on the Internet

The Internet can be a major source of study-skills and self-help materials. Handouts prepared by many college centers are available on-line. Check out the following:

- The CalREN Project, a series of tips and exercises to help develop better study strategies and habits.
  http://128.32.89.153/CalRENHP.html

- College of Saint Benedict and Saint John's University Study Skills Guides.
  http://www.csbsju.edu/advising/helplist.html

- Dartmouth Study Skills Guide Menu.
  http://www.dartmouth.edu/admin/acskills/index.html#study

- Study Tips—a collection of some of the handouts used in the University of Texas at Austin, Learning Skills Center.
  http://www.utexas.edu/student/lsc/handouts/stutips.html

- Virginia Polytechnic Institute Study Skills Self-Help Information.
  http://www.ucc.vt.edu/stdysk/stdyhlp.html

- University of Minnesota Duluth Study Strategies Homepage.
  http://www.d.umn.edu/student/loon/acad/strat/study_strat_enr.html

What information did you find that you will be able to use?

_____

_____

_____

_____

_____

_____

EXERCISE 5.2 Participating in Classroom Thinking

How much do your classes require or encourage you to develop the four general critical thinking skills? The answer will vary with the teaching ability of your instructor and with how much preparation you yourself bring to class. It may also vary according to the size and format of the class. Yet even in a lecture with many students, a talented teacher can stimulate your ability to form abstractions, think creatively, think systematically, and communicate well.

Consider several courses you are taking now. In a group, discuss the following issues.

A Compare your classroom experiences with different instructors.

Forming Abstractions

Do they expect or encourage students to raise questions?

Do they present evidence and challenge you to interpret it?

Do they challenge class members to restate or paraphrase the main idea of a lecture?

Creative Thinking

Do they help you practice looking at several sides of an issue?

Do they ask for your ideas on an issue?

Do they ask you to keep an open mind on a question that you at first think has an obvious right answer?

Do they use brainstorming strategies in which ideas can be generated without being prejudged?

Systematic Thinking

Do they give you practice in following a careful line of reasoning?

Do they ask you to fill in the missing steps in an argument?

Do they ask you to judge whether an idea is adequately supported by logic or data?

Communication

Do they have a process for encouraging students to speak—even shy students?

Do they ask a member of the class to clarify a point for the benefit of other students?

B Compare your own participation in classes with that of other students.

Forming Abstractions

Have you asked an instructor to clarify the main idea of a lecture or discussion?

Have you asked other questions about a lecture or the reading?

Have you volunteered to answer a question posed by the instructor?

Have you gotten lost or confused in a lecture? What did you do to get back on track?

Creative Thinking

Have you volunteered an idea?

Have you made an effort to keep an open mind about something about which you already had a strong opinion?

Have you participated in a group or classroom brainstorming effort?

Systematic Thinking

Have you outlined in your notes the general argument that an instructor is making in class?

Have you asked a question when you were uncertain about the reasoning behind an argument that is made in the lecture or in the reading?

Communication

Have you talked with the instructor before or after class or during office hours?

Have you discussed ideas from the course or asked questions of other students in the class?

C Use the goal-setting process in Chapter 1 to expand your critical thinking participation in at least one of your classes. If something makes it hard for you to participate in class, make an office appointment to talk with your instructor or a counselor about the problem.

Take Effective Notes

Now that you are listening effectively, you can make class time as productive as possible by using your listening skills to take effective notes. Here's how:

1. Identify the main ideas. Good lectures always contain certain key points. The first principle of effective note-taking is to identify and write down the most important ideas (usually four or five) around which the lecture is built. Although supporting details are important as well, focus your note-taking on the main ideas. These main ideas may be buried in details, statistics, anecdotes, or problems to be solved, but you need to locate and record them for further study.

Instructors sometimes announce the purpose of a lecture or offer an outline, thus providing you with the skeleton of main ideas, followed by the details. Some lecturers change their tone of voice or repeat themselves at each key idea. Some ask questions or promote discussion. These are all clues to what is important. If a lecturer says something three times, it is probably essential information! Ask yourself, "What does my instructor want me to know at the end of today's session?"

You certainly don't need to write down everything. Because of insecurity or inexperience, some first-year students try to do just that. They stop being thinkers and become stenographers. Learn to avoid that trap. If you're an active listener, always searching for the main ideas and the connections between them, you will ultimately have shorter but better notes.

As you take notes, leave some space so that you can fill in additional details later that you might have missed during class. But remember to do it as soon after class as possible; remember the forgetting curve!

Unfortunately, some of your instructors may teach in a manner that makes it difficult to take good notes. You can still use the same techniques, however, to organize the lectures for your own use. Even though some of your teachers may not teach as you would like them to, you are still ultimately responsible for making sense of what they say.

When a lecture is disorganized, you need to try to organize what is said into general and specific frameworks, and, when this order is not apparent, you need to take notes on where the gaps lie in the lecture's structure. After the lecture, you may need to consult your reading material or classmates to try to fill in these gaps.

You might also consult your instructor. Most instructors have regular office hours when they are available to meet students, yet it is amazing how few students use these opportunities for one-on-one instruction. You can also raise questions in class; if something is not clear to you, chances are that others are also puzzled. Asking such questions may help your instructor discover which parts of his or her presentation need more attention and clarification.

2. Leave space for a recall column. This is a critical part of effective note-taking. In addition to helping you listen well, your notes become an important study device for tests and examinations. In anticipation of using your notes later, treat each page of your notes as part of an exam-preparation system.

Here's how to create a recall column. Using one side of the paper only, draw a vertical line to divide the page into two columns (see Figure 5.2 on page 91). The column on the left, about 2 to 3 inches wide, is called the "recall column," and it remains blank while you are taking notes during class in the wider

A good lecture is an exploration. As part of the expedition, think critically about the direction of a teacher's thought. Try to predict where the lecture is heading and why. What are the major landmarks and key ideas along the way?

column on the right. The recall column is essentially the place where, as you sift through your note materials after class, you highlight the main ideas and important details. Completing the blank recall column, you will discover, is a powerful study device that reduces forgetting, helps you warm up for class, and promotes understanding in class. It also lets you review efficiently right after class.

Computer Notes in Class?

More and more students bring laptop computers to class. Laptops are often poor tools for note-taking. Computer screens are not conducive to making marginal notes, circling important items, or copying diagrams. And, although most students can scribble coherently without watching their hands, few are really good keyboarders. Finally, notes on a computer are often harder to access or scan when it comes time to review.

Entering notes onto a computer can provide an opportunity to review and reflect on your notes after class. On the other hand, if you enter them verbatim, you may be simply wasting time that could be spent more productively.

AFTER CLASS

Remember and Respond

Relate new information to other things you already know. Tie together similar kinds of information. Fit new facts into your total system of knowledge. Make a conscious effort to remember. One way is to repeat important data to yourself every few minutes. Another approach is to tie one idea to another idea, concept, or name, so that thinking of one will prompt recall of the other.

Often, the best way to learn something is to teach it to someone else. You will understand something better and remember it longer if you try to explain it. This process helps you discover your own reactions and uncover gaps in your comprehension of the material. (Asking and answering questions in class also provides you with the feedback you need to make certain your understanding is accurate.)

Before the next class, get ready to listen again. Listening is an ongoing activity. It does not start and stop. You have already learned how to prepare yourself to listen well. You must maintain that readiness so that you are prepared to listen daily.

EXERCISE 5.3 Using Critical Thinking to Determine Main Ideas and Major Details

Divide a piece of paper as shown in Figure 5.2. Read the following excerpt from a psychology lecture on memory. Take notes on the right side of the paper, leaving the recall column blank. When you are done, use the critical thinking process to abstract the main ideas and write them in the recall column. Think about those ideas and jot down in the same recall column any thoughts, or possibilities, that occur to you. For example, your possibilities may include, "I wonder what I can attach this information about memory to so I can recall it later?" Or, "Maybe if I break my American lit notes into small chunks, I'll recall them easier."

> Today we will continue our discussion of memory and treat the idea of distributed practice—an important aspect of memory. This is the practice of learning a little bit at a time, as opposed to a lot at a time. Cramming for a test is an example of the opposite kind of practice known as massed practice. Distributed practice is what you need to develop as you study for your classes.
>
> Further, what you learn tends to be remembered easily if you can attach it to similar knowledge. This is the third term I want to discuss today—the depth-of-processing principle. That is, information is stored in the brain on various levels. If it is stored superficially, the material cannot attach itself to rich associations. If it is stored deeply, the knowledge finds a series of associations to attach itself to. Storing material deeply allows for retention of it, while, as you would guess, storing superficially tends to lead to forgetting.

Fill in the Recall Column, Recite, and Review

Don't let the forgetting curve take its toll on you! As soon after class as possible, review your notes and fill in the details you still remember, but missed writing down, in those spaces you left in the right-hand column. Then it's time to go through three important steps for remembering the key points in the lecture.

Figure 5.2 Sample Lecture Notes

Recall Column	Take Notes Here
Sept. 21 How to take notes	
Problems with lectures	Lecture not best way to teach. Problems: Short attention span (may be only 15 minutes!). Teacher dominates. Most info is forgotten. "Stenographer" role interferes with thinking, understanding, learning.
Forgetting curves	Forgetting curves critical period: over ½ of lecture forgotten in 24 hours.
Solution: Active listening	Answer: Active listening, really understanding during lecture. Aims— (1) immediate understanding, (2) longer attention, (3) better retention, (4) notes for study later
Before: Read Warm up	BEFORE: Always prepare. Read: Readings parallel lectures & make them meaningful. Warm up: Review last lecture notes & readings right before class.
During: main ideas	DURING: Write main ideas & some detail. No stems. What clues does prof give about what's most important? Ask. Ask other questions. Leave blank column about 2½" on left of page. Use only front side of paper.
After: Review Recall Recite	AFTER: Left column for key recall words "tags." Cover right side & recite what tags mean. Review/Recall/Recite

Answers to Exercise 5.1: All statements are false.

1. Write the main ideas in the recall column. For 5 or 10 minutes, quickly review your notes and select key words or phrases that will act as labels or tags for main ideas and key information covered in the notes. Highlight the main ideas and write them in the recall column next to the material they represent.

2. Use the recall column to recite your ideas. Cover the notes on the right and use the prompts from the recall column to help you recite *out loud* a brief version of what you understand from the class you have just participated in. If you don't have a few minutes after class to review your notes, find some other time during that day to review what you have written. You might also want to ask your teacher to glance at your recall column to determine whether you have noted the major ideas.

3. Review the previous day's notes just before the next class session. As you sit in class the next day waiting for the lecture to begin, use the time to quickly review the notes from the previous day. This action will put you in tune with the lecture that is about to begin and also prompt you to ask questions about material from the previous lecture that may not have been clear to you. These three "engagements" with the material will pay off later, when you begin to study for your examinations.

EXERCISE 5.4 Using a Recall Column

Suppose the information in this chapter had been presented to you as a lecture rather than a reading. Using the system described previously, your lecture notes might look like those in Figure 5.2. Cover the right-hand column. Using the recall column, try reciting in your own words the main ideas from this chapter. Uncover the right-hand column when you need to refer to it. If you can phrase the main ideas from the recall column in your own words, you are well on your way to mastering this note-taking system for dealing with lectures. Does this system seem to work? If not, why not?

Why Is This Process So Powerful?

The key to this system is that you are encountering the same material through four different approaches: active listening, writing effective notes, reviewing and summarizing in the recall column, and reciting aloud what you understand from class. Your whole person, mind and body, is involved. All of these actions promote active learning and retention.

Recitation is a particularly effective way to avoid forgetting. The very act of speaking and listening to concepts gives your memory sufficient time to grasp them. You move material from short-term memory to long-term memory, where you can call upon it when you need it.

What if you have three classes in a row and no time for recall columns or recitation between them? You should recall and recite as soon after class as possible. Review the most recent class first. Never delay recall and recitation longer than one day: it will then take you longer to review, make a recall column, and recite. With practice, you can complete your recall column in only a few moments, perhaps between classes or while eating lunch or riding a bus. Recitation will only take a few more minutes. If you recall and recite faithfully, you will find these processes to be great aides to understanding and remembering.

MORE ON NOTE-TAKING

Tips for Using Your Notes

1. **Find a note-taking format that works for you and follow it consistently.** If you switch from one format to another, even though you are dealing with different kinds of material, you will be more confused and may spend more time writing notes than listening for what is important.

2. **Leave some blank space in your notes.** This will allow you to add additional material later, to provide your own explanations and to recreate your outline if you find the instructor repeats an idea or example that helps you understand earlier material.

3. **Take notes in a style that is best for you.** Many good students purposely take their notes in pen so they cannot erase but can still make easy corrections during classes: drawing lines to connect various ideas, scratching out incorrect statements, adding supplemental material in the spaces left in notes, highlighting with a colored marker, underlining, using stars to identify important points, and so forth.

EXERCISE 5.5 / Apply an Active Listening and Learning System

Examine the study schedule on page 50 in Chapter 3, and then answer the following questions:

1. Where do you see evidence of plans to use the recall column?

   _____

   _____

   _____

2. What problems might you have in performing review/recall/recite as soon after class as possible?

   _____

   _____

   _____

3. How might these problems be addressed and solved?

   _____

   _____

   _____

   Share your answers with other students in a small group.

Taking Notes in Nonlecture Courses

Sometimes you must be flexible about how you take notes. Many classes are not in lecture format, but instead may be question–answer sessions, group

# Kinds of Notes

1. **Outline notes are the most widely used.** Try to determine the instructor's "outline" and recreate it in your notes. Supplement it with details, definitions, examples, applications, and explanations. Be careful not to confuse the supporting information with the main points. The main points are the major divisions of the course, of the day's lecture, or of the overall topic. The next level should follow the logical divisions of the main topics. Then you can add the more detailed explanatory material in successive levels.

2. **Definitional notes work in some, but not all, courses.** Using this method, you enter the major terms on the left edge of the page. Then place all material for that term—definitions, explanations, examples, and supporting evidence—beside and under it.

3. **Paragraph notes work for some people and in some situations.** These comprehensive paragraphs contain a summary of an entire topic. This approach may work better for you in summarizing what you have read rather than for class notes, where it may be difficult to summarize the topic until it has been covered completely, by which time it may be too late to recall some of the critical information.

4. **Fact notes include only important items,** usually the more critical facts from the lecture or discussion. The major problem with this note-taking method is trying to organize the facts into meaningful groups. Too often they wind up as a collection of terms with little organization, reason, or rationale.

Keep in mind that you can also take notes on your notes. It is often helpful to go back through your course notes, reorganize your thoughts, highlight the essential items, and then write new notes. You will find the revised notes are easier to follow and understand, which will aid your ability to remember them.

discussions, workshops, laboratories, seminars, and so forth. So always be ready to adapt your note-taking methods to match the situation. In fact, group discussion is becoming a popular way to teach in college, replacing the traditional lecture, because it involves active participation, which usually leads to better learning. In discussion groups, you still must keep in mind the two basic types of information transmitted, general and specific.

Assume you are taking notes in a problem-solving group assignment. You would begin your notes by asking yourself the question, "What is the problem?" and writing down the answer. As the discussion progresses, you would list the solutions offered. These would be main ideas. The important details might include the positive and negative aspects of each view or solution.

The important thing to remember when taking notes in nonlecture courses is that you need to record the information presented by your classmates as well as from the instructor. You must be sure to consider all reasonable ideas, even though they may differ from your own.

Sometimes a course will have both lecture and discussion elements. You will need to make certain how the discussion elements augment and correlate with the lectures. If different material is covered in each section, ask for guidance in organizing your notes. If similar topics are covered, be sure to combine your notes so that you have comprehensive coverage of each topic.

In a class discussion, begin your notes by stating the aspects of each issue addressed. You can then divide your notes into comments in favor of and against the issue at hand. Details would include reasons for supporting each perspective or argument. It is important that you record all reasonable arguments, but not every offhand remark. Even if you do not agree with others, you need to understand their views and rationale, and your teacher may ask you to defend your own opinions in light of the others.

Comparing Notes

You may be able to improve how you use your notes by comparing notes with another student. See whether your notes are as clear and concise as the other person's and whether you both find the same important points. Share how you take and organize your notes with one another.

If you use the recall column in your notes, share notes after class and take turns reciting to each other what you have learned.

When you know that you are going to compare notes, you will tend to take better notes. Knowing that your notes will be seen by someone else will prompt you to make your notes well-organized, clear, and accurate.

Incidentally, comparing notes is not the same as copying somebody else's notes. You simply cannot get the course material from someone else's notes, no matter how good they are. If you have not heard the original lecture and discussion, have not experienced the same examples, and have not learned the same details, you will not have the background information to make the notes complete and meaningful. The most sensible way to get through college is to go to class every day. If you must miss because of illness or other legitimate reasons, talk with the instructor as soon as you can. Maybe you can use the instructor's notes or at least get the lecture outline. Certainly you can ask for any handouts or assignments that were given in class. But never assume that you can replicate a class by copying someone else's notes. If you do, chances are you will wind up confused and perform poorly.

EXERCISE 5.6 ## Comparing Notes

Pair up with another student and compare your class notes for this course. Are your notes clear? Do you agree on what is important? Take a few minutes to explain to each other your note-taking systems. Agree to use a recall column during the next class meeting. Afterward, share your notes again and check on how each of you used the recall column. And again, compare your notes and what each of you deemed important.

Using Notes in Your Homework

No matter what subject you are studying, good class notes can help you with your homework. Too many times, we think that homework assignments are separate and distinct from class lectures and discussions, but they usually complement one another. Following these steps will help ensure that you successfully complete your homework assignments.

1. **Take 10 minutes to review your notes.** Skim the notes and put a question mark next to anything you do not understand at first reading. Put stars next to topics that warrant special emphasis. Try to place the material in context: What has been going on in the course for the last few weeks? How does today's class fit in?

2. **Do a warm-up for your homework.** Before doing the assignment, look through your notes again. Use a separate sheet of paper to rework examples, problems, or exercises. Now read through the assigned material in the textbook. Go back to the examples, one at a time. Cover the solution, and attempt to answer each question or complete each problem on your own. Look at the author's work only after you have made a serious personal effort.

3. **Do any assigned problems and answer any assigned questions.** Now you are actually starting on your homework. As you read each question or problem, ask: "What am I supposed to find or find out?" "What is essential and what is extraneous?" Read the problem several times and state it in your own words. The last sentence may be where you will find the essential question or answer.

4. **Persevere.** Don't give up too soon. When you encounter a problem or question that you cannot readily handle, move on only after a reasonable effort. After you have completed the entire assignment, come back to those items that stumped you. Try once more, then take a break or work on another subject. You may need to mull over a particularly difficult problem for several days. Think about the problem at odd moments. Let your unconscious mind have a chance, too, by not concentrating on that problem all the time. Inspiration may come when you are waiting for a stoplight or just before you fall asleep.

5. **Complete your work.** When you finish an assignment, talk to yourself about what you learned from this particular assignment. Generalize about how the problems and questions were different from one another, which strategies were successful, and what form the answers took.

You may be thinking, "That all sounds good, but who has the time to do all that extra work?" In reality, this approach does work and actually helps save you time. Try it for a few weeks. You will find that you can diminish the frustration that comes when you tackle your homework "cold."

SUGGESTIONS FOR FURTHER READING

Pauk, Walter. *How to Study in College,* 6th ed. Boston: Houghton Mifflin, 1997. See Chapter 9, "Listening to Take Good Notes," and Chapter 10, "Taking Good Notes."

Schumm, Jeanne S., and Post, Shawn A. *Executive Learning: Successful Strategies for College Reading and Studying.* Upper Saddle River, NJ: Prentice Hall, 1997.

Wolff, Florence I., and Marsnik, Nadine C. *Perceptive Listening,* 2nd ed. Orlando: Harcourt Brace Jovanovich, 1992.

RESOURCES

Throughout the book, we've mentioned the helpfulness of study groups for your success in college. Use this resource page to list names, numbers, and meeting times for the study groups you are in. Keep the list handy, especially close to test time.

Study Group _____ meets _____

Name	Phone number	e-mail

Study Group _____ meets _____

Name	Phone number	e-mail

Study Group _____ meets _____

Name	Phone number	e-mail

Library Hours

Library	Regular hours	Hours during finals	Phone number

JOURNAL

NAME _____

DATE _____

Try at least three approaches to taking notes, either from approaches discussed in this chapter or that you develop on your own. Which methods seem to work best with which subjects? (Remember the different learning styles from Chapter 4.)

....

....

....

....

....

How does your learning style affect your listening (that is, what you listen for)? How can you use this information to listen more actively and effectively?

....

....

....

....

....

How might your note-taking be altered to match the needs of a particular course? How might it be fine-tuned to match the presentation approaches of a particular instructor?

....

....

....

....

....

How might you improve your note-taking and study habits by working with a study group?

....

....

....

....

What would it take to form such a group, and how would you begin working together?

....

....

....

....

CHAPTER

Reading Textbooks for Clarity and Understanding

Mary Walz-Chojnacki

Johanna Dvorak
University of Wisconsin—Milwaukee

I've read this paragraph five times and I still don't understand it. How am I supposed to be ready to discuss this chapter tomorrow when I can't even get through the first page? There's gotta be a better way. Can't someone just drill a hole in my head and pour it in?

This chapter will help you turn the following keys to success:

6. **Assess and improve your study habits.**

7. **Join at least one study group.**

9. **Develop critical thinking skills.**

Chapter Goals   *After reading this chapter, you should be able to*

- *know how to use a reading method that promotes concentration and comprehension.*

- *learn the basic reading steps of overviewing, reading, marking, monitoring, and reviewing.*

- *understand how to prepare to read.*

- *improve your concentration and understanding.*

- *understand the process of study reading your textbooks.*

- *become more proficient in marking your textbook.*

- *develop a method for recycling your study reading.*

- *learn the advantages of monitoring and reviewing.*

- *develop a talent for maintaining flexibility.*

- *develop and broaden your vocabulary*

■ PREPARING TO READ

Reading college textbooks is a more challenging activity than reading high school texts or general interest books. College texts are loaded with new concepts and terms that you are expected to learn on your own in a short period of time. These demands on your time and your reading skills require that you use a study reading method such as the one presented in this chapter.

EXERCISE 6.1   Evaluating Your Reading Strengths and Weaknesses

Before you read further, it's a good idea to consider your "study reading" strengths and weaknesses. Answer the questions in this self-report inventory to assess your college reading skills.

1. Do you overview your chapter before you begin to read?

   Yes _____   No _____

2. Do you often lose concentration while reading your texts?

   Yes _____   No _____

3. Do you highlight or mark your text *after* you read?

   Yes _____   No _____

4. Do you take notes *after* you read?

   Yes _____   No _____

5. Do you pause at the end of each section or page to note what you have read?

   Yes _____   No _____

6. Do you have different reading styles depending on your purpose for reading?

   Yes _____   No _____

7. Do you recite key ideas to yourself or with a partner?

   Yes _____   No _____

8. Do you review what you have read at least once a week?

   Yes _____   No _____

A "yes" to any question, except 2, indicates a strength. A "no" indicates an area of weakness. Look for strategies that will improve your concentration and your comprehension as you study this chapter.

The following plan for study reading will increase your focus and concentration, promote your understanding, and prepare you to study for tests and exams. The system is based on four steps: overviewing, reading, marking, and reviewing.

■ OVERVIEWING

Overviewing is an important first step in preparing to read. Begin by reading the title of the chapter. Ask yourself, "What do I already know about this subject?" Next, quickly read through the introductory paragraphs and then turn to the end of the chapter and read the summary paragraphs. Then take a few minutes to page through the chapter headings and subheadings. Note if there are any study exercises at the end of the chapter. As part of your overview, note how many pages the chapter contains. (It is a good idea to decide how many pages you will cover in your first 50-minute study period before you begin to *actively* read. This strategy helps build your concentration and develop a purpose for reading.)

Mapping

Mapping the chapter as you overview it will give you a visual guide of how the different chapter ideas fit together. About 75 percent of students identify themselves as visual learners; mapping is an excellent way to create a visual learning tool that will be useful for test preparation as well as active reading. How do you map a chapter? While you are in the process of overviewing, use either a wheel or branching mapping structure (see the examples in Figure 6.1). In the wheel structure, you should place the central idea of the chapter in the circle, place secondary ideas on the spokes emanating from the circle, and offshoots of those ideas on the lines attached to the spokes. In the branching map, the main idea goes at the top, followed by supporting ideas on the second tier, and so forth. Fill in the title first. Then as you skim

Figure 6.1 Wheel and Branching Maps

Wheel Map

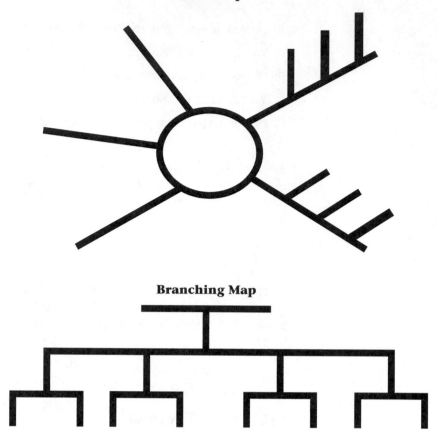

Branching Map

through the rest of the chapter, use the headings and subheadings to fill in the key ideas on the type of map you have chosen.

This active learning step may require more time up front, but you will save time later because you have created an excellent review tool to use when you prepare for quizzes and tests. Also, you will be using your visual learning mode as well as creating "advance organizers" to help you associate details of the chapter with the larger ideas. These associations will be essential for later recall.

As you overview the text material, look for connections between the text and the related lecture material. Call to mind the related terms and concepts that you recorded in lecture. Use these strategies to warm up and create a plan for reading. Ask yourself, "Why am I reading this?" and "What do I want to know?"

EXERCISE 6.2 **Overviewing and Creating a Visual Map**

Overview this chapter and create a visual map, noting the following information: title, key points from the introduction, any graphics (maps, charts, tables, diagrams), study questions or exercises built into or at the end of the chapter, introduction and summary paragraphs. Fill in either the wheel or branching maps in Figure 6.1. (Add spokes or tiers as necessary.)

■ READING YOUR TEXTBOOK

After you have completed your overview, you are ready to actively read the text. Having created a "skeleton" cognitive map or outline, you now will be able to read the text more quickly and with greater comprehension. Read the first section of the text, up to the next heading or subheading, and then stop. To avoid overmarking or marking the wrong information, read first without using your pencil or highlighter. When you have reached the end of a section, ask yourself, "What are the key ideas in this section?" and "What do I think I'll see on the test?" Then, and only then, decide what to mark.

Building Concentration and Understanding

Two common problems that students report are their lack of concentration and their inability to understand what they are reading. They often feel unable to complete reading assignments and become frustrated when they don't understand the material. Many factors may affect one's ability to concentrate and understand the texts. These factors can vary a great deal, depending on such things as the time of day, one's interest in the material, and one's study location.

Consider these suggestions for promoting optimal concentration or "flow," and decide which of these would work for you to increase your reading focus:

- Find a study location, preferably in the library, that is removed from traffic and distracting noises.
- Read in 50-minute blocks of time, with short breaks between. By reading more frequently during the day, in 50-minute blocks, instead of cramming all your reading in at the end of the day, you should be able to process material more easily.
- Set goals for your study period, such as, "I will read 20 pages of my psychology text in the next 50 minutes." Reward yourself with a 10-minute study break after each 50-minute study period.
- If you are having trouble concentrating or staying awake, take a quick walk around the library or down the hall. Take some deep breaths and talk to yourself positively about your study goals.
- To keep your focus, use study questions in the margin, take notes, or recite the key ideas. Reread confusing parts of the text and make a note to ask your instructor for clarification.
- Experiment with your reading rate. Try to move your eyes more quickly over the material by focusing on a phrase at a time.
- Focus on the high-yield portions of the text: pay attention to the first and last sentences of paragraphs and to words in italics or bold print.
- Use the glossary in the text to define unfamiliar terms.

■ MARKING YOUR TEXTBOOK

Think for a moment about your goals for marking in your texts. Some students report that marking is an active reading strategy that helps them focus and concentrate on the material as they read. In addition, most students expect to use their text notations when studying for tests. To meet these goals, some students like to underline, some light to highlight, and others like to use margin notes. Look at Figure 6.2 for examples of different methods of marking. You can also combine methods.

Figure 6.2 Sample Marked Pages

IMPROVEMENT, LOSS, AND DISTORTION OF MEMORY

How improve memory?

How can we improve memory?
Why do we sometimes forget?
Why do we sometimes think we remember something, when in fact we are wrong?

At one point while I was doing the research for this book, I went to find an article that I remembered reading, which I thought would very nicely illustrate a particular point I wanted to make. I was pretty sure I remembered the author, the name of the journal, and the date of the article within a year. So I was certain it would not take me long to find the article.

About four hours later I finally located it. I was right about the author, but I was wrong about the journal and the year. Worst of all, I discovered that the results the article reported were quite different from what I remembered. (The way I *remembered* the results made a lot more sense than the *actual* results!)

Why does my memory—and probably yours as well—make mistakes like this? And is there any way to improve memory?

IMPROVING MEMORY BY IMPROVING LEARNING

"I'm sorry. I don't remember your name. I just don't have a good memory for names." "I went to class regularly and did all the reading, but I couldn't remember all those facts when it came time for the test."

When people cannot remember names or facts, the reason is generally that they did not learn them very well in the first place. To improve your ability to remember something, be very careful about how you learn it.

Distribution of Practice

Distribution
- over time

You want to memorize a part for a play. Should you sit down and study your lines in one long marathon session until you know them? Or should you spread your study sessions over several days? Research indicates that **distributed practice**—that is, a little at a time over many days—is generally better than **massed practice**, the same number of repetitions over a short time. One reason is that it is hard to maintain full attention when you repeat the same thing over and over at one sitting. Another is that studying something at different times links it to a wider variety of associations.

Depth of Processing

Depth
- associations

Once again, how well you will remember something depends on how well you understood it when

"Alas! poor Yorick. I knew him, Horatio." Hamlet delivers some two dozen soliloquies (solo speeches) of hundreds of words each. (In comparison, the Gettysburg Address is 266 words.) Actors generally use distribution of practice to learn their parts, memorizing a little daily over weeks. They also associate their lines with emotional motivations, physical movements, cues from other actors, and their own memories to help them remember.

IMPROVEMENT, LOSS, AND DISTORTION OF MEMORY 295

SOURCE: Pages reproduced with permission from James W. Kalat, Introduction to Psychology, *2nd ed. Belmont, Calif.: Wadsworth, 1990.*

Figure 6.2 *(continued)*

you learned it and how much you thought about it at the time. According to the **depth-of-processing principle** (Craik & Lockhart, 1972), information may be stored at various levels, either superficially or deeply, depending on the number and type of associations formed with it.

Repetitions –shallow

At the most superficial level, a person merely focuses on the words and how they sound. If you try to memorize a list by simply repeating it over and over, you may recognize it when you see or hear it again, but you may have trouble recalling it (Greene, 1987). Actors and public speakers who have to memorize lengthy passages soon discover that mere repetition is an inefficient method.

Associations

A more efficient way to memorize is to deal actively with the material and to form associations with it. For example, you read a list of 20 words. At a slightly deeper level of processing than mere repetition, you might count the number of letters in each word, think of a rhyming word, or note whether the word contains the letter *e*. Such activities require a more active involvement on your part and establish more connections among the words on the list and other items in your experience. At a still deeper level of processing, you might consider the meaning of each word and try to think of a synonym for it. According to this theory (and according to many experimental results), the deeper the level of processing, the more you will remember. *(How can you use this principle to develop good study habits?)*

Deeper associations → meaning

The depth-of-processing principle resembles what happens when a librarian files a new book in the library. Simply to place the book somewhere on the shelves without recording its location would be a very low level of processing, and the librarian's chances of ever finding it again would be slight. So the librarian fills out file cards for the book and puts them into the card catalog. To fill out just a title card for the book would be an intermediate level of processing. To fill out several cards—one for title, one for author, and one or more for subject matter—would be a deeper level of processing. Someone who came to the library later looking for that book would have an excellent chance of finding it. Similarly, when you are trying to memorize something, the more "cards" you fill out (that is, the more ways you link it to other information), the greater your chances of finding the memory when you want it.

Association like multiple listings

You can improve your memorization of a list by attending to two types of processing that are largely independent of each other (Einstein & Hunt, 1980; McDaniel, Einstein, & Lollis, 1988). First, you can go through the list thinking about how much you like or dislike each item or trying to recall the

Remembering lists: two types of processing ① Each item

last time you had a personal experience with it. That will enhance your processing of *individual items.* Second, you can go through the list and look for relationships among the items. That will enhance your processing of the *organization* of the list. You might notice, for example, that the list you are trying to memorize consists of five animals, six foods, four methods of transportation, and five objects made of wood. Even sorting items into such simple categories as "words that apply to me" and "words that do not apply to me" will enhance your sense of how the list is organized and therefore your ability to recall it (Klein & Kihlstrom, 1986).

*② Relation- ships *organization*

Concept Check

4. Here are two arrangements of the same words:
a. Be a room age to the attend ball will over party across be there 18 you after wild in the class must.
b. There will be a wild party in the room across the ball after class; you must be over age 18 to attend. Why is it easier to remember b than a—because of processing of individual items or because of processing of organization? (Check your answer on page 312.)

Self-Monitoring of Reading Comprehension

What is the difference between good readers (those who remember what they read) and poor readers (those who do not)? One difference is that good readers process what they read more deeply. But how do readers know when they have processed deeply enough? How do they know whether they need to slow down and read more carefully?

Good readers monitor their own reading comprehension; that is, they keep track of whether or not they understand what they are reading. Occasionally in reading, you come across a sentence that is complicated, confusing, or just badly written. Here is an example from the student newspaper at North Carolina State University:

Keep track of under- standing

He said Harris told him she and Brothers told French that grades had been changed.

What do you do when you come across a sentence like that? If you are monitoring your own understanding, you notice that you are confused. Good readers generally stop and reread the confusing sentence or, if necessary, the whole paragraph. As a result, they improve their understanding and their ability to remember the material. When poor readers come to something they do not understand, they generally just keep on reading. Either they do not notice their lack of understanding or they do not care.

Write as you read. Taking notes on your reading helps you focus on the key ideas and summarize as you go. You take in and digest the material rather than skim it.

Tom Jorgenson/photo courtesy of The University of Iowa

No matter what method you prefer for collecting the key ideas in a section, remember these two important guidelines:

1. **Read Before You Mark.** Wait until you have finished reading a section before you mark it. After you have completed a section, decide what are the most important ideas and concepts. Then mark only those ideas, using your preferred method (highlighting, underlining, circling key terms, and/or making margin notes).

2. **Think Before You Mark.** Another key to effective marking is to be very selective. When you read through a text for the first time, everything may seem important. Only after you have completed a section and reflected on it will you be ready to identify the key ideas. Ask yourself, "What are the most important ideas?" and "What will I see on the test?" This strategy can help you avoid the common problem of marking too much material. An overzealous use of highlighting can convert a text to pages of dayglo yellow, orange, or pink, in which nothing stands out as important.

One caution about only marking in your textbooks, as opposed to creating an outline, a concept map, or taking notes in your notebook as well, is that you are committing yourself to at least one more viewing of all the pages that you have already read—all 400 pages of your anatomy or art history textbook! Instead, consider using margin notes or creating a visual map or outline as you read your text. These study reading methods take more time initially, but they are active reading techniques that promote concentration while you are reading and also promote easy, regular review of the material.

Monitoring

An important step in a study reading method is to monitor your comprehension. As you read and collect information from the text, ask yourself "Do

Analyzing and Thinking Critically About Texts

When we analyze an argument we have read, we first must understand its parts and then see how they combine. Is the argument a good one? Suppose someone alleges that *the rise in the number of violent crimes is caused by the increase in violence on television.* Although it may at first appear easy to agree or disagree with this idea, the following analysis makes us think more carefully about it:

1. **Define the terms.** Which crimes are considered violent? Is destruction of property a violent crime, or do people have to be physically harmed? Under one definition, graffiti might be a violent crime but not armed robbery. What does violence consist of on television? Are the NBA playoffs an example of violence on TV? Is a horror movie that terrifies viewers but contains no physical violence okay?

2. **Examine the premises (the assumptions).** Has the number of violent crimes actually risen, or are they simply reported more frequently? Has there actually been an increase in violence on television (as you defined it), or have viewers been more sensitive to violence on television recently?

3. **Examine the logic.** If those who commit violent acts also watch violence on television, can we conclude without seeking further evidence that watching violence causes their violent acts? More data will be needed to rule out the possibility that people who are already violent simply tend to watch violent television. Certainly there are those who watch violent programs who do not become violent. Perhaps we need to find evidence showing that the more violence an individual watches, the more likely he or she is to become violent.

Try applying these critical thinking strategies when you read.

I understand this information?" and "Am I able to connect this new information with what I have heard in lecture or what I read in the last chapter?" If so, you can proceed with the next section. If not, it is important to stop and reread the material. Try to identify the troublesome terms or concepts. If possible, ask someone to clarify the material for you.

Another way to check your comprehension is to try to recite the material aloud. If you are able to talk yourself or your study partner through the concepts, you can be pretty sure that you understand the material. Using a study group to monitor your comprehension gives you immediate feedback and is very motivating. Once way that group members can work together is to divide up a chapter for pre-reading and studying and get together later to teach the material to one another.

Recycle Your Reading

After you have read and marked key ideas from the first section of the text, proceed to each subsequent section until you have finished the chapter. After you have completed each section, again ask, "What are the key ideas?"

Internet

Activity 6.1
Reading Web Pages Critically

Just as you must read textbooks critically, so you should read material on the Internet with a critical eye.

Examine the "Checklist for an Informational Web Page" offered by the Widener University Wolfgram Memorial Library (http://www.science.widener.edu/~withers/inform.htm). This page offers questions to ask about an informational Web page.

Evaluate that Web page using its own five criteria.

Is the site authoritative? _____

_____

Is the site accurate? _____

_____

Is the site objective? _____

_____

Is the site current? _____

_____

Is the coverage complete? _____

_____

See also "Evaluating World Wide Web Information" presented by the Libraries of Purdue University (http://thorplus.lib.purdue.edu/library_info/instruction/gs175/3gs175/evaluation.html), which includes an Internet Evaluator Checklist and "Thinking Critically about World Wide Web Resources" at http://www.library.ucla.edu/libraries/college/instruct/critical.htm.

or "What will I see on the test?" before you move on to the next section. At the end of each section see if you can guess what information the author will present in the next section. Good writing should lead you from one section to the next, with each new section adding to your understanding of the material.

■REVIEWING

The final step in a study reading method is reviewing. Many students expect the improbable—that they will read through their text material one time and be able to remember the ideas 4, 6, or even 12 weeks later, at test time. Rather, you will need to include regular reviews in your study process. Here is where your margin notes, study questions, and visual maps or outlines will be most useful. Your study goal is to review the material from each chapter every week.

MAINTAINING FLEXIBILITY

With effort, you can improve your reading dramatically, but remember to be flexible. How you read should depend on the material. Assess the relative importance of the assigned readings and adjust your reading style accordingly. Connect one important idea to another by asking yourself, "Why am I reading this?" and "Where does this fit in?" When the textbook material is virtually identical to the lecture material, you can save time by concentrating mainly on one or the other. Remember that to read textbook materials and other assigned readings with good understanding and recall requires a planned approach. So always keep in mind the following rules:

1. Plan to read in your prime study time.
2. Use warm-up time to prepare to read and to set a purpose for reading.
3. Set a specific number of pages to read within a specific amount of time.
4. Organize your work into short tasks for high concentration.
5. Take notes, recite, and review for each section of the reading.
6. Reward yourself.

VOCABULARY DEVELOPMENT

Textbooks are full of new terminology. In fact, one could argue that learning chemistry is largely a matter of learning the language of chemists and that mastering philosophy or history or sociology requires a mastery of the terminology of each particular discipline. Experts argue that students will learn 20,000 new words in four years of college. Since words are such a basic and essential component of our knowledge, what is the best way to learn them? Follow these basic vocabulary strategies.

1. During your overview of the chapter, notice the terms at the beginning of the chapter, in the margins, and in bold print or italics in the body of the text.
2. When you encounter these terms in your reading, review their definitions and devote a section in your notebook to collecting and defining them. Or create flash cards for these terms and incorporate them in your weekly review.
3. For other challenging words that you encounter in your texts, first consider the words surrounding the unfamiliar term—the context. See if you can predict the meaning of the unfamiliar term using the surrounding words.
4. If this strategy seems to leave a gap in your comprehension, see if you can analyze the term to discover the root or meaningful part of the word. For example, *emissary* has the root *to emit* or *to send forth,* so we can guess that an emissary is someone sent forth with a message.
5. If your comprehension is still incomplete, turn to the glossary of the text or to a collegiate dictionary to locate the definition. Be sure to note if there are multiple definitions for the word and then search for the meaning that seems to fit this usage.
6. To increase your vocabulary, employ these strategies for your reading and listening experiences. Then, take every opportunity to use these new terms in your writing and speaking. If you are able to use a new term,

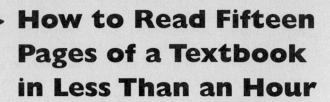

How to Read Fifteen Pages of a Textbook in Less Than an Hour

It takes practice—but it can be done!

Pages 1–3	Read and mark	10 minutes
	Review and recite	2 minutes
Pages 4–7	Read and mark	10 minutes
	Review and recite	2 minutes
Pages 8–12	Read and mark	10 minutes
	Review and recite	2 minutes
Pages 13–15	Read and mark	10 minutes
	Review and recite	2 minutes
Review and recite for all fifteen pages. Answer aloud the questions "What did I learn? How does it relate to the course?"		8 minutes
	Total	56 minutes

Done. Take a break—you've earned it!

then you'll know it! In addition, studying new terminology for a course is a very effective way to prepare for exams. Prepare flash cards or study sheets based on new terms.

SUGGESTIONS FOR FURTHER READING

Gross, Ronald. "Improving Your Learning, Reading, and Memory Skills." Chapter 6 in *Peak Learning*. Los Angeles: Jeremy R. Tarcher, 1991.

Pauk, Walter. *How to Study in College*, 6th ed. "Learning from Your Textbook," Chapter 11; "Noting What Is Important," Chapter 12; "Thinking Visually," Chapter 13. Boston: Houghton Mifflin, 1997.

Phillips, Anne Dye, and Peter Elias Sotiriou. *Steps to Reading Proficiency*, 4th ed. Belmont, Calif.: Wadsworth, 1996.

Smith, Richard Manning. *Mastering Mathematics: How to Be a Great Math Student*, 2nd ed. Belmont, Calif.: Wadsworth, 1994.

Sotiriou, Peter Elias. *Integrating College Study Skills: Reasoning in Reading, Listening, and Writing*, 4th ed. Belmont, Calif.: Wadsworth, 1996. See Chapters 3–8.

Van, Blerkom, Dianna L. *College Study Strategies: Becoming a Strategic Learner*, 2nd ed. "Reading Your Textbook," Chapter 6, and "Marking Your Textbook," Chapter 7. Belmont, Calif.: Wadsworth, 1997.

RESOURCES

One way to improve your study reading is to read more. The more reading you do on your own, for pleasure, unrelated to school or study, the more you will begin to absorb information about writing, presentation, and vocabulary, in addition to whatever the material is about. Reading anything (almost) can contribute to your success in college—as long as you keep up with your study reading as well. Use this resource page to brainstorm a list of extra-curricular reading materials.

Use the second half of the page to list 10-minute rewards that you can give yourself when you finish a 50-minute study reading session.

Things I would enjoy reading for pleasure. Need ideas? Wander through the library or a good bookstore. *(Try spending at least 1 hour a week reading something just for you.)*

Fiction books	Nonfiction books	Magazines	Newspapers	Internet pages

Make a list of 10-minute rewards that you can give yourself after a 50-minute study reading session. Include a few bigger rewards for a week of successful studying.

10-minute rewards:

End-of-the-week rewards:

JOURNAL

NAME _____

DATE _____

Compare the planned approach to textbook reading presented in this chapter with ways that you have previously read textbooks (in high school or previously in college).

....

....

....

....

....

Which aspect of this study reading approach is most appealing to you? Why?

....

....

....

....

....

Which aspect is least appealing? Why?

....

....

....

....

....

What problems do you foresee in using the entire study reading plan? How might you overcome these problems?

....

....

....

....

....

....

CHAPTER →

Making the Grade—Taking Exams and Giving Speeches

Johanna Dvorak

Mary Walz-Chojnacki
University of Wisconsin—Milwaukee

Constance Courtney Staley
University of Colorado—Colorado Springs

Robert Stephens Staley III
Colorado Technical University

*T*hree tests and a speech in the
next two days! I am never
going to live through this week. I
mean, I did everything they said
about how to read and how to take
notes. I've written my speech outline
and driven my roommate crazy
practicing all the main points. Help!

This chapter will help you turn the follow-ing keys to success:

2. **Learn what helping resources your cam-pus offers and where they are located.**

6. **Assess and improve your study habits.**

7. **Join at least one study group.**

8. **See your instructors outside class.**

9. **Develop critical thinking skills.**

12. **Improve your writing and speaking skills.**

20. **Show up for class.**

21. **Try to have realistic expectations.**

Chapter Goals *This chapter has been designed to help you*

- *learn to be prepared physically, emotionally, and mentally for tests and speaking assignments.*

- *collect and organize all the materials you will need to study from.*

- *determine when and for how long you need to study for a test.*

- *use academic support or learning centers for additional help.*

- *employ recall sheets and mind maps to help you remember facts and ideas.*

- *use critical thinking to write a précis or summary as a study guide.*

- *learn the difference between studying for essay exams and for objective exams.*

- *overcome anxiety about public speaking.*

- *learn how to prepare and give a speech.*

When we say "making the grade," we're talking about preparing yourself to do your best in every college course, whether it be studying to "ace" a quiz or major exam or earning a top grade on a speech or presentation. Truth is, you'll probably be graded on more exams than speeches, yet the preparations are similar. So we'll begin with preparing for exams and follow that with some speaking tips to help you feel more comfortable addressing a group.

■ STUDYING FOR EXAMS

The days and hours immediately prior to a test (or speech) are critical. However, it is equally important to realize that your preparation really began on the first day of the semester. All the lecture notes you have recorded, the text pages you have read, and the homework problems you have done are essentially preparation. As you approach the big day, it is important to know how much additional time you will need to review materials, what material the test will cover, and what format the test will take.

Good communication with your instructor, effective time management, and organization of your materials will support your study efforts.

Place a check mark in front of the sentence in each pair that best describes you.

_____ 1a. I always study for essay tests by developing questions and outlines.

_____ 1b. I rarely study for essay tests by developing questions and outlines.

_____ 2a. I always begin studying for an exam at least a week in advance.

_____ 2b. I rarely begin studying for an exam a week in advance.

_____ 3a. I usually study for an exam with at least one other person.

_____ 3b. I rarely study for an exam with another person.

_____ 4a. I usually know what to expect on a test before I go into the exam.

_____ 4b. I rarely know what to expect on a test before I go into the exam.

_____ 5a. I usually finish an exam early or on time.

_____ 5b. I sometimes do not have enough time to finish an exam.

_____ 6a. I usually know that I have done well on an exam when I finish.

_____ 6b. I rarely know whether I have done well on an exam when I finish.

_____ 7a. I usually perform better on essay tests than on objective tests.

_____ 7b. I usually perform better on objective tests than on essay tests.

Write a paragraph about yourself as a test-taker based on your answers to this inventory and your feelings about test-taking in general.

_____

_____

_____

■PLANNING YOUR APPROACH

Physical Preparation

1. **Maintain your regular sleep routine.** Don't cut back on your sleep in order to "cram" in additional study hours. Remember that most tests will require you to apply the concepts that you have studied, and in order to do that effectively, you must have all your brain power available.

2. **Maintain your regular exercise program.** Walking, jogging, swimming, or other aerobic activities are effective stress reducers and provide positive breaks from studying.

3. **Be sure to eat right.** Avoid drinking more than three or four caffeinated drinks a day, and avoid eating foods that are high in sugar. Eat fruits, vegetables, and foods that are high in complex carbohydrates so that you won't experience highs and lows in your energy level.

Internet

Activity 7.1
Stress, Anxiety, and Relaxation

When you prepare for and take tests or give speeches,

do your hands get cold? _____

does your breathing speed up? _____

does your mouth go dry? _____

do your muscles tense? _____

do you sweat? _____

If you said "yes" to any of the questions above, you are probably experiencing performance-related stress.

Read "How to Master Stress" (http://www.mindtools.com/smpage.html). What did you find there that you will be able to use to help manage your stress?

_____

_____

_____

_____

_____

_____

_____

Emotional Preparation

1. **Know your material.** If you have given yourself adequate time to review terms, concepts, and formulas, you will find that you can enter the classroom believing that you are "in control."

2. **Practice relaxing.** Some students have "learned" to feel anxious about taking a test. They have associated it with failure and often experience an upset stomach, sweaty palms, a racing heart, or other unpleasant physical symptoms. These students can benefit by learning a relaxation technique. Your counseling center probably offers such sessions. Use them!

3. **Use positive self-talk or affirmation.** Students can pay attention to the negative statements they are saying to themselves, such as "I never do well on math tests," or "I'll never be able to learn all the information for my history essay exam," and replace them with positive statements, such as "I have attended all the lectures, done my homework, and passed the quizzes. Now I'm ready to pass the test!"

Personal Emergency? Your Instructor Needs to Know

Emergencies do happen. Even if your instructor has warned you that there is no excuse for missing a quiz or turning in a paper late, he or she may bend the rules in a true emergency. Here are some things you can do to soften the consequences of missing class or an exam:

1. *For a recurring medical condition that you know may keep you home unexpectedly on some days:* Let the instructor know about it early in the term. Make it clear you are not asking for relief from required work, but for some allowance for turning in work late if necessary.

2. *For an emergency:* Get phone numbers and/or e-mail addresses in advance. If possible, leave word. Many faculty have answering machines and will get your message even if they're not in the office when you call. Leave a number where you can be reached. If you don't know where you'll be, leave the number of a friend or relative who could relay the message to you.

At some colleges your academic advisor or counselor or the student services office can distribute a memo to all of your instructors to inform them of an emergency, especially if you will be missing classes for a week or more.

3. *For a situation when you know in advance you can't make a class:* Tell the instructor as soon as you know. Even if the excuse seems unimportant to everyone but you, it's always worth asking. There's a possibility that you can turn in work early or make up work when you return.

Even if you missed an important quiz or deadline for dubious reasons, let your instructor know anyway. It's better to make a fool of yourself by admitting you overslept or even forgot a paper was due or left the essay at home than to get a zero. If you are polite and reasonable in your approach, you may be surprised how willing your instructor is to help you in your dilemma.

Find Out About the Test

It is at best inefficient and could be disastrous to prepare for the wrong type of exam. Ask whether it will be essay, multiple choice, true-false, or other kind of test. Find out how long the test will last, and how it will be graded. If you don't know, ask your instructor. Sometimes your instructor may let you see copies of old exams. By finding out and practicing the same types of questions, you will be more confident. Instructors vary as to how much information they will provide. Never miss the last class before an exam, because your instructor may summarize valuable information that you will need to know. Some instructors will provide you with review guides or sample questions that will help you focus on the key ideas.

Note: Although you will take objective (multiple-choice, matching, and true-false) exams in college, the editors of this book have a strong preference for the essay exam for a simple reason: it promotes higher-order critical thinking, whereas other types of exams tend to be exercises in memorization. Why do some instructors use objective tests, then? It may have to do with the size of the class. Grading over 100 essay exams might take days, while "objective" exams can be machine scored and returned quickly. Generally, the closer you are to graduation, the more essay exams you'll take.

EXERCISE 7.2 Designing an Exam Plan

Consult the Master Plan you created in Chapter 3. Use the following guidelines to design an exam plan for one of your courses.

1. What are the characteristics of the exam?

   _____

   What material will be covered?

   _____

   What type of questions will it contain?

   _____

   How many questions will there be?

   _____

   What is the grading system?

   _____

2. Identify the approach you intend to use to study for this exam.

   _____

   _____

3. How much time and how many study sessions will you need to complete your studying?

   _____

4. Using your "To Do List" format, list all material to be covered.

   _____

   _____

   _____

   What still needs to be read?

   _____

   _____

5. Using the timetable you created in Chapter 3, create a study schedule for the week prior to the exam, allowing as many one-hour blocks for review as you need and specifically stating what you need to do.

Your Resources for Exam Success

STUDY GROUPS

Research has shown that study groups help students develop better study techniques. In addition, students benefit from different views regarding instructors' goals, objectives, and emphasis; have partners to quiz on facts and concepts; and gain the enthusiasm and friendship of others to help sustain their motivation.

Study groups can meet all semester, or they can form to review for midterms or final exams. If your study group decides to meet just before exams, allow enough time to share notes and ideas. Together, devise a list of potential questions for review. Then each of you should spend time studying alone to develop answers, outlines, and mind maps. The group should then reconvene shortly before the test to share answers and review.

Joining a study group or finding a study partner is a key to success. Ask your instructor, advisor, or tutoring center to help you identify other interested students and decide on guidelines for the group.

Group members should complete their homework or assignments before the group meets and prepare study questions or points of discussion ahead of time. Study groups also can help students reduce their isolation on campus, one of the leading causes of academic failure, and can share information about which course sections to enroll in, where to study, and where to find good reference material.

TUTORING

Large lecture classes are the norm for first-year general education requirements. Students have a limited opportunity to ask the instructor questions. Tutors know the highlights and pitfalls of the course. A tutor may have taken the course from the same instructor. Most are A students who are trained to explain difficult concepts and show you good study techniques.

If you think tutoring is just for failing students, you're wrong! Often excellent students seek tutorial assistance to insure their A's. Struggling students can benefit greatly by modeling their studying techniques after tutors. Many tutoring services are free. Ask your academic advisor/counselor or campus learning center.

COMPUTER LABS AND ACADEMIC SUPPORT CENTERS

Most academic support centers or learning centers have computer labs that can provide assistance for course work. Some offer walk-in assistance for help in using word processing, spreadsheet, or statistical computer programs. Often computer tutorials are available to help students refresh basic skills. Math and English grammar programs may also be available, as well as access to the Internet.

Some labs may have CD-ROMs on such subjects as chemistry, anatomy, and physiology that visually display course content. Other media, such as videotapes, interactive videos, and audiotapes are also available in many centers. Many have other text resources and handouts on study techniques.

EXERCISE 7.3 Forming a Study Group

Use the goal-setting process from Chapter 1 to form a study group for at least one of your courses this term. As you do this, think about your strengths and weaknesses in a learning or studying situation. For instance, do you excel at memorizing facts but find it difficult to comprehend theories? Do you learn best by repeatedly reading the information or by applying the knowledge to a real situation? Do you prefer to learn by processing information in your head or by participating in a "hands-on" demonstration? Make some notes about your learning and studying strengths and weaknesses here.

Strengths: _____

_____

Weaknesses: _____

_____

In a study group how will your strengths help others? What strengths will you look for in others that will help you?

How you can help others: _____

_____

How others can help you: _____

_____

In your first study group session, suggest that each person share his or her strengths and weaknesses and talk about how abilities might be shared for everyone's maximum benefit.

EXERCISE 7.4 **On-line Exam Schedules**

Find out whether your school publishes examination schedules on-line as a World Wide Web page or in some other electronic form. If it does, get access to the schedule for the next examination period on your own computer or on a campus computer. Record the information for your exams on your calendar.

■HOW TO STUDY FOR EXAMS

If you have been using the suggested note-taking and study reading methods, you will be able to make the best use of the critical time in the days before a test, provided you have recorded the key ideas from the text using a map or an outline and have created a recall column with study questions in your notebook or margins of your text.

Through the steady use of recall columns and recite-and-review techniques, you already will have processed and learned most of what you will need to know. As you prepare for the test, you can focus your study efforts on the most challenging concepts, practice recalling information, and familiarize yourself with details.

Recall Sheets and Mind Maps

As you prepare for an exam covering large amounts of material, you need to condense the volume of notes and text pages into manageable study units. Review your materials with these questions in mind: "Is this one of the key ideas in the chapter or unit?" "Will I see this on the test?" Some students like to highlight the most important ideas; others like to create recall sheets and mind maps containing only the key ideas.

Recall sheets summarizing main ideas can be organized chapter by chapter or according to the major themes in the course. Look for relationships between ideas. Consider time order for events and look for similarities and differences among concepts. Review terms and concepts and look for connections. Recall sheets can be condensed to one page of essential information. Key words on this page can call up blocks of information previously studied.

A mind map is essentially a recall sheet with a visual element. Its word and visual patterns provide you with highly charged clues to "jog" your memory. Mind maps help in the visual recall of material, because it is easier to remember material you can visualize. Cues from the mind map evoke information needed on the exam.

Figure 7.1 shows what a mind map might look like for Chapter 5, "Listening and Learning in the Classroom." Note the use of lists, arrows, and circles—all powerful aids to memory. Take time to study and recite from the map to put the information in your long-term memory. Visualizing the mind map during the test will help recall the information you will need. Working with a study partner to recite key ideas and quiz each other is another excellent preparation technique.

Summaries

One of the best techniques for improving memory and recall is to write a summary. This technique is especially helpful when preparing for essay and short-answer exams. By condensing the main ideas of a longer document or from several sources into a concise written summary in your own words, you store this information in your long-term memory so it can be retrieved to answer an essay question. Here is the process:

1. **Predict a test question** from your lecture notes or other resources

2. **Read the chapter, article, notes, or other resources.** Use a combination of materials, if needed. Underline or mark main ideas as you go or make notations on a separate sheet.

3. **Analyze and abstract.** What is the purpose of the material? Does it compare, define a concept, or prove an idea? What are the main ideas?

4. **Make connections between main points and key supporting details.** Reread to identify each main point and supporting evidence. Analyze the author's argument for bias or insufficient details.

5. **Select, condense, order.** Review underlined material and begin putting the ideas into your own words. Number your underlinings in a logical order.

6. **Write your ideas precisely in a draft.** In the first sentence, state the purpose of your summary. Follow with each main point and its supporting ideas.

7. **Rewrite.** Read it over, adding missing transitions or insufficient information. Check the logic of your summary. Annotate with the material you used for later reference.

8. **Make a brief outline of key ideas of your summary.** Start with your posed question or purpose statement. Number each main point. Associate supporting evidence with each main idea. Use flash cards for your outline. Memorize your outline to help you recall the information.

Figure 7.1 Sample Mind Map on Listening and Learning in the Classroom

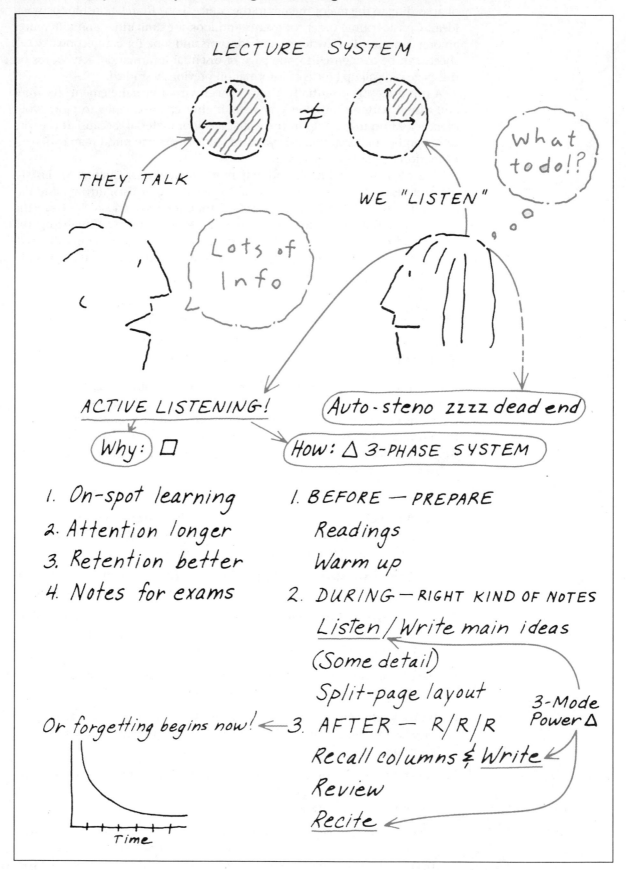

Hard to Remember?
Tips on Memory

Thirty days hath September, April, June, and November. . . .
Doe a deer, a female deer. Ray, a drop of golden sun. . . .
A pint's a pound, the world around.

The human mind has discovered ingenious ways to remember information. Here are some methods that may be useful to you when you're nailing down the causes of the Civil War, trying to remember the steps in a physics problem, or absorbing a mathematical formula.

1. **Use mnemonics.** Create rhymes, jingles, sayings, or nonsense phrases that repeat or codify information. "Homes" is a mnemonic word for remembering the five Great Lakes: Huron, Ontario, Michigan, Erie, and Superior. "Spring forward, fall back" tells many Americans how to set their clocks.

   Setting a rhyme to music is one of the most powerful ways to make words memorable.

2. **Associate.** Relate the idea to something you already know. Make the association as personal as possible. If you're reading a chapter on laws regarding free speech, pretend your right to speak out on a subject that's important to you may be affected by those laws. In remembering the spelling difference between *through* and *threw,* think of walking through something "rough," and that "threw" comes from "throw."

3. **Peg.** Visualize in order a number of locations or objects in your home. To remember a list of things, associate each item in the list with one of the locations or objects. For example, let's memorize three classic appeals of advertising (appetite, fear, and sexual attraction):

   - *Appetite:* The first peg is the corner countertop. Visualize some creature devouring your favorite chocolate cake.

   - *Fear:* The second peg is the coat rack. Visualize a menacing coat rack running after you.

   - *Sexual attraction:* The third peg is a sofa. Use your imagination.

4. **Visualize.** Make yourself see the things that you've associated with important concepts. Concentrate on the images so they'll become firmly planted in your memory.

5. **Overlearn.** Even after you "know" the material, go over it again to make sure you'll retain it for a long time.

6. **Use flashcards.** Write the word or information to be learned on one side and the definition or explanation on the other. Review the cards often. Prepare them early and spend more time on the hard ones.

7. **Categorize.** If the information seems to lack an inherent organization, impose one. Most information can be organized in some way, even if only by the look or sound of the words.

8. **Draw a mind map.** (See the previous discussion in this chapter.) Arrange the main topics on a single sheet of paper and connect the points in logical fashion by arrows, dots, and so forth. Large points are written in large boxes or circles, smaller points in smaller ones. Subgroups are placed under major headings. Drawing relationships on paper—even faces, objects, or stick figures—can help you visualize them later.

Internet

Activity 7.2
Memory

Which of the following statements are true?

The more you use your memory, the better it gets. _____

Memory is improved by organization. _____

Imagination is helpful for improving memory. _____

You can actively improve your memory. _____

Pleasant images help you remember. _____

Humor helps you remember. _____

For answers to these questions, and for extended information on memory and memorizing, see "Memory Techniques and Mnemonics" (http://www.gasou.edu/psychweb/mtsite/memory.html).

What information did you learn at this Web site that you can use to improve your memory?

_____

_____

_____

_____

_____

_____

_____

EXERCISE 7.5 **Writing a Summary**

Using underlining, highlighting, and margin notes for reference, write a summary of this chapter (or some other material) following the directions for summary writing. Exchange your summary with another student to discuss how well you summarized the material.

■SUGGESTIONS FOR TAKING THE TEST

1. Focus on the test.
   - Read all the directions so that you understand what to do.
   - Ask for clarification if you don't understand something.
   - Be confident.
   - Don't panic! Just answer one question at a time.

2. **Make the best use of your time.** Quickly survey the entire test and decide how much time you will spend on each section.

3. **Answer the easy questions first.** Expect that you'll be puzzled by some questions. Make a note to come back to them later.

4. **If you finish early, keep your seat and check your work.**

Strategies for Taking Essay Exams

1. **Budget your exam time.** Quickly survey the entire exam and note the questions that are the easiest for you, along with their point values. Take a moment to weigh their values, estimate the approximate time you should allot to each question, and write the time beside each number. No rule says you must answer the questions in chronological order. To build confidence, start with the questions that are easiest for you. It can be a costly error to write profusely on easy questions of low value, which takes up precious time you may need on more important questions. Be sure to wear a watch so you can monitor your time for each question. Allow time at the end for a quick review of your writing.

2. **Write focused, organized answers.** The summary writing process should help you stay organized during an essay exam. In your quick survey of the test, did you find questions that you were prepared to answer? If so, quickly jot down your memorized outline for such questions. This action both relieves pressure to remember and also saves time; the answer is now waiting for your full attention later. Many well-prepared students write fine answers to questions that may not have been asked. This problem stems from not reading a question carefully. Others hastily write down everything they know on a topic. Answers that are vague and tend to ramble will be downgraded by instructors. Avoid these pitfalls by learning to write focused, organized answers.

3. **Know the key task words in essay questions.** Being familiar with the key question word in an essay test will help you answer the question more specifically. The following key task words are most frequently asked on essay tests. Take time to learn them, so that you can answer essay questions more accurately and precisely.

KEY TASK WORDS

Analyze: to divide something into its parts in order to understand it better. Be sure to show how the parts work together to produce the overall pattern.

Compare: to look at the characteristics or qualities of several things and identify their similarities. "Compare" is often intended to imply that you may also contrast them.

Contrast: to identify the differences between things.

Criticize/Critique: to analyze and judge something. Criticism can be either positive or negative. A criticism should generally contain your own judgments (supported by evidence) and those of other authorities who can support your point.

Define: to give the meaning of a word or expression. Giving an example of something sometimes helps to clarify a definition, but giving an example is not in itself a definition.

Describe: to give a general verbal sketch of something, in narrative or other form.

Discuss: to examine or analyze something in a broad and detailed way. Discussion often includes identifying the important questions related to an issue and attempting to answer these questions. A good discussion explores as much of the evidence and information as is relevant.

Evaluate: to discuss the strengths and weaknesses of something. Evaluation is similar to criticism, but the word *evaluate* places more stress on the idea of how well something meets a certain standard or fulfills some specific purpose.

Explain: to clarify or interpret something. Explanations generally focus on why or how something has come about.

Illustrate: to give one or more examples of something, either in words or in diagrams. Providing a good example is a way of showing you know your course material in detail.

Interpret: to explain the meaning of something. For instance, in science you may be asked to explain what the evidence of an experiment shows and what conclusions can be drawn from it. In a literature course you may be asked to explain—or interpret—what a poem means beyond the literal meaning of the words.

Justify: to argue in support of some decision or conclusion, by showing sufficient evidence or reason in its favor. Whenever possible, try to support your argument with both logic and concrete examples.

Narrate: to relate a series of events in the order in which they occurred. Generally, you are also asked to explain something about the events you are narrating.

Outline: to present a series of main points in appropriate order, omitting lesser details. An outline shows the correct order and grouping of ideas.

Prove: to give a convincing logical argument and evidence in support of the truth of some statement.

Review: to summarize and comment on the main parts of a problem or a series of statements. A review question usually also asks you to evaluate or criticize.

Summarize: to give information in brief form, omitting examples and details. A summary is short, yet covers all of the most important points.

Trace: to narrate a course of events. Where possible, you should show connections from one event to the next.

EXERCISE 7.6 Key on Task Words

Essay questions may require quite different responses, depending on their key task words. Discuss the following in class. In your discussion, include what each task word is asking you to do, and how it differs from the other two listed here.

1. How would you define the purposes of this chapter?

   _____

   _____

   _____

   _____

2. How would you evaluate the purposes of this chapter?

_____

_____

_____

_____

3. How would you justify the purposes of this chapter?

_____

_____

_____

_____

Strategies for Taking Multiple-Choice Exams

Preparing for multiple-choice tests requires the student to actively review all of the material covered in the course. Actively reciting the course material that has been organized on flash cards, summary sheets, or mind maps is a good way to review large amounts of material.

Take advantage of the many cues that multiple-choice questions contain. With careful reading, you will find that the correct answer is frequently apparent. Always question choices that use absolute words such as *always, never,* and *only.* These choices are often incorrect. Also, read carefully for terms such as *not, except,* and *but* that are introduced before the choices. Be sure to choose the answer that is the most inclusive of the choices after carefully reading them all.

Strategies for Taking True-False Exams

Since true-false questions contain only two answers, your chances for choosing the right one are better than on a multiple-choice exam. Here are some hints that may help you:

For the question to be true, every detail of the question must be true. Questions containing words such as *always, never,* and *only* are usually false, while less definite terms such as *often* and *frequently* suggest the statement will be true.

As with multiple-choice questions, read through the entire exam to see if information in one question will help you answer a question whose answer you are unsure of.

Strategies for Taking Matching Exams

The matching question is the hardest to answer by guessing. In one column you will find the term, in the other the description of it. Before answering any question, review all of the terms or descriptions. Match those terms you are sure of first. As you do so, cross out both the term and its description.

■SUCCESSFUL SPEAKING

The *Book of Lists* reports that speaking in front of others is the number one fear of Americans. It's more frightening for most of us than death, sickness, deep water, financial problems, insects, or high places.

Basics of Public Speaking

Speaking in front of others may be one of our most prevalent fears, but it doesn't have to be. Here are some essentials you may not have considered:

- **Once you begin speaking, your anxiety is likely to decrease.** Anxiety is highest right before or during the first 2 minutes of a presentation.
- **Your listeners will generally be unaware of your anxiety.** Although your heart *sounds* as if it were pounding audibly or your knees *feel* as if they were knocking visibly, rarely is this the case.
- **Having some anxiety is beneficial.** Anxiety indicates that your presentation is important to you. Think of your nervousness as *energy,* and harness it to propel you before and during your talk.
- **Practice is the best preventive.** The best way to reduce your fears is to prepare and rehearse *thoroughly.* World-famous violinist Isaac Stern is rumored to have once said, "I practice 8 hours a day for 40 years, and they call me a genius?!"

EXERCISE 7.7 Introduce Yourself

To try your hand at speaking in front of the class, prepare a 3-minute presentation introducing yourself to your classmates. Bring or wear a "prop" that characterizes or caricatures you. For example, if you like to ski, wear your goggles; if you flip burgers on the weekends, wear your apron and carry a spatula. You can talk about your hometown, your high school days, your family, your reasons for going to college, or some other topic your instructor suggests.

Six Steps to Success

If you're assigned a speaking task in class, how should you proceed? Successful speaking involves six fundamental steps:

- **Step 1:** Clarify your objective.
- **Step 2:** Analyze your audience.
- **Step 3:** Collect and organize your information.
- **Step 4:** Choose your visual aids.
- **Step 5:** Prepare your notes.
- **Step 6:** Practice your delivery.

Step 1: Clarify Your Objective

You need to identify what you are trying to accomplish. To *persuade* your listeners that your campus needs additional student parking? To *inform* your listeners about student government's accomplishments? *What* do you want your listeners to know, believe, or do when you are finished?

Step 2: Analyze Your Audience

You need to understand the people you'll be talking to. Ask yourself:

1. What do they already know about my topic?
2. What do they want or need to know?
3. What are their attitudes toward me, my ideas, and my topic?

In other words, consider the audience members in terms of their *knowledge, interest,* and *attitudes.*

KNOWLEDGE
During your preliminary analysis, discover how much your audience knows about your topic. If you're going to give a presentation on the health risks of fast food, you'll want to know how much your listeners already know about fast food so you don't risk boring them or wasting their time.

INTEREST
How much interest do your classmates have in nutrition? Would they be more interested in some other aspect of college life?

ATTITUDES
Recognize that your listeners will respond with both head and heart (and in this case, stomachs) to your message. How are they likely to feel about the ideas you are presenting? What attitudes have they cultivated about fast food?

Step 3: Collect and Organize Your Information

Now comes the critical part of the process: "building" your presentation by selecting and arranging "blocks" of information.

One useful analogy for this step is to think of yourself as *guiding* your listeners through the ideas they already have to the new knowledge, attitudes, and beliefs you would like them to have.

Imagine you've been selected as a guide for next year's prospective first-year students and their parents visiting campus. Picture yourself in front of the administration building with a group of people assembled around you. You want to get their attention and keep it in order to achieve your *objective:* raising their interest in your school. Let's be more specific by discussing the GUIDE checklist in Figure 7.2.

[G]   GET YOUR AUDIENCE'S ATTENTION
In order to guide your audience, you must get their attention right away. There are many ways to do so. For example, you can relate the topic to your listeners:

> *"Let me tell you what to expect during your college years here—at the best school in the state."*

Or you can state the significance of the topic:

> *"Deciding on which college to attend is one of the most important decisions you'll ever make."*

Figure 7.2 The GUIDE Checklist

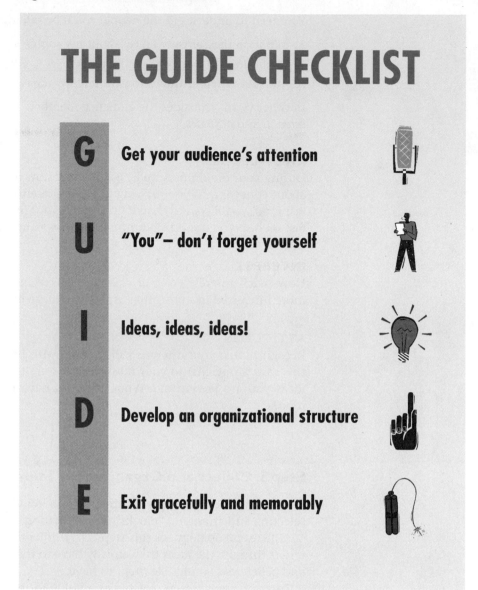

THE GUIDE CHECKLIST

G — Get your audience's attention

U — "You"– don't forget yourself

I — Ideas, ideas, ideas!

D — Develop an organizational structure

E — Exit gracefully and memorably

Or you can arouse their curiosity:

"Do you know the three most important factors students and their families consider when choosing a college?"

Or you can begin with a compelling quotation or paraphrase:

"Alexander Pope once said, 'A little learning is a dangerous thing; Drink deep or taste not the Pierian spring.' That's what a college education is all about."

You can also tell a joke, startle the audience, question them, tell a story, or ask a rhetorical question. Regardless of which method you select, remember that a well-designed introduction must do more than simply get the audience's attention. You must also develop rapport with your audience, motivate them to continue listening, and preview what you are going to say in the rest of your speech.

Think of a speech as a guided tour, with things you want your audience to see and experience along the way. Let them know where the tour is going and what you hope they'll get out of it. Choose a path of ideas that stimulates interest along the way and leads to a satisfying destination.

Photo by David Gonzales

EXERCISE 7.8 Writing an Opening

Assume you've been assigned to give a speech at another college or university on the value of your first-year seminar class. Write an introductory paragraph using one of the methods outlined.

_____

_____

_____

_____

_____

_____

[U] "YOU"—DON'T FORGET YOURSELF

In all this talk of objectives, audience analysis, and "guides," don't exclude the most important source of your presentation—YOU. You might think that speaking in front of others means assuming a role, being someone other than who you really are. Even in a formal professional presentation, you will be most successful if you develop a comfortable style that's easy to listen to. Don't play a role. Let your wit and personality shine through.

[I] IDEAS, IDEAS, IDEAS!

This brings us to the "meat" of your presentation. Create a list of all the possible points you might want to make. Then write them out as conclusions you want your listeners to accept. For example, let's imagine that in your campus tour for prospective new students and their parents you want to make the following points:

1. Tuition is reasonable.
2. The faculty is composed of good teachers.
3. The school is committed to student success.
4. College can prepare you to get a good job.
5. Student life is a blast.
6. The library has adequate resources.
7. The campus is attractive.
8. The campus is safe.
9. Faculty members conduct prestigious research.
10. Our college is the best choice.

For the typical presentation, five main points are the most that listeners can process. After considering your list for some time, you decide that the following five points are critical:

1. Tuition is reasonable.
2. The faculty is composed of good teachers.
3. The school is committed to student success.
4. The campus is attractive.
5. The campus is safe.

Try to generate more ideas than you think you'll need so that you can select the best ones. Don't be critical at first. Then, from the many ideas you come up with, decide what is relevant and critical to your objective.

As you formulate your main ideas, keep these guidelines in mind:

Main points should be parallel, if possible. Each main point should be a full sentence with a construction similar to the others. A non-parallel structure might look like this:

1. Tuition. (*a one-word main point*)
2. Student life is a blast. (*a full-sentence main point*)

Main points should each include a separate, single idea. Don't crowd main points with multiple messages, as in the following:

1. Tuition is reasonable and the campus is safe.
2. Faculty are good teachers and researchers.

Main points should cover relatively equal amounts of time in your presentation. If you find enough material to devote 3 minutes to point 1 above, but only 10 seconds to point 2, rethink your approach.

Ideas rarely stand on their own merit. To ensure that your main ideas work, use a variety of supporting materials. The three most widely used forms of supporting materials are *examples, statistics,* and *testimony.*

Examples include *stories* and *illustrations, hypothetical events,* and *specific cases.* They can be powerful, compelling ways to dramatize and clarify main ideas, but make sure they're relevant, representative, and reasonable.

Statistics are widely used as evidence in speeches. Of course, numbers can be manipulated, and unscrupulous speakers sometimes lie with statistics. If you use statistics, make sure they are clear, concise, accurate, and comprehensible to your listeners.

Testimony includes quoting outside experts, paraphrasing reliable sources, and generally demonstrating the quality of individuals who agree with your main points. When you use testimony, make sure that it is accurate, qualified, and unbiased.

Finally, since your audience members are each unique individuals, you are most likely to add interest, clarity, and credibility to your presentation by varying the types of support you provide.

[D]   DEVELOP AN ORGANIZATIONAL STRUCTURE

Now that you've decided on the main points you want to make in your presentation, you must decide how to arrange your ideas. You'll be able to choose from a variety of structural formats, depending on the nature and objective of your presentation. For example, you may decide to use a *chronological narrative* approach by discussing the history of the college from its early years to the present or you may already have chosen some other procedure. Or you might wish to use a *problem–solution* format in which you describe a problem (such as choosing a school), present the pros and cons of several solutions (or other schools), and finally identify your school as the best solution.

Begin with your most important ideas. Writing an outline might be one of the most useful ways to spend your preparation time. List each main point and subpoint separately on a 3 × 5 or 4 × 6 notecard. This allows you to work on a large surface (such as the floor) arranging, rearranging, adding, and deleting cards until you find the most effective format. Then simply number the cards, pick them up, and use them to prepare your final outline.

As you organize your presentation, remember that your overall purpose is to **GUIDE** your listeners. That means you must not neglect connectors between your main points. For example:

Now that we've looked at the library . . .

The first half of my presentation has identified our recreational facilities. *Now let's look* at the academic hubs on campus.

So much for the academic buildings on campus. *What about* the campus social scene?

In speaking as in writing, transitions make the difference between keeping your audience "with" you and losing them at an important juncture.

[E]   EXIT GRACEFULLY AND MEMORABLY

Someone once commented that "a speech is like a love affair. Any fool can start it, but to end it requires considerable skill." Most of the suggestions for introductions also apply to conclusions.

Whatever else you do, go out with style, impact, and dignity. Don't leave your listeners asking, "So that's it?" Subtly signal that the end is in sight (without the overused "So in conclusion"), summarize your major points, and then conclude.

Step 4: Choose Your Visual Aids

When visual aids are added to presentations, listeners can absorb 35 percent more information—and over time they can recall 55 percent more. Should you prepare a chart? Show a videotape clip? Write on the blackboard? Distribute handouts? You can also make excellent overhead transparencies on the computer using large and legible typefaces. As you select and use your visual aids, consider these rules of thumb:

Rehearse your talk with a friend. Ask for feedback about your words, your posture, your gestures, and anything else that contributes to the total effect of your presentation. Practicing erect and out loud will help you much more than memorizing with your head bowed.

Photo by Hilary Smith

1. Make visuals clear and easy to follow—use readable lettering and don't crowd information.
2. Introduce each visual before displaying and explaining it.
3. Allow your listeners enough time to process visuals.
4. Proofread carefully—misspelled words hurt your credibility as a speaker.
5. Maintain eye contact with your listeners while you discuss visuals.

Step 5: Prepare Your Notes

If you are like most speakers, you will find having an entire text before you to be an irresistible temptation and end up reading much of your presentation. A second temptation to avoid is memorizing your presentation and eliminating notes altogether. Your memory may fail you. And even if it doesn't, your presentation could sound "canned." A better strategy is to memorize only the introduction and conclusion so that you can maintain eye contact and therefore build rapport with your listeners.

The best notes are a minimal outline from which you can speak extemporaneously. You will rehearse thoroughly in advance, but since you are speaking from brief notes, each time you give your presentation, your choice of words will be slightly different, causing you to sound prepared but natural. You may wish to use notecards, since they are unobtrusive. (Make sure you number them just in case you accidentally drop the stack on your way to the front of the room.)

After you become more experienced, experiment with other methods of preparing notes. Eventually, you may want to let your visuals serve that purpose. A handout listing key points may also serve as your basic outline. As you become even more proficient, you may find you no longer need notes.

Step 6: Practice Your Delivery

As you rehearse, form an image of success rather than failure. Practice your presentation aloud several times beforehand—harnessing that energy-producing anxiety we've been talking about.

Begin a few days before your target date, and continue until you're about to go "on stage." Make sure you rehearse aloud; *thinking* through your speech and *talking* through your speech have very different results. Practice before an "audience"—your roommate, a friend, your dog, even the mirror. Talking to something or someone helps simulate the distraction listeners cause. Consider audiotaping or videotaping yourself, to pinpoint your own mistakes and to reinforce your strengths. If you ask your "audience" to critique you, you'll have some idea of what those changes should be. Beginning this process early leaves enough time to make changes if something isn't working.

Using Your Voice and Body Language

Speakers should allow hands to hang comfortably at the sides, reserving them for natural, spontaneous gestures.

Don't lean over the lectern. Plan to move comfortably about the room, without pacing nervously. Some experts suggest changing positions between major points, in order to punctuate your presentation. The unconscious message is "I've finished with that point; let's shift topics." Face your audience as much as possible, and don't be afraid to move toward them while you're speaking.

Eye contact is even more important. Make contact with as many listeners as you can by looking at individuals as directly as possible. This also helps you read their reactions and establish command.

A smile helps to warm up your listeners, although you should avoid smiling excessively or inappropriately. Smiling through a presentation on "World Hunger" would send your listeners a mixed message.

As you practice, also pay attention to the pitch of your voice, your rate of speech, and your volume. Project confidence and enthusiasm by varying your pitch within your natural range. Speak at a rate that mirrors normal conversation—not too fast and not too slow. Consider varying your volume for the same reasons you vary pitch and rate—to engage your listeners and to produce special effects.

Pronunciation and word choice are important, too. A poorly articulated word (such as "gonna" for "going to"), a mispronounced word (such as "nucular" for "nuclear"), or even a misused word can quickly erode credibility. Check meanings and pronunciations in the dictionary if you're not sure, and use a thesaurus for word variety. Fillers such as "uhm," "uh," "like," and "you know," are distracting, too. If your practice audience hears you overusing these fillers, then, uh, like, cut them out, you know?

Finally, consider your appearance. Convey a look of competence, preparedness, and success. As Lawrence J. Peter, author of *The Peter Principle*, says, "Competence, like truth, beauty, and a contact lens, is in the eye of the beholder."

■ THINK POSITIVELY!

What if you plan, organize, prepare, and rehearse, but calamity strikes anyway? What if your mind goes completely blank, you drop your notecards, or say something totally embarrassing?

For the most part, we're sure you'll find that things will go smoothly and your preparation will pay off. If you make a mistake, the most important factor is not *that* the mistake occurred, but rather that you as the speaker *handled* and *minimized* the problem. Don't forget that your audience has been in your position and probably empathizes with you. Accentuate the positive; rely on your wit; use the opportunity to emphasize that you're not perfect. Your recovery is what they are most likely to recognize; your success is what they are most likely to remember.

Finally, remember that quizzes, exams, and speeches are not intended to punish you but to offer proof that you learned something during the course of the term. Think of them positively. Essay exams allow you a rare chance to discuss key issues from the class with your instructor, and objective tests prompt you to review important details from the course. In a speech you can share your insights, thoughts, and feelings about a subject with your peers. And when you do any of these, and prepare well for them, you're a better educated person as a result.

SUGGESTIONS FOR FURTHER READING

Adams, James L. *Conceptual Blockbusting: A Guide to Better Ideas,* 3rd ed. Reading, Mass.: Addison-Wesley, 1986.

Burk, Carol, and Molly Best Tinsley. *The Creative Process.* New York: St. Martin's Press, 1993.

Buzan, Tony. *Use Both Sides of Your Brain.* New York: Dutton, 1974.

Cahn, S. M. *Saints and Scamps: Ethics in Academia.* Totowa, N.J.: Rowman & Littlefield, 1986.

Longman, Debbie Guice, and Rhonda Holt Atkinson. *College Learning and Study Skills,* 3rd ed. "Tests: Preparing for and Taking Them," Chapter 7. Minneapolis/ St. Paul: West Publishing, 1993.

McKowen, Clark. *Get Your A out of College: Mastering the Hidden Rules of the Game.* Los Altos, Calif.: Crisp Publications, 1979.

Paul, Walter. *How to Study in College,* 8th ed. "Mastering Objective Tests," Chapter 15. Boston: Houghton Mifflin, 1997.

Smith, Richard Manning. *Mastering Mathematics: How to Be a Great Math Student,* 2nd ed. Belmont, Calif.: Wadsworth, 1994.

Stone, Janet, and Jane Bachner. *Speaking Up: A Book for Every Woman Who Wants to Speak Effectively.* New York: McGraw-Hill, 1977.

Van Blerkom, Dianna L. *College Study Strategies: Becoming a Strategic Learner,* 2nd ed. "Improving Memory," Chapter 10, "Taking Objective Exams," Chapter 11, and "Preparing for Final Exams," Chapter 14. Belmont, Calif.: Wadsworth, 1997.

Williams, Joseph M. *Style: Ten Lessons in Clarity and Grace,* 3rd ed. Glenview, Ill.: Scott, Foresman, 1989.

Wydro, Kenneth. *Thinking on Your Feet: The Art of Thinking and Speaking Under Pressure.* Englewood Cliffs, N.J.: Prentice-Hall, 1981, pp. 64–69.

RESOURCES

Motivation and confidence are key to success on exams and in speeches. Building on the reward idea from the resource list in Chapter 6, think of some really nice ways to congratulate yourself for exams and speeches well done.

Write a list of celebrations and rewards for finishing quizzes, exams, papers, and speeches.

....

....

....

....

....

Make a list of your exams, quizzes, papers, and speeches here. For each one, add one of the celebration ideas.

....

....

....

....

....

....

....

Go to the calendars you made in Chapter 3, "Time Management." Put your celebrations into your calendars. Make sure that you actually do them, too. Sometimes, highly motivated students put off rewarding themselves for a job well done for so long that they burn themselves out, or forget why they want to be in college, or lose touch with their successes. Even if it's only a mental affirmation, right after the test or speech, pat yourself on the back; it's important.

Another help for performance success is inspiration from others. Make a list of speakers you admire.

....

....

....

....

....

Watch a video, hear a recording, or see live one of your admired speakers before your presentation. Imagine yourself speaking with ease and confidence, connecting with your audience and inspiring them, as your admired speaker has inspired you. (And when you're giving your speech, remember to breathe, not to lock your knees, and to have fun.)

JOURNAL

NAME _____

DATE _____

If you have already taken at least one exam and/or given one speech in college, reflect on how it went.

What strategies did you use to prepare? How well did they work?

....

....

....

....

....

Did you get the results you were aiming for? If not, why not?

....

....

....

....

....

What specific strategies from this chapter might you want to apply on your next exam or next speech?

....

....

....

....

Think about yourself as a speaker. How do you prepare for and present a speech?

....

....

....

....

How well does your method work? What suggestions have instructors made to you about your speaking?

....

....

....

....

Thriving in the Information Age: The Campus Library, Computing, and You

Marilee Birchfield
University of South Carolina

Faye A. Chadwell
University of Oregon

Steven W. Gilbert
American Association for Higher Education

Kenneth C. Green
Claremont Graduate School

*I*t looks like I'll be spending more time in the library and using my computer for more things, like finding information on the World Wide Web, creating databases and spreadsheets, and sending e-mail. Will I be able to learn the system and find the information I need?

This chapter will help you turn the following keys to success:

2. **Learn what helping resources your campus offers and where they are located.**

6. **Assess and improve your study habits.**

8. **"See" your instructors outside class (using e-mail).**

9. **Develop critical thinking skills.**

11. **Know how to find information in your campus library, on the Internet, and through other sources.**

19. **Polish your computer skills.**

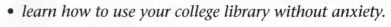

This chapter has been designed to help you

- *learn how to use your college library without anxiety.*
- *select and survey a topic.*
- *define what you need to know about that topic.*
- *speak comfortably with librarians about what you need.*
- *understand the various types of library resources.*
- *do a keyword or title search for information.*
- *use CD-ROM databases and other electronic sources for information.*
- *develop a strategy for using computers.*
- *find out what to do if you "hate" computers.*
- *learn about computer keyboarding, getting help, and preventing disasters.*
- *identify the major computer applications: word processing, spreadsheets, databases, graphics, personal productivity, e-mail, the Internet, and the World Wide Web.*

T he growth of computer technology has had a tremendous impact on campus. Nowhere is this more evident than in the library, a central information resource. Most campus libraries now are using computerized library catalogs or networks rather than the traditional card catalog. Many libraries also provide access to resources like the Internet, on-line computer databases, and CD-ROMs, in addition to the library's typical printed sources.

The growth of your critical thinking skills in college will depend a great deal on how much and how well you learn to use your campus library and a computer.

■ GET A GRIP ON THE LIBRARY

The first step is to familiarize yourself with your library system *before* you have to use it. Is there more than one library on campus? If so, is one geared toward helping undergraduates? Does your library offer tours? (Your class may be able to schedule one.) Try taking a tour to discover what some of the services and various departments offer you. Maybe your library offers an orientation via a computer system.

Look over the following list of common concerns and misconceptions about libraries and librarians:

- I should automatically know how to use the library.
- The library is too big, and I never find what I need.
- Librarians speak a language that only they understand.
- Librarians look too busy to help me.
- I don't know how to use the library's materials; its computers just make it more complicated.
- Librarians in the past haven't helped me, so campus librarians won't either.
- I hate doing research and writing papers, and I always will.
- Doing research usually requires having to talk to someone and ask for help, which can be tough.

Think about you own experiences using libraries—both the rewarding and the challenging or frustrating ones. What are some of your concerns or feelings? Discuss them with others in a group. Of the items listed above, are there any that you would not consider misconceptions?

Does your library have handouts describing various services and different library departments and their hours? Get these handouts. Note the different library departments that might interest you—for example, government documents, reserve, interlibrary loan, or a special collection devoted to one subject area.

Defining Your Need for Information

You can begin to gather information on a research topic or idea by asking yourself several questions even before you physically or electronically enter the library. The following questions will give you ideas on how to think about your topic before actually searching for information.

1. **What Do You Already Know About Your Topic?** Consider names, events, dates, places, terms, and relationships to other topics.
2. **Who Would Be Writing About Your Topic?** For example, which scholars, researchers, professionals in what specific fields or disciplines might be interested? Disciplines are broadly classified as the *arts, humanities, social sciences,* and *natural sciences.*
3. **What Do You Want to Know About This Topic?** Asking this question further focuses your research or your assignment. Sometimes your first question may be too general and not easily answered.
4. **What Is the Vocabulary of Your Topic?** What words describe it? Are there specialized terms that you could search for?
5. **What Do You Want to Do with This Information?** Are you writing a research paper, giving a speech, or preparing for a debate or an interview? Knowing how you plan to use the information you find will help you determine how much information you need and where to look.

Libraries everywhere have been computerizing their catalogs. In many cases, however, not all resources are listed yet in the computer. Ask a librarian about sources that may not show up on the screen.

Photo by Angela Mann

6. **What Are the Characteristics of the Information You Need to Find?** Characteristics or qualities of information don't necessarily fall into discrete categories, but can occur in combinations or along a continuum:

- **Introductory:** general information on a topic; written for an audience without prior or special knowledge in an area
- **In-depth:** specialized and detailed information on a topic; written for an audience with prior or special knowledge in an area
- **Biographical:** about someone but by another person
- **Autobiographical:** about someone and by that same person
- **Current:** about an event or idea that just occurred
- **Contemporary:** a perspective at the time an event occurred
- **Retrospective:** written by someone reflecting on a topic
- **Summative:** summarizing or giving an overview of a topic
- **Argumentative or persuasive:** expressing a strong point of view
- **Analytical:** breaking an idea down into its components

Answering these six questions will help you to clarify the information you want and to explain your needs to a librarian.

Tips on Talking to Librarians

"A problem without a solution is usually a problem that is put the wrong way."

1. Recognize that librarians are usually more than willing to help you and that they can save you time and effort.
2. When a librarian uses a term you do not know, ask for clarification.
3. Accept responsibility for your work. Librarians will expect you to know what your assignment is, to ask questions, and to discuss what steps you have already taken.
4. Not all librarians are alike. Different librarians have different communication styles and areas of expertise. If you are not satisfied after talking to one librarian, seek another.

Research Tips

WRITING THE "WRITE" WAY

1. Come prepared with the necessary supplies: paper, notecards, pen or pencil, computer disks for downloading, your college ID, and cash for photocopying.

2. Be clear in your notes if you are taking down information verbatim (direct quotes) or if you are paraphrasing. Be wary of plagiarizing. Plagiarism is using someone else's work without giving that person credit.

3. Write down all the appropriate information about sources to avoid unnecessary and frustrating backtracking when it comes time to write up your bibliography or cite your sources.

AVOIDING FRUSTRATION

1. If the necessary sources are not on the shelf, ask for help. They may be misshelved, checked out, or available in another library through interlibrary loan, a service that finds the material in another library and then borrows it for you.

2. Start early. Allow yourself the time it will take to gather sources before you have to write the paper.

5. Ask as many questions as you need to. Librarians do not have a quota for the number of questions you may ask.

6. Word your requests carefully. Ask for what you want and be descriptive. In most cases the librarian will interview you to determine how to meet your needs.

7. Don't worry if your topic is of a controversial or personal nature. Librarians have a professional responsibility to treat your request confidentially.

▮FINDING YOUR WAY

General Encyclopedias

Although encyclopedias are useful tools for getting you started, instructors will not want you to rely on them as the major source for the papers you submit. Using an encyclopedia as a starting point, you should make an effort to find information in other sources.

Following are some sample titles that may be available in your library. Encyclopedias are not all equal, and which is best will depend on your topic.

Encyclopedia Americana

World Book Encyclopedia

Collier's Encyclopedia

Compton's Encyclopedia

Encyclopaedia Britannica

Grolier's (on compact disc; need a computer to search)

Information Finder (on compact disc)

Subject Encyclopedias

Subject encyclopedias are constructed the same way as general encyclopedias, but they are more specialized. They concentrate on a narrower field of knowledge and cover it in greater depth.

The subject encyclopedias listed here are grouped by general areas. This is not a comprehensive list. If you cannot find a title that fits your area of interest, ask a librarian to suggest one.

Arts
The New Grove Dictionary of Music and Musicians

Encyclopedia of World Art

McGraw-Hill Encyclopedia of World Drama

Humanities
Encyclopedia of Philosophy

Encyclopedia of Bioethics

Encyclopedia of Religion

Handbook of American Popular Culture

History
Encyclopedia of American Social History

The African American Encyclopedia

Dictionary of American History

Social Sciences
International Encyclopedia of the Social Sciences

Encyclopedia of Educational Research

International Encyclopedia of Communications

Encyclopedia of American Economic History

Encyclopedia of American Foreign Policy

Encyclopedia of Psychology

Encyclopedia of Sociology

Guide to American Law

Natural Sciences
McGraw-Hill Encyclopedia of Science and Technology

Encyclopedia of Computer Science

Catalogs

A catalog is a list of books and periodicals (magazines, newspapers, or journals) owned by the library. The catalog may also list other materials such as films, videos, audiotapes, manuscripts, and government documents. Your library's catalog may be the traditional card catalog; it may be computerized; it could be a combination of cards and computers; or it could even be available on microform (microfiche or microfilm) or in another format. You also may be able to gain electronic access or "log on" to your catalog without even going to the library. Whatever the format, it is important to familiarize yourself with the library's catalog and the particulars of looking for a book or other materials by its author, title, or subject.

KEYWORD SEARCHING

Most computerized sources also provide searching by "keyword." Here, the computer searches the entire record of an item for the words or phrases you entered. The word you entered might appear somewhere in the title, might be a subject term, or might be in another part of the description of the item. When you search by keyword, you can specify how to combine the terms you want it to search, how to position a word in relation to other words, and where to look for a word in the record (for example, only in the title).

Activity 8.1
Finding Information on the World Wide Web

Searching the Internet, like searching the card catalog, is an art. Experienced searchers use a variety of techniques to save time and ensure the desired results.

A Keyword Search Programs

Choose a topic to search: _____

Using the keyword search program Infoseek (www.infoseek.com), execute a search. List the first four items returned.

_____   _____   _____   _____

Restrict the search by requiring that two keywords be present at the same time. A search for +Lincoln, +Gettysburg, for instance, would include pages that had both Lincoln and Gettysburg present.

New search term: +_____ ,   +_____

First four items returned:

_____   _____   _____   _____

Repeat the search, this time restricting the search by requiring that a second keyword *not* be present. A search for +Lincoln, −Gettysburg would require that Lincoln be present but eliminate all pages with Gettysburg.

Search term: +_____ ,   −_____

First four items returned:

_____   _____   _____   _____

Do this exercise again using another search program discussed in "Top Keyword Resources of the Web" (http://www.december.com/web/top/keyword.html).

First four items returned:

_____   _____   _____   _____

How are the results different? _____

_____

When might you use one program over the other? _____

_____

To learn how to restrict searches with other search programs, see "Tips on Popular Search Engines" (http://www.hamline.edu/library/bush/handouts/slahandout.html), as well as "Internet Searching Strategies" (http://www.rice/edu/fondren/netguides/strategies.html).

B Subject-Oriented Search Programs

To search a topic using the subject-oriented search program YAHOO (http://www.yahoo.com), you continually choose from lists of subcategories until you locate the specific topic you seek—much as you would search in a card catalog. Find your original topic from part A above using YAHOO.

When might you wish to use a subject-oriented search program, such as YAHOO, instead of a keyword search program? _____

Indexes

Using an index to locate articles saves time. Indexes identify articles in periodicals, which may be published daily, weekly, monthly, bimonthly, or quarterly. The most common periodicals you will use for research are newspapers, magazines, and journals. Because articles are published more frequently and more quickly than books, they often contain more current information. When you look in an index, you do not actually find the article itself. You find a citation listing the author(s), title of the article, title of the magazine or journal, date of the issue, and volume and page numbers. Some indexes, called abstracts, also provide a short summary of the article's content, which can tell you if the article is relevant. Your library may also have a computerized version of a particular index.

SUBJECT OR SPECIALIZED INDEXES

Specialized subject indexes list articles in journals that cover a narrow subject field. Instructors may specifically request that you look for journal articles rather than magazine articles. Below is a useful, but not comprehensive list of subject indexes. Ask a librarian for specialized indexes for the subject you're interested in.

MAGAZINE INDEXES

Magazine indexes list articles in magazines on a wide variety of topics. Some frequently used magazine indexes include the following:

> *Readers' Guide to Periodical Literature*
> *Infotrac* (computerized)
> *Magazine Index* (computerized)
> *Academic Index* (computerized)
> *Periodical Abstracts* (computerized)

Finding Periodicals in Your Library

Some libraries keep a separate list of their journals and magazines. However, the library's catalog may not indicate which specific issues of a periodical the library actually contains. Ask a librarian for help.

Periodicals may be shelved by call number with the books, or they may be organized alphabetically. If they are shelved by call number, you will have to look in the catalog, or possibly another list, to discover what the correct call number is. Most libraries will have the back issues of these periodicals bound into hardcover volumes by year. The more current issues are usually not bound until a volume is complete. Some periodicals are available on microform. Newspapers are almost always kept on microfilm, except for the most recent issues.

World Wide Web Resources

The World Wide Web is rapidly becoming a resource of choice for students doing research for class papers. For many kinds of information, this can be a productive approach. However, the information available on the Internet may not have the authority or authenticity of material available in the library or from databases such as Lexis/Nexis, Data-Star, and Dialog.

In its quiet way, having explored the "stacks" of the library may become one of your fondest memories of college. But you'll get the most out of your exploration if you've prepared well beforehand by exploring catalogs and indexes.

Photo courtesy of University of Connecticut

■ COMPUTING FOR COLLEGE SUCCESS

What You Need to Know

For most people, using a computer has become like driving a car: You don't really need to know what's under the hood. Rather, you need a general sense of how the car works—and how to make it work well for you. You also must know what to do if the computer won't do what you need it to do.

One reassurance and a caution: In normal use, it is almost impossible for you to damage a computer—unless, of course, you spill a drink on the keyboard or hit the machine angrily because it "ate" or "destroyed" some of your work. Although you cannot break a computer through normal use, you should understand that a computer can do major damage to your work: For example, it can quickly (and completely) erase the term paper you labored on late at night and through several weekends.

EXERCISE 8.2 Rating Your Computer Skills

A Rate your current computer skills from 1 (low) to 5 (high) for each of the following:

_____ 1. Keyboarding or typing

_____ 2. Word processing

_____ 3. Electronic mail

_____ 4. The Internet and the World Wide Web

_____ 5. Computerized library/card catalog search

_____ 6. Spreadsheets/budgeting software

Internet Resources

Finding information on the Internet depends on knowing where to look for it. It helps to know the existence and uses of a number of electronic resources—both in general and in your field of interest:

Databases (both public and commercial)

Abstract services (which provide summaries of journal articles or other information)

Specialized on-line library collections

Professional associations

State and government agencies

Nonprofit organizations

Usenet newsgroups and Listserver discussion groups

Anonymous software archives, known as FTP (File Transfer Protocol) archives.

You also need to know how to gain access to the above resources by using various other services and programs. Each service accesses different resources. Depending on what you are looking for, you select the appropriate service:

E-mail: for contacting specific people, or posting a message to a discussion group or newsgroup.

Listserv/Discussion Groups: for locating and communicating with individuals as representatives of an organization or sharing a specific interest.

Newsgroups: for discussion of a particular topic or issue, or to identify individuals with a specific interest.

FTP/Archie: for sending or receiving specific computer files, especially programs related to the Internet. If you are not sure where to find specific files, the associated search program, Archie, is a useful tool.

Gopher/Veronica: for locating documents, files, information, or data from or about a specific education, governmental, or non-profit organization or association. The search program Veronica can be of service here.

WAIS: for specific documents or to search the content of a certain type of document or database.

World Wide Web: for locating documents, files, information, or data from or about a specific commercial enterprise or other institution. The same is true for product information and technical assistance. The Web is the choice for most multimedia presentations, whether sound, movies, or simply graphics, as well as for the site of homepages for popular issues and concerns.

The World Wide Web is an easy place to start, because many World Wide Web search programs include references to other services of the Internet and often provide direct links to them.

To use the Internet—and your own time—effectively, be careful to distinguish between active discovery and idle diversion, between productive research and sheer busywork.

SOURCE: Adapted with permission from Daniel J. Kurland, *The 'Net, the Web, and You: All You Really Need to Know About the Internet and a Little Bit More*. Belmont, CA: Wadsworth, 1996.

_____ 7. Presentation graphics

_____ 8. Computer programming

Where do your answers cluster? Mostly 3's, 4's, or 5's suggest you have some advanced skills. Mostly 1's or 2's suggest you're just getting started and should think carefully about ways to acquire skills that will help you during and after college.

B Next, identify the technology skills that are important for students in your major. Which skills are important for people in the career field you intend to pursue? If you don't know, find out. Ask an academic advisor, a faculty member, or a career counselor about the key technology skills for your major and intended career. Match their answers about key skills against your self-assessment of your skills.

My Current Skills	My Planned Major	My Intended Career	
_____	_____	_____	Keyboarding or typing
_____	_____	_____	Word processing
_____	_____	_____	Electronic mail
_____	_____	_____	The Internet and the World Wide Web
_____	_____	_____	Computerized library/ card catalog search
_____	_____	_____	Spreadsheets/ budgeting software
_____	_____	_____	Presentation graphics
_____	_____	_____	Computer programming
_____	_____	_____	Other: _____
_____	_____	_____	Other: _____

C Use the goal-setting process from Chapter 1 to address any needs suggested by step B.

What If You Really Hate Computers?

Face the facts—technology skills will play a significant role in the twenty-first-century job market. So meet this issue head on. You might begin with a book about computers intended for people who are not interested in technology and would rather avoid it. You might also look into workshops for beginners where you will learn with others who might share your concerns. You also could make a pact with a friend who shares your attitudes about computers. Agree that you will help each other. Attend the same training class, review the class activities and exercises, work together after your classes, and push (and pull) each other along.

A growing number of colleges provide computer instruction and give computer-based assignments in first-year courses, especially writing classes. Often, lab sessions for these classes take you into a computer classroom to learn the basics: how to use a computer and to develop word processing

Ask for help. Good helpers will know what to do but will show you how rather than doing it themselves. They will also know how to explain things to you in a way that you can understand. If they don't, ask questions. If questions don't get through, look for a different helper.

Photo by Angela Mann

skills. Many residence halls or libraries have computer labs staffed with troubleshooters who can help you with your learning.

If possible, develop your basic word processing skills several weeks before your first paper is due. Use the preparation of that paper as a practical objective to focus your efforts and distract you from your fears and discomfort. Look forward to the reward of a professional-looking paper.

■GETTING STARTED

Keyboarding

Keyboarding still remains the core skill for using a computer. If you can type, you're in good shape for working with a computer. If you can't type, you need to learn. Find a keyboarding course that fits into your schedule, or learn on your own with an inexpensive "typing tutor" software package. (To find the right one, look at ads in a computer magazine or ask someone in a computer store or your campus bookstore for suggestions.)

Accessing Computers

Does your college sell computers through the bookstore? Will you have to pay a lab fee for computer time and access for some of your classes? Will you be charged printing fees? The answers to these questions may depend on your major or your courses.

A small number of schools require (or strongly encourage) all students to own computers. These institutions have committed themselves to bringing information technology into nearly every aspect of academic life—from wiring residence halls into a campus network to including the cost of a computer as part of total college costs.

Many campuses encourage computer use in other ways: selling computers in the bookstore, providing campus labs for student use, offering e-mail accounts to students, establishing a campus "home page" on the World Wide Web, allowing students to set up their own home pages, and offering various support services such as training classes and computer consultants to help solve specific problems.

EXERCISE 8.3   Campus Strategies and Access

A As a class find out what steps your school has taken to make information technology available to students and faculty. What seems to be its overall plan, if any? Be sure to check for any booklets and guides, intended for students and faculty, that describe services and resources.

B Place a check mark next to each of the following that is available on your campus.

_____ 1. "Intro to Computers" classes

_____ 2. Training seminars/workshops on specific computer applications such as word processing, graphics, e-mail, and Internet/World Wide Web

_____ 3. A computer support center for assistance

_____ 4. A call-in phone number for computer assistance

_____ 5. Computers for sale in the bookstore

_____ 6. Dial-up access to the campus network from a computer in campus living quarters or at off-campus locations such as your home or place of work

_____ 7. Resources to help you construct your own home page on the campus World Wide Web site

_____ 8. Something else: _____

_____

Finding the Right Kind of Help

Even as you become comfortable doing routine computing tasks, you'll still have occasional problems or questions. Most often, you'll want to ask questions such as "Now that I'm doing X, how can I get the computer to do Y?" Some questions may concern the kinds of information sources and services available through your computer and telecommunications options. Here are some sources of help:

- **FAQs.** When you're getting started using computers, most of the help you will need will be what insiders call "frequently asked questions," or FAQs. Your campus may have a source of FAQs and answers "on-line." ("On-line" means that you can locate answers via the computer itself. See the section "On-line Services, the World Wide Web, and the Internet" later in the chapter.)

- **Support for academic computing.** Many campuses have a group or department responsible for *academic computing*—the use of computing and information technology for instruction and research. This unit often includes a "user support service" that can help you. If you have trouble finding the right place, someone in the computer science department can probably tell you where it is.

- **A few good souls.** Find a few people with whom you feel comfortable asking questions about computing. Also, try to find at least one librarian who is able and willing to answer questions about computer-related information resources in the library and through your campus network (if you have one) and the Internet and World Wide Web (if you have access to it).

- **A few good notes.** Don't assume that you will automatically be able to remember the magic words and motions each time. Write down the steps necessary to perform important tasks. Keep handouts where the information will be handy when you need it.

- **A few good books.** In almost any bookstore, you will find dozens of books about computing, information technology, and computer software.

Preventing Disaster

Whether you're using your own computer or another one, take precautions to avoid the most serious catastrophes.

1. **Don't do anything silly to a computer.** Don't spill things on it. Don't drop it. Don't hit it.

2. **Learn how to start, stop, and restart the computer you are using.** Two common problems are (1) a computer gets "hung up" so that no matter what you do, absolutely nothing changes on the screen, and (2) you get "lost" in an application program and suddenly don't know what you're doing. In both cases, the last (and very desperate) option is to turn the computer off and restart it. Usually, you will lose whatever work you had done since the last time you saved or filed your work. But at least you will be back in operation.

3. **Learn how to make "backups."** Be sure you understand the different ways to make backup copies and know where you can save and store copies of your computer work (your computer files). Learn what *diskettes, hard drives, internal memory,* and *network server shared storage* are and whether each is available to you. For most projects, you should probably:

   a. *Save* the document at least every 5 or 10 minutes while you work on it. Give the file or document a name that you can easily recognize and remember. Use numbers to help identify the version number of the document. (Is it your first draft or your fourth rewrite?)

   b. *Make a backup copy.* Most computers allow you to copy documents (*files*) from the hard drive of the computer to a diskette (and vice versa). Be sure you save your work on the document frequently and also at the end of a work session.

   c. *Print a "hard" (paper) copy* of the most up-to-date version at the end of each work session and keep it in a safe place. Use it to make corrections for future revisions.

Computer graphics aren't only for art and video commercials. They are also revolutionizing how computers help us see, share, and analyze complex information.

Photo courtesy of University of Utah

■SPECIAL APPLICATIONS

Spreadsheets

A spreadsheet program divides the computer screen into "cells" arranged in rows and columns. In each cell, you can type a number, a short bit of text, or a formula that performs some calculation on the contents of other cells. Spreadsheets are most widely used for budgeting and financial analysis. They are also useful wherever there is a need to experiment and calculate with numerical data. One great advantage of a spreadsheet is that, once you have typed in the data, the computer does all the calculations, such as finding the total of a column of numbers. Spreadsheets are better than calculators in that the spreadsheet stores the data so that it never has to be retyped. One way to learn about spreadsheets is to use one to work out your personal budget.

Databases

A database can be used to manage, sort, summarize, and print out large amounts of systematic alphabetic or numerical data. Businesses use databases to keep records of things such as inventory, customers, and transactions. The electronic catalog in your campus library is a database. Researchers use databases to record and manipulate research data, such as survey results. One way to get started with a database is to use it in place of an old-fashioned personal address book.

Graphics and Presentation Software

Graphics and presentation software lets you capture, create, and display words and visual images, maps, and other graphic data on the computer monitor, on projection screens, and in printed form. Computer graphics are everywhere you look today in art and advertising. They also have many uses on campus. For example, medical schools are now creating and using graphics software to teach human anatomy and medical diagnosis.

Personal Productivity Software

Personal productivity software includes personal information managers (PIMs) such as electronic phone books, calendars, and other tools that help you manage information about your activities and contacts. Sometimes these come as bonus products when you buy computers.

EXERCISE 8.4 **Knowing What Can Be Done**

Review the software descriptions you've just read. If you're already familiar enough with an application to know how it might be useful to you, place a check mark by it. For the rest, consult someone else or a magazine or other source for some fairly simple explanations and write them down. Exchange your explanations with others in your class until each of you understands these terms. Add more of your favorite new applications, if any (or ones you are curious about), and do the same thing.

■WRITING PAPERS WITH WORD PROCESSING

For most first-year students, word processing is by far the most important application of information technology. Learning to use word processing with a spelling checker is essential. It is equally important to learn the limitations of most word processing software: It cannot help you pick the right word, cannot supply the ideas, and cannot do the research for you. But if you learn to use a word processor, your papers will look better and require less effort to write and revise. Some word processing packages can even take care of the placement and numbering of footnotes.

Word processing involves some risks and costs. If you are careless, you can lose the results of your work. You can find yourself exploring features that you don't really need, getting too fancy with choosing type sizes and styles, and changing the appearance of your documents instead of working on the content. If you can produce a nice-looking paper in a few hours and can make changes right up until you are ready to print, you may be inclined to put off starting, and the quality of your writing may suffer.

When you use a spelling checker, keep in mind that such programs don't end the need for your own intelligent proofreading. For example, spelling checkers won't pick up errors such as typing "there" for "their" or "too" for "to." Thus you will need to continue to proof your own work.

The main advantage of word processing over other forms of writing is that you can revise with much less effort. With practice, you can find your own most effective techniques and "rhythm" of writing—but this will work only if you also learn how to plan your time to let yourself do more than one draft before the final version. "Sleeping on it" is one of the best things you can do between drafts.

EXERCISE 8.5　Word Processing—Beginning and Advanced

A *For those not already using word processing:* Learn by doing a real task. Pick an assignment in one of your courses in which you must produce a paper, preferably not too long and due somewhere between one and five weeks from now.

If your campus offers some sort of noncredit or nominal credit workshops to introduce word processing, sign up and go. If you can find a tutorial disk or video, try it.

Use the computer to write, save, revise, and print your paper. Remember that famous computer advice "If all else fails, try reading the manual." If the manual is impenetrable, buy another, easier book about your particular software package. Learn the basics of how to make your report look nice, but don't try to get too fancy this time. Keep your design simple.

B *For those already using word processing:* Mark each of the following either T (true) or F (false).

1. When I use the computer to prepare a paper, I routinely use a spell-checking program.

2. I never turn in work with spelling errors that I have done on a computer.

3. I know how to use advanced features of my word processing program such as headers, footers, and footnotes, and I actually use them fairly often.

4. I always save my work regularly and never lose long or important pieces of my work.

5. From session to session, I back up my work on disk.

6. I rarely waste much time getting fancy with fonts, paragraph formats, and other superficial stuff.

7. When I write a paper, I always go through a stage in which I focus hard on deciding what I want to say and how I plan to organize my thoughts (perhaps more than once).

8. I don't procrastinate. Whenever possible, I start writing a paper early and leave time to think about it between drafts. I always plan time to revise.

9. I always proofread work before I turn it in or share it with others.

Do your answers suggest any need for improvement? Discuss this in a group.

■ON-LINE SERVICES, THE WORLD WIDE WEB, AND THE INTERNET

The Internet

What is the Internet? At its simplest level, the *Internet* is many thousands of computers connected by telephone lines used to exchange messages and find or offer other forms of information. There is no recognized governing body, just widespread agreement among users on some standard ways of packaging and sending information.

Most colleges and universities have computer networks of their own and access to the Internet. The personal computer that you now own or may soon own can be hooked up to the Internet through a direct connection to your campus network or through a *modem,* a small device that lets your computer communicate with other computers via telephone lines. If your institution has a Campus Wide Information System (CWIS), you may, through a microcomputer, find information about course offerings, campus policies and regulations governing students and faculty (perhaps including an "acceptable use" policy or guidelines suggesting appropriate on-line behavior), phone numbers, faculty ratings, course schedules, other institutional publications, and the campus events calendar.

The World Wide Web

The World Wide Web is simply the most recent, exciting, powerful way of linking information within the Internet. What makes it different is both the kind of information that can be packed together and how it can be linked.

The Web permits packaging information on individual computers in a way that allows the inclusion of pictures, sounds, and other formats as well as text. Individuals can set up their own personal sets of information—home pages—once they have learned a little about the language of the Web (Hyper Text Mark-up Language, or "HTML").

Most important, the Web enables people to build "hot links" into their home pages. Usually, these appear as buttons or words underlined in color. When you are "browsing" someone's home page, you may "click" on any hot link and immediately find that you are reading a different section or a completely different home page or Web site.

Right now, the World Wide Web is a little like an old-fashioned library card catalog in which someone dumped all the cards on the floor, and then thousands of individuals strung threads between those cards that they personally believe should be connected. But no one is in charge of the overall arrangement of all those strings. And these same individuals can change their minds any time and remove or change the connections of the threads—with no notice to anyone. You can't be sure that what you find today will be in the same place or at the end of the same links tomorrow.

EXERCISE 8.6 Learning About the World Wide Web

A Find out whether your college or university offers some form of access to the World Wide Web.

Are there publicly accessible workstations with direct connections to the Internet and Web browser software? Where are they located, and what are the rules governing your use of them?

_____

_____

_____

_____

If you have your own computer, does your campus offer a way of dialing in to a modem that will enable you to connect to the Internet? If so, what software is recommended to permit you to explore the Web from your home or anywhere else? What fees are involved?

_____

_____

_____

Note: The most popular software for Web use is available free on the Web. Get some help from the computing people on your campus on how to obtain the Web browser they recommend.

B Once you figure out how to get on the World Wide Web, "browse"! You'll probably need to figure out how to use one of the "search" tools. (See Internet Activity 8.1 on page 145 in this chapter.) Ask for some help. Find out if your library has someone on staff who helps students learn to use the Web and to find things on it. See if you can find a home page for your own college.

C Try to use the Web for your next research paper. See how quickly you can find sources relevant to your topic. Ask for a model of the format for citing references found on the Web.

Electronic Mail—Some Basics

Like many business networks, your campus network may have a system of electronic mail (e-mail) that lets you send and receive messages via computer. These messages may be local—on your campus to other students and to faculty—and they also may be sent out on the Internet to people at other campuses and to off-campus organizations and firms.

More and more faculty members are using e-mail to communicate with their students. It may be easier for you to get a faculty member to answer a question via e-mail than to wait in line after a class to try to schedule time during office hours. Indeed, you might well view e-mail as just another way to communicate with your teachers.

COMPUTER ETIQUETTE: REPLYING, PAUSING, AND FLAMING

One nice feature of most e-mail systems is that you don't have to look up someone's e-mail address every time. Usually, there is an easy way to reply to an incoming message. Unfortunately, people often use the "reply" feature too quickly or without thinking carefully. Be sure that you understand how your "reply" option works in general and that each time you use it you know where your reply will *really* go.

One common mistake occurs when you reply to a message that came from a "Listserv"—a kind of on-line information service that relays messages provided by one person to all others on the service. When you respond to a message forwarded from a Listserv, it is easy to think you are replying to the original author. However, the local e-mail system may send your message to the address that sent it to you—which may be someone other than the author and may even be a list of hundreds of people. It's usually easy to find out how your "reply" feature works and easy to check that your outgoing reply is going where you intend, to one or two or three people, rather than to ten or fifty or hundreds.

Internet

Activity 8.2
The Web Versus
Usenet Newsgroups

The keyword search program Infoseek (www.infoseek.com) can be directed to search either a database of World Wide Web pages or archives of postings to Usenet Newsgroups.

Select an area of interest (such as sports, travel, or a contemporary social or political issue). Then conduct searches using each of these options.

Search term: _____

First four items returned using newsgroup option:

_____ _____ _____ _____

First four items returned using Web option:

_____ _____ _____ _____

How are the results different?

_____

When might you wish to search Usenet Newsgroups postings instead of the World Wide Web?

_____

_____

Flaming refers to sending highly emotional, highly critical messages via e-mail. Sometimes this is exactly what you want and need to do, but most "flames" result from someone having an immediate strong emotional reaction to a message just received, writing an almost stream-of-consciousness response, and sending it without thinking about the consequences. The problem is that with most e-mail systems, once you have sent a message you cannot "unsend" it. Unfortunately, an apology offered afterward rarely undoes the harm or takes away the hurt.

The real solution is to pause and take a deep breath before you send any e-mail message. Take a few seconds to review what you have written and to ask yourself if what you intended to say will be clear from what you have typed. If you aren't sure, fix it! Remember that e-mail makes it very difficult for the reader to know when you are joking or when you are extremely serious. AND IF YOU TYPE ANYTHING IN ALL CAPS, IT HAS THE EFFECT OF MAKING IT SEEM LIKE YOU ARE YELLING AT THE RECIPIENT! Use these techniques sparingly.

One last reminder about e-mail: It is usually easy to "forward" e-mail—to send a copy of a message you receive to someone else or to a list of e-mail addresses.

- The possibility always exists that an e-mail message that you send to one person will be seen by others. Pause and think about that before you send it.

- It not only reflects common courtesy but may be a legal requirement that you get permission from the author (or copyright holder) before forwarding a message or document. Pause before sending it, and consider the likely wishes of the author or publisher.

Be careful to avoid publicizing what was intended as a private message. If you have any doubt about the author's wishes (or any doubt about maintaining a friendship), check with the author before sending a copy to someone else.

EXERCISE 8.7 Learning to Use E-Mail

A Is e-mail available to students on your campus? If so, learn how to use it. Find out if and how you will be charged for using e-mail. If available, get an account and an e-mail address. Write your e-mail address here:

_____

Write your password, if any, somewhere else where you won't lose it.

B Exchange e-mail addresses with another student enrolled in this course and also with the faculty member teaching this course. Write in the e-mail addresses below:

Teacher name _____   E-mail address _____

Student name _____   E-mail address _____

Student name _____   E-mail address _____

Send some messages to each other. Learn how to use the "reply" and "forward" features and practice them together.

1. Learn how to use your e-mail system in conjunction with your word processing package. (If the process is too difficult, save it for special occasions that involve very long messages.)

2. Try exchanging messages with someone else on your campus and with someone at another campus who also has an e-mail account.

C Find out if any of your own teachers are using e-mail, and make a point of asking an intelligent question via e-mail and making use of the answer.

D Send an e-mail message to the publishers of this book. Tell them how you like the book and how you think it could be improved for future first-year students. Address your message over the Internet to the editor:

karen_allanson@wadsworth.com

E Use e-mail to speak out on an issue that is important to you. Send a letter, via e-mail, to any of the following:

NBC's *Dateline* news program, in response to a story: *dateline@nbc.news.com*

The White House: *president@whitehouse.gov*

Newsweek magazine in response to a recent article: *letters@Newsweek.com*

Internet

Activity 8.3
Myths and Misconceptions
About the Internet

Indicate whether each of the following statements is true or false:

E-mail is private.

The Internet is free.

No one can tell what Internet sites I have visited.

If it's on the Internet, you can find it.

New Internet search engines and databases make library research unnecessary.

There is no censorship on the Internet.

Discussion of myths such as these can be accessed at "Myths and Truths and the 'Net" (http://www.underground-online.com/archive/issue4/myths/index.html).

■ETHICAL AND LEGAL ISSUES

Your campus may have materials or courses explaining local policy on computing and relevant law. You are responsible for knowing enough to avoid breaking the law. Old laws may not address all the new situations, at least not in obvious ways. You may be tempted to do things with computers that would seem clearly wrong in other situations.

The best advice is to maintain your ethical principles and to learn enough of the relevant law to be comfortable. Learn whom you can go to on campus for reliable advice about what is and is not permitted. The library and the computing center are good places to start.

SUGGESTIONS FOR
FURTHER READING

Gaffin, Adam. Preface to *The Big Dummy's Guide to the Internet*. Cambridge: MIT Press, 1994. (This source is also available on the Internet; ask for help.)

Kurland, Daniel J. *The 'Net, the Web, and You: All You Really Need to Know About the Internet and a Little Bit More*. Belmont, Calif.: Wadsworth, 1996.

Lubar, Steven D. *InfoCulture: The Smithsonian Book of Information Age Inventions*. Boston: Houghton Mifflin, 1993.

Roszak, Theodore. *The Cult of Information: The Folklore of Computers and the True Art of Thinking*. New York: Pantheon, 1986.

Tehranian, Majid. *Technologies of Power: Information Machines and Democratic Prospects*. Norwood, N.J.: Ablex, 1990, p. 155.

Wriston, Walter B. *The Twilight of Sovereignty: How the Information Revolution Is Transforming Our World*. New York: Scribner, 1992, p. 21.

Wurman, Richard Saul. *Information Anxiety Is Produced by the Ever-Widening Gap . . .* New York: Doubleday, 1989.

RESOURCES

LIBRARY DATABASES

At your campus library or at a computer that is linked to the library, find out what databases are available on-line or on CD-ROM at the library. Fill out the following for each base:

Name of the database:	How to reach it:	What materials it includes:	Nature of its output (i.e. citations only, abstracts, on-screen text, down-loadable computer files):

USER SUPPORT

Locate the user-support services of the academic computing office (it may have another name). Fill in the following information:

Office name

Location

User support hours

User support phone number

Ask the academic computing office if there is a list of FAQs and their answers, and, if so, how to get it.

Fill in the following information about people who can answer basic and advanced computer questions:

Name:	Phone number:	Hours available:	Beginning/advanced?

JOURNAL

NAME _____

DATE _____

What do you need to do now to improve your information retrieval skills?

....

....

....

....

....

What else might you do to learn about information resources on your campus that might be of help to you?

....

....

....

....

....

....

How many computer applications are you already comfortable with? Which ones are they?

....

....

....

....

....

Which other applications should you be using to help you become more productive? What steps should you take to become more comfortable with them?

....

....

....

....

....

CHAPTER

Values: Setting Standards for Academic and Personal Integrity

Richard L. Morrill
University of Richmond

Debora Ritter-Williams
South Carolina Educational TV Network

I t amazes me to hear people talk about what's important to them. Two of my friends think nothing of spending the night together. Someone else I know admits to cheating on an exam to raise his grade. Another friend feels guilty if he misses church, and someone else says she's plagiarized material for her term paper. I thought people here were going to feel more like I do.

This chapter will help you turn the following keys to success:

3. **Understand why you are in college.**

15. **Make at least one or two close friends among your peers.**

17. **Get involved in campus activities.**

21. **Try to have realistic expectations.**

Chapter Goals *This chapter has been designed to help you*

- *define values and discover what your values are.*
- *prioritize your values.*
- *become aware of college challenges to your personal values.*
- *become aware of how your intellectual values change in college.*
- *identify types of academic misconduct.*
- *understand how cheating hurts everyone.*
- *take specific steps to avoid the likelihood of academic dishonesty.*

Discussions about values often generate more heat than light because the word *values* means different things to different people. For some the word refers to specific positions a person holds on controversial moral issues such as capital punishment. For others it refers to whatever might be most important to a person, such as a good job, a fancy car, or the welfare of the family. For still others it refers to abstractions such as truth, justice, or success. In this chapter, we offer a definition of values and explore ways to discover your values and apply them to the college experience.

■ DEFINING VALUES

Perhaps we can best define a *value* as an important attitude or belief that commits us to taking *action,* to doing something. We may not necessarily act in response to others' feelings, but when we truly hold a value we act on it. For instance, we might watch a television program showing starving people and feel sympathy or regret but take no action whatsoever. If our feelings of sympathy cause us to take an action to help those who are suffering, then those feelings qualify as values. Actions do not have to be overtly physical. Actions may involve thinking and talking continually about a problem, trying to interest others in it, reading about it, or sending letters to officials regarding it. The basic point is that when we truly hold a value, it leads us to *do* something.

Let us also define values as beliefs that we accept *by choice,* with a sense of responsibility and ownership. Much of what we think is simply what others have taught us. Many things we have learned from our parents and others close to us will come to count fully as our values, but only once we fully embrace them for ourselves. You must personally accept or reject something before it can become a value.

Finally, the idea of *affirmation* or *prizing* is an essential part of values. We are proud of our values and the choices to which they lead. We also find ourselves ready to sacrifice for them and to establish our priorities around them. Our values draw forth our loyalties and commitment. In other words, a real aura of pressure or "oughtness" surrounds the values we have chosen.

In summary, then, our values are those important attitudes or beliefs that we

- accept by choice,
- affirm with pride, and
- express in action.

Photo by Angela Mann

■DISCOVERING VALUES

You probably already have at least a fair sense of what your values are. Yet one of your key tasks in college is to more consciously define your own approach to life and articulate your values. College is an opportunity to locate and test those values by analyzing their full implications, comparing them with the values of others, and giving voice to your beliefs.

Identifying your values is at once simple and complex. One way to start is by asking yourself directly what your most important values are.

EXERCISE 9.1   **Prioritizing Your Values**

Consider the following list of twenty-five values. Rank-order these values (1 for the most important value, 2 for the second-most important value, and so on down to 25 for the least important one).

_____   1. companionship

_____   2. family life

_____   3. security

_____   4. being financially and materially successful

_____   5. enjoying leisure time

_____   6. work

_____   7. learning and getting an education

_____   8. appreciation of nature

Values: Setting Standards for Academic and Personal Integrity   **165**

_____ 9. competing and winning

_____ 10. loving others and being loved

_____ 11. a relationship with God/spirituality

_____ 12. self-respect and pride

_____ 13. being productive and achieving

_____ 14. enjoying an intimate relationship

_____ 15. having solitude and private time to reflect

_____ 16. having a good time and being with others

_____ 17. laughter and a sense of humor

_____ 18. intelligence and a sense of curiosity

_____ 19. opening up to new experiences

_____ 20. risk taking and personal growth

_____ 21. being approved of and liked by others

_____ 22. being challenged and meeting challenges well

_____ 23. courage

_____ 24. compassion

_____ 25. being of service to others

Look at your top three choices on the list. What was the source for each of these values? We usually "learn" values from important people, peak events, or societal trends. List each value and try to indicate where you "learned" it.

NOTE: List used with permission from Gerald Corey and Marianne Schneider Corey, _I Never Knew I Had a Choice,_ 5th ed. (Pacific Grove, Calif.: Brooks/Cole, 1993).

Value   **Source**

1._____   _____

                            _____

2._____   _____

                            _____

3._____   _____

                            _____

Review the values and their sources. Can you detect an overall pattern? If so, what does the pattern tell you about yourself? Were there any surprises?

_____

_____

_____

_____

_____

_____

EXERCISE 9.2　Evidence of Values

Another way to start discovering your values is by defining them in relation to some immediate evidence or circumstances. In the space below, list fifteen items in your room (or apartment or house) that are important or that symbolize something important to you.

_____	_____	_____
_____	_____	_____
_____	_____	_____
_____	_____	_____
_____	_____	_____

Now cross out the five items that are least important—the ones you could most easily live without. Of the remaining ten, cross out the three that are least important. Of the remaining seven, cross out two more. Of the remaining five, cross out two more. Rank-order the final three items from most to least important.

What has this exercise told you about what you value?

_____

_____

_____

Another way to begin discovering your values is by looking at some choices you have already made in response to life's demands and opportunities. Many students will say that they chose a certain college because of its academic reputation. How much do you value your school's reputation? And more precisely, what does the word *reputation* mean to you? Are you interested in the prestige that comes from enrolling in the college? Does this signify an interest in high achievement and in meeting demanding standards? Obviously, a value such as prestige can run in several directions, one being social, another intellectual. Finding the values that stand behind your choices requires continual exploration of the implications of those choices.

Many students say they have chosen a college because it offers the best opportunity for a good job in the future. Is this true for you? The choice to seek education in terms of your future career suggests any number of possible values. Does this mean that economic security is one of your top values, or does it suggest that you are defining personal success or power in terms of wealth? And once again, what are the implications of the choice? How much are you willing to sacrifice to achieve the goals connected with this economic value? How will your obligations to family and to society relate to this particular value?

EXERCISE 9.3　Shared Values?

List all the reasons you chose to attend college. (Look back at your responses to Chapter 1, Exercises 1.1 and 1.2, regarding your reasons for attending college.) Share your reasons in a small group. Attempt to arrive at a consensus about the five most important reasons for people in general to choose college. Then rank the top five, from most important to least important.

Share your final rankings with other groups in the class. How similar were the results of the groups? How different? How easy or hard was it to reach a consensus in your group? In other groups? What does the exercise tell you about the consistency or inconsistency of values among members of the class?

_____

_____

_____

In exploring your values, you may also ask how you became committed to this value in the first place and how it relates to other values. Conflict in values is a frequent, sometimes difficult problem. How far are you willing to go in service to this value? What sacrifices do you accept in its name? How do the values you have chosen provide you with a meaning for your future? Few of us ever stop trying to give a sharper and clearer account of exactly what our values mean and what implications they have for ourselves and those around us.

The previous exercises present ways to begin identifying values. Of course, this is not a one-time task—strongly held values may change with time and experience. Thus you should not only develop a sense of your present values but also gain some sense of how they are evolving in a variety of areas: personal, moral, political, economic, social, religious, and intellectual.

EXERCISE 9.4 Your Values and Your Family's Values

The process by which we assimilate values into our own value systems involves three steps: (1) choosing (selecting freely from alternatives after thoughtful consideration of the consequences), (2) prizing (cherishing the value and affirming it publicly), and (3) acting (consistently displaying this value in behavior and decisions). List three values your family has taught you are important. For each, document how you have completed the three-step process to make their value yours.

Value	Choosing	Prizing	Acting
1. _____	_____	_____	_____
	_____	_____	_____
2. _____	_____	_____	_____
	_____	_____	_____
3. _____	_____	_____	_____
	_____	_____	_____

If you haven't completed the three steps, does it mean you have not chosen this value as your own? Explain your thoughts about this.

_____

_____

_____

_____

Choice shows value. What you choose to do with a few free minutes or hours of your time may say more about your values than what you spend long hours doing because you have to.

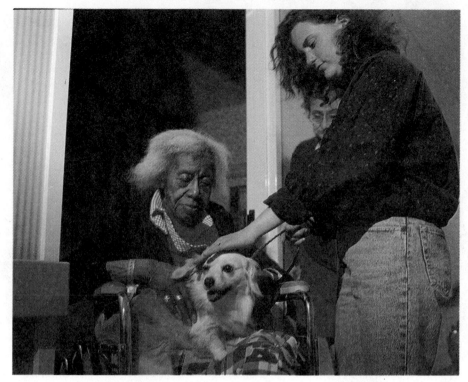

Photo courtesy of Earlham College

■COLLEGE CHALLENGES TO PERSONAL VALUES

Almost all students find that college life challenges their existing personal and moral values. The challenge typically comes through friendships and relationships with new people whose backgrounds, experiences, goals, and desires run counter to their own. This clash with diversity can be unsettling, threatening, exciting; it can also produce positive change.

Students differ from one another in everything from sleep and study habits to deep philosophical beliefs about the purposes of life. First-year students are often startled at the diversity of personal moralities to be found on any campus. For instance, some students have been taught at home or in church that it is wrong to drink alcohol. Yet they may find that friends whom they respect and care about see nothing wrong with drinking. Likewise, students from more liberal backgrounds may be astonished to discover themselves forming friendships with classmates whose personal values are very conservative.

How do you react when you do not approve of some aspects of a friend's way of life? Do you try to change his or her behavior, pass judgments on the person, or withdraw from the relationship? Often, part of the problem is that the friend demonstrates countless good qualities and values that make the conduct itself seem less significant. In the process, your own values may begin to change under the influence of a new kind of relativism: "I don't choose to do that, but I'm not going to make any judgments against those who do." A similar pattern often develops regarding sexual involvements. People become friends with others whose behavior and values differ from their own, and the result can be personal turmoil.

Values: Setting Standards for Academic and Personal Integrity

Photo by Hilary Smith

You probably get along most easily with people who dress and act like you do. You expect to have a lot in common. At the same time, you may find that you learn a lot from friends whose backgrounds and values are very different from yours.

EXERCISE 9.5 **Friends and Values**

Consider several friends and think about their values. Pick one who really differs from you in some important value. Write about the differences here.

_____

_____

_____

_____

In a small group, discuss this difference in values. Explore how it's possible to be friends with someone so different.

In cases where a friendship is affected by differing values, tolerance is generally a good goal. Tolerance for others is a central value in our society and one that often grows during college. Even so, it is easy to think of cases in which tolerance becomes indulgence of another's destructive tendencies. It is one thing to accept a friend's responsible use of alcohol at a party, and quite another to fail to challenge a drunk who plans to drive you home. Sexual intimacy in an enduring relationship may be one thing; a never-ending series of one-night stands is quite another. Remember, the failure to challenge destructive conduct is no sign of friendship.

Read the situation and discuss your responses in a small group. Describe any similar situations you've experienced. How did you respond to the situation? Were you successful? How did you define success?

> You have become good friends with your roommate since the beginning of the term. You know he or she uses drugs once in a while, which usually results in some rowdy behavior you're not always comfortable with. He or she certainly doesn't use drugs every day, but you wonder if even occasional use is healthy. You've tried to discuss the topic with him or her and received very little response.
>
> Last night, while under the influence of drugs, your roommate set fire to a number of flyers and posters on the hallway walls. Today, your resident assistant (or house supervisor or landlord) wants an explanation and demands to know who is responsible. Your roommate doesn't seem willing to come forward.

Which of your values may come into play here? Will any of your values conflict with one another? How might your values conflict with those of your roommate? Your resident assistant, supervisor, or landlord? How would you resolve the situation?

_____

_____

_____

_____

Discuss how changing one part of the scenario might change your response. (For instance, what if your friend burned _your_ posters on the door to _your_ room?)

Are there better and worse ways to deal with these challenges to personal and moral values? As we saw earlier, true values must be freely chosen and cannot be accepted simply on the authority of another person. After all, the purpose of values is to give active meaning to our lives. Trying to make sense out of the complex circumstances of our own lives by using someone else's values simply doesn't work.

At the same time, it is appropriate to talk about values with those whose values seem to be in conflict with our own. What are the other person's true values (consciously identified, freely chosen, and actively expressed)? Do his or her current behaviors correspond to those values? Much can be learned on both sides.

Many people make the mistake of fleeing from the challenge of diversity and failing to confront conflicting value systems. The problem with this strategy is that at some time in their lives, often within a year or two, these people find themselves unable to cope with the next set of challenges to which they are exposed. They do not grow as persons because they do not prize their own values enough to speak for them and their behaviors are not consistent with what they say they value. Although it's only a first step, you must work through challenges to your own personal values by finding answers that truly make sense to you and help you to move ahead with your life.

■CHANGING INTELLECTUAL VALUES

Intellectual values such as clarity, accuracy, rigor, and excellence cluster around the central value of truth. One of the most striking transitions that occurs during the college years has to do with the way in which a person's notion of truth changes.

Many students enter college assuming the process of education is one in which unquestioned authorities "pour" truth into the students' open ears. Some students believe that every problem has a single right answer and that the instructor or the textbook will always be the source of truth. However, most college instructors don't believe this, and their views on truth may initially shock these students.

It's not that the teacher is cynical about the possibility of truth, but rather that he or she is seeking as many valid interpretations of the information as can be found. College instructors continually ask for reasons, for arguments, for the assumptions on which a given position is based, and for the evidence that confirms or discounts it.

Just as with personal and moral values, college-level education assumes that as a student you will become a maker of your own meaning, with the ultimate responsibility for judgments of truth and falseness resting in your hands. The whole system of intellectual values—openness, freedom of inquiry, tolerance, rigor, and excellence—is based on this approach, and there is no escaping it.

EXERCISE 9.7   Applying Your Values in College

Recall Chapter 3 on time management, which discussed prioritizing activities by their importance to you. This is a way of expressing your values through actions. For the following two values, list a variety of actions that would express those values.

Achieving Excellence in College

1. Reading one book each week not required for class but related to my major
2. _____
3. _____
4. _____
5. _____

Maintaining a Great Social Life

1. Spending weekends out of town with friends
2. _____
3. _____
4. _____
5. _____

Although achieving excellence and maintaining a social life may not seem like conflicting values, the actions that express the values may cause conflict. In other words, acting on one value may prevent you from staying true to the other. Which of the actions you've listed in each column might conflict with one another? If you held these two values, how would you reconcile each of these conflicts?

The Right to Vote

No matter what their political preference, college students have a poor record of showing up to vote. Government data suggest that voting in presidential elections among 18- to 21-year-olds has dropped steadily since 1972, the first year persons under 21 were allowed to vote. Americans ages 18–24 have the lowest levels of voter turnout of any age group.

How would you explain this apparent lack of interest in voting?

_____

_____

_____

■ACADEMIC HONESTY

Higher education in America evolved with a strong commitment to the search for truth, to uncover new knowledge and to solve problems to benefit society. The commitment to search for truth was accompanied by the concept of academic freedom—the freedom of faculty and students to pursue whatever inquiry they believe to be important and to speak about it in classrooms without fear of censorship.

Honesty and integrity are crucial to the search for truth and academic freedom. Imagine where our society would be if researchers reported fraudulent results that were then used to develop new machines or medical treatments. The integrity of knowledge is a cornerstone of higher education, and activities that compromise that integrity damage everyone.

Colleges and universities have academic integrity policies or honor codes that clearly define cheating, lying, plagiarism, and other forms of dishonest conduct, but it is often difficult to know how those rules apply to specific situations. For example, is it really lying to tell an instructor you missed class because you were "not feeling well" (whatever "well" means) or because you were experiencing that conveniently vague and all-encompassing malady "car trouble"? Some people would argue that car trouble includes anything from a flat tire to difficulty finding a parking spot!

Types of Misconduct

Institutions vary widely in how specifically they define broad terms such as *lying* or *cheating*. For instance, one university's code of student academic integrity defines cheating as "intentionally using or attempting to use unauthorized materials, information, notes, study aids or other devices . . . [including] unauthorized communication of information during an academic exercise." This would apply to all of these:

- Looking over a classmate's shoulder for an answer
- Using a calculator when it is not authorized
- Procuring or discussing an exam without permission
- Copying lab notes
- Duplicating computer files

Plagiarism is especially intolerable in the academic culture. *Plagiarism* means taking another person's ideas or work and presenting them as your own. Just as taking someone else's property constitutes physical theft, taking credit for someone else's ideas constitutes "intellectual theft."

Rules for referencing (or "citing") another's ideas apply more strictly to the papers you write than to your responses on a test. On tests you do not have to credit specific individuals for their ideas. On written reports and papers, however, you must give credit any time you use (1) another person's actual words, (2) another person's ideas or theories—even if you don't quote them directly—and (3) any other information not considered common knowledge. Check with your instructors about how to cite material they've covered in classroom lectures. Usually you do not need to provide a reference for this, but it is always better to ask first.

Many schools prohibit other activities besides lying, cheating, and plagiarism. For instance, the University of Delaware prohibits fabrication (intentionally inventing information or results); the University of North Carolina outlaws multiple submission (earning credit more than once for the same piece of academic work without permission); Eastern Illinois University rules out tendering of information (giving your work or exam answer to another student to copy during the actual exam or before the exam is given to another section); and the University of South Carolina prohibits bribery (trading something of value in exchange for any kind of academic advantage). Most schools also outlaw helping or attempting to help another student commit a dishonest act.

Some outlawed behaviors do not seem to fall within any clear category. Understanding the mission and values of higher education will help you make better decisions about those behaviors that "fall through the cracks."

Reducing the Likelihood of Problems

In order to avoid becoming intentionally or unintentionally involved in academic misconduct, consider the reasons it *could* happen.

Ignorance is one reason. In a survey at the University of South Carolina, 20 percent of students incorrectly thought that buying a term paper wasn't cheating. Forty percent thought using a test file (a collection of actual tests from previous terms, usually kept by an organization such as a fraternity or sorority) was fair behavior. Sixty percent thought it was all right to get answers from someone who had taken an exam earlier in the same or in a prior semester.

This may not be so unusual in light of the fact that in some countries students are encouraged to review past exams as practice exercises. In other countries, it is also acceptable to share answers and information for homework and other types of assignments with friends. In some countries, these behaviors are not only acceptable, they are considered acts of generosity and courtesy.

Instructors also may vary in their acceptance of such behaviors. Because there is no universal code that dictates such behaviors, you should ask your instructors for clarification. When a student is caught violating the academic code of a particular school or teacher, pleading ignorance of the rules is a weak defense.

Internet

Activity 9.1
Institutional Values

Many colleges and universities post campus rules and regulations on their Internet sites. One such college is Southern Methodist University, whose Student Code of Conduct is found at http://www.smu.edu/~stulife/studentcode.html.

What policies and/or infractions does SMU provide for the following cases?

keeping bicycles in dormitory rooms _____

drinking alcohol in public _____

(any other area of interest to you) _____

Are these policies more or less strict than those at your institution?

_____

_____

Would you prefer to live under the Code of Conduct at Southern Methodist? Give your reasons.

_____

_____

Compare SMU's regulations with the listing of "Student Rights and College Regulations of Brooklyn College of the City University of New York" (http://146.245.2.151/bc/info/right.html).

_____

_____

A second reason some people cheat is that they overestimate the importance of grades, apart from actual learning, and fall into thinking they must "succeed" at any cost. This may reflect our society's competitive atmosphere. It also may be the result of pressure from parents, peers, or teachers. The desire for "success at any cost" is often accompanied by a strong fear of failure that is hard to confront and deal with.

A third common cause of cheating is a student's own lack of preparation or inability to manage time and activities. The problem is made worse if he or she is unwilling to ask an instructor to extend a deadline so that a project can be done well.

Here are some steps you can take to reduce the likelihood of problems:

1. **Know the Rules.** Learn the academic code for your school. If a teacher does not clarify his or her standards and expectations, ask exactly what the rules are.

2. **Set Clear Boundaries.** Work with a partner or study group to prepare for a test, but refrain from discussing past exams with others unless it is

Does Cheating Hurt Anyone?

WHAT ABOUT THE INDIVIDUAL?

- **Cheating sabotages academic growth.** Cheating confuses and weakens the process by which students demonstrate understanding of course content. Because the grade and the instructor's comments apply to someone else's work, cheating prevents accurate feedback, thus hindering academic growth.

- **Cheating sabotages personal growth.** Educational accomplishments inspire pride and confidence. What confidence in their ability will individuals have whose work is not their own?

- **Cheating may have long-term effects.** Taking the "easy way" in college may become a habit that can spill over into graduate school, jobs, and relationships. And consider this: Would you want a doctor, lawyer, or accountant who had cheated on exams handling your affairs?

WHAT ABOUT THE COMMUNITY?

- **Cheating jeopardizes the basic fairness of the grading process.** Widespread cheating causes honest students to become cynical and resentful. This is especially true when grades are curved and the cheating directly affects other students.

- **Widespread cheating devalues the college's degree.** Alumni, potential students, graduate schools, and employers learn to distrust degrees from schools where cheating is widespread.

specifically permitted. Tell friends exactly what is acceptable or unacceptable if you lend them a term paper. Refuse to "help" others who ask you to help them cheat. In test settings, keep your answers covered and your eyes down, and put all extraneous materials away. Help friends to resist temptation. Make sure your typist understands that he or she may not make any changes in your work.

3. **Improve Self-Management.** Be well prepared for all quizzes, exams, projects, and papers. This may mean *un*learning some bad habits (such as procrastination) and building better time management and study skills. Keep your own long-term goals in mind.

"The Only A"

As a student at a large, predominantly white university, I enrolled in an advanced composition course. The class of twenty-five or so was all white with the exception of me and another black student. As part of the writing process, the instructor required the class to read each other's papers. After the first peer critiquing session, the other black student and I compared notes and thought we saw a pattern. Not only did our student critics seem to be critical of our writing, but their comments carried what we perceived as racial overtones. Needless to say we were both bothered by this, but decided to dismiss it as oversensitivity on our part—until we encountered the same sort of comments on our drafts the next week. The other student decided that our classmates were racially biased and dropped the class. I searched for a different approach, especially since I needed the course to complete my degree requirements in time.

I carefully considered the comments my classmates were making and decided that some of them were unfounded and probably motivated by personal bias. Many of their comments, however, were based upon instructions from the professor and appeared to be valid. I then sifted through their comments, discarding the obvious personal ones and paying attention to those that seemed justified. And each time the peer critique session was held, I wrote and rewrote my papers, basing many of my changes on the comments of my peer critics.

When grades were posted that semester, I made the traditional trek to the professor's office door, where he had promised to post the final grades. When I arrived, four or five of my classmates were perusing the grade roster, and I could tell that they were trying to decipher who had made what grade. Since only Social Security numbers appeared on the sheet, figuring out who was who was a little difficult. I approached the grade roster and looked for my grade. When I saw what it was, I placed my finger at the top of the list and ever so gently let it slide down the page, where, residing beside my Social Security number, was the only A in the class. The other students at the professor's door congratulated me, and I thanked them—both for their kind comments and for their help in netting me that A.

So what was an unbearable situation for one student became a success story for another, all because the two of us chose to react to a negative situation differently. Yes, I still think that some of the comments my classmates made on my papers were unnecessarily personal and harsh, but I also recognized the worthwhile comments. This approach allowed me to glean from a negative situation the positive elements that I used to my advantage.

—John Slade, Humanities Division of Arts and Sciences, Forsyth Technical Community College, Winston-Salem, North Carolina.

4. **Seek Help.** Find out what is available for assistance with study skills, time management, and test-taking—and take advantage of it. If your methods are in good shape but the content of the course is too difficult, consult with your instructor.

5. **Withdraw from the Course.** Consider cutting your losses before it's too late. Your school has a policy about dropping courses and a "last day to drop without penalty" (drop date). You may choose this route and plan to retake the course later. Some students may choose to withdraw

from all their classes and take some time off before returning to school. This may be an option if you find yourself in over your head, or if some unplanned event (a long illness, a family crisis) has caused you to fall behind with little hope of catching up.

6. **Reexamine Goals.** You need to stick to your own realistic goals instead of giving in to pressure from family or friends to achieve impossibly high standards. What grades do you *need,* and what grades do you have the potential to earn? You may also feel pressure to enter a particular career or profession. If this isn't what you want, your frustration is likely to appear in your lack of preparation and your grades. It may be time to sit down with others—perhaps professionals in your career and counseling centers—and explore alternatives.

■ CHOOSING VALUES

We have stressed that the essential first step in developing a value system is for you to become your own maker of meaning. But it is only a first step; you must be aware not only of making meaning but also of making a meaning that can lead to a coherent and fulfilling life. As crucial as it is to develop your own values, it is equally important that you find ethical values. Little is accomplished if you develop a genuine system of values that leads to egocentric, dishonest, cruel, and/or irresponsible conduct.

The question of what ethical values are cannot be answered simply. There are no automatic criteria (though perhaps the "Golden Rule" will serve as well as any). Yet clearly all of us who have accepted life in a democratic society and membership in an academic community such as a college or university are committed to many significant values. To participate in democratic institutions is to honor such values as respect for others, tolerance, equality, liberty, and fairness. Members of an academic community are usually passionate in their defense of academic freedom, the open search for truth, honesty, collegiality, civility, and tolerance for dissenting views.

SUGGESTIONS FOR FURTHER READING

Bellah, R., R. Madsen, W. M. Sullivan, A. Swidler, and S. M. Tipton. *Habits of the Heart.* Berkeley: University of California Press, 1985.

Corey, G., and M. S. Corey. *I Never Knew I Had a Choice,* 5th ed. Pacific Grove, Calif.: Brooks/Cole, 1993.

Kolak, Daniel, and Raymond Martin. *Wisdom Without Answers: A Guide to the Experience of Philosophy,* 3rd ed. Belmont, Calif.: Wadsworth, 1996.

Lewis, Hunter. *A Question of Values.* New York: Harper & Row, 1990.

Morrill, R. L. *Teaching Values in College.* San Francisco: Jossey-Bass, 1980.

Niebuhr, H. R. *Faith on Earth.* New Haven, Conn.: Yale University Press, 1989.

Pojman, Louis P. *Ethics: Discovering Right and Wrong,* 2nd ed. Belmont, Calif.: Wadsworth, 1995.

Rokeach, M. *The Nature of Human Values.* New York: Free Press, 1973.

Simon, S., L. Howe, and H. Kirschenbaum. *Values Clarification.* New York: Hart, 1972.

RESOURCES

In keeping with this chapter's emphasis on values as chosen, affirmed, and acted upon, think about how you have acted, and can act in the future, on the values that you hold. Use this resource page to make a list of activities and organizations that you can work with to express the values that you hold.

Look in the phone book, on the Internet, on bulletin boards, and so on, and make a list of organizations whose work you agree with and support.

Name of organization: Phone number:

....

....

....

....

....

....

....

....

....

....

....

....

....

Call several organizations that you are most interested in working with. Ask about volunteer opportunities. (Remember that volunteering can take many different forms: a daily or weekly commitment, helping out once a month or whenever needed, bringing in donations, working on newsletters, and so on. There are probably more possibilities than you realize.) Make a list of the opportunities or kinds of support that you could give at each organization.

Organization:	Support I can give:

JOURNAL

NAME _____

DATE _____

Describe your current system of "true values" (chosen, affirmed, and acted upon).

....

....

....

....

....

....

In what ways has college already tested or changed these values?

....

....

....

....

....

....

....

Are you facing any issues related to academic honesty? What are they? What are you doing about them?

....

....

....

....

....

....

How are your actions serving your own best interests? The interests of other students? Your institution?

....

....

....

....

....

....

CHAPTER

Choosing Courses and Careers

Linda B. Salane
Columbia College

Mary Stuart Hunter
University of South Carolina

*G*ot the results of my career inventory today. It said I might
want to go into the funeral business! And I thought I was interested
in computers. Think I'd better see
my advisor and see what it all
means. Better check the catalog,
too, to see if there are any courses in
Mortuary Science. I just got here
and I'm already confused!

This chapter will help you turn the follow-ing keys to success:

1. **Find and get to know one individual on campus who cares about your survival.**

2. **Learn what helping resources your cam-pus offers and where they are located.**

8. **See your instructors outside class.**

10. **Choose instructors who involve you in the learning process.**

13. **Find a great academic advisor or counselor.**

14. **Visit the career center early in your first term.**

21. **Try to have realistic expectations.**

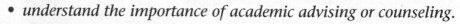

Chapter Goals *This chapter has been designed to help you*

- *understand the importance of academic advising or counseling.*
- *find the best advisor or counselor for your needs.*
- *organize a procedure for preparing to meet with your academic advisor or counselor.*
- *change advisors or counselors if you feel you are not getting the help you seek.*
- *learn how to use your college catalog.*
- *learn what information in your college catalog will be of help to you.*
- *understand that your academic major may lead to a career far different from what you expected.*
- *learn the factors involved in career planning.*
- *explore the possibility of new career fields, especially if you are a returning student.*

One of the most important individuals you will meet in college is your academic advisor or counselor. This person can guide you through the complexities of choosing courses that will follow your interests and meet the requirements in your major. Your counselor probably will point you to resources such as the college catalog—where you'll find important information on degree requirements, an academic calendar of important dates, tuition costs and other financial information, general academic regulations, and a complete listing of all courses on your campus, with descriptions and prerequisites. If you have doubts about the major you have chosen, your counselor may advise you to visit the career center, where you can explore other majors through career inventories, career data, and guidance from a career counselor.

■ YOUR ACADEMIC ADVISOR OR COUNSELOR

We already know that when a student has one person on campus who cares about his or her survival, that student stands a better chance of succeeding than the student who lacks a relationship with a significant other person. A mounting body of evidence has convinced colleges and universities that poor academic advising is one major reason students drop out of college. Thus academic advising has become one of the most important ingredients for student success. Although your "significant other" person may be an instructor, a staff member, an upper-class student, or a counselor, it might also be none other than your academic advisor.

Academic advising is a systematic process for obtaining the critical information you need to make the most important decisions about college, decisions af-

What Are You Looking for in Your Academic Advisor?

This graph from a study of students at Harvard shows that men and women tend to seek different qualities in advisors.

When asked about advising, men want an advisor who "knows the facts." Or "if he doesn't know the data, he knows where to get it or to send me to get it." Or one who "makes concrete and directive suggestions, which I'm then free to accept or reject."

Women more often want an advisor who "will take the time to get to know me personally." Or who "is a good listener and can read between the lines if I am hesitant to express a concern." Or who "shares my interests so that we will have something in common." The women's responses focus far more on a personal relationship.[*]

What do you plan to look for in your advisor? What can you do to ensure that you get the advisor who is best for you?

[*]Richard J. Light. The Harvard Assessment Seminars, First Report (Cambridge, Mass.: Harvard University Graduate School of Education and Kennedy School of Government, 1990).

What Students Want from Academic Advisors
(percentage indicating "very important")

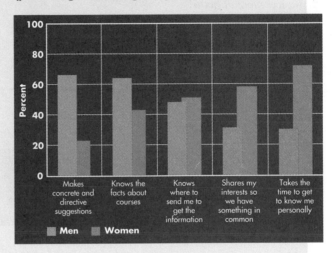

fecting your academic major, career goals, elective courses, secondary fields of study, and co-curricular activities. Academic advising is also a one-to-one, highly personal, out-of-class form of learning. Academic advising includes periodic assistance in scheduling courses that you will take the following term and is inextricably related to the process of career planning and decision making. But beyond decision-making and scheduling considerations, it represents a relationship between two human beings who care about, understand, and respect each other and share a common goal: your education.

Even if you have no serious problems, you may want to talk with your advisor for any number of reasons: to get advice on applying for a job, to get a reaction to a piece of writing or a project, to ask for the names of books in a given field that might be helpful to you, to share some good news about grades or job interviews, or to check on academic rules and regulations.

At many colleges, academic advisors are full-time faculty. At some schools they may be educators whose sole professional responsibility is advising. At other schools, you'll find a combination of faculty and professional staff members as advisors.

In many community colleges, academic advising is done by counselors in the college counseling/advising center. These counselors are trained in and

The best academic advisor is someone who really wants to get to know you and welcomes your questions and concerns. If these qualities seem to be missing, think about whether there is something you can do to improve communication. Or consider looking for an advisor with whom you feel more at home.

© Brian Smith/Stock Boston

responsible for assisting students with both academic and personal issues. If you haven't declared a major, you may be assigned to an advisor who specializes in dealing with undecided students. You may be attending an institution that, as a matter of policy, does not initially assign new students to advisors in their intended major field, but does so later on. Even if you are not assigned a faculty member from your special area of interest, your advisor is usually expected to be familiar with the requirements of your program. If your advisor is not familiar with them, there may be a center on campus where a staff advisor can give specific program information.

EXERCISE 10.1   Who's Your Academic Advisor?

Find out and record the name of your academic advisor, along with his or her office location, phone number, and normal advising hours. If you have not already done so, arrange to meet this person.

Name: _____

Office location: _____

Phone(s): _____

_____

Hours: _____

Arranging to Meet with Your Advisor

At many institutions, academic advising takes place in advisement centers. These centers may also include offices for personal counseling, career planning and placement, financial aid, and study skills. Or you may have a faculty member as an advisor. One of the many differences between high school and college is that most college faculty have private offices where they can meet with you during their posted office hours.

Generally, at least once a term, students are notified to sign up for appointments with their advisors to discuss the selection and scheduling of courses for the next term. This advising period may last up to two weeks and is usually widely publicized on campus. It is very important that you be aware of these periods and schedule a conference to discuss your course selections for the coming term.

EXERCISE 10.2 ## Advising Process and Schedules

To prepare for your basic academic advising sessions, do the following:

1. Find out when the course selection and scheduling process for next term begins, and record the date here: _____

2. Record what you need to do to prepare for this process (include any important dates):

   _____

   _____

   _____

   _____

Don't forget to transfer the important dates to your calendar so you'll be prepared!

Relating to Your Advisor

Advising is likely to be much more successful for you if you take the relationship seriously and work hard to make it meaningful. Ask for advice on course prerequisites, interesting courses to take, good teachers to study under, or other options.

Discuss any major decisions—such as adding or dropping a course, changing your major, or transferring or withdrawing from school—*before* making them. You may also need to discuss personal problems with your advisor. If he or she can't help you with a certain problem, ask for referral to a professional on campus who can. Your advisor should be someone you can always turn to. Will your advisor respect your request for confidentiality on such matters? That's something you will need to clarify.

Your advising sessions will be more productive if you are already familiar with your college catalog. Make up a list of questions before your appointment and also arrive with a tentative schedule of courses and alternate choices for the coming term.

Is Your Advisor Right for You?

The key word here is *trust*. You will know you have the right academic advisor if you establish good rapport with this person. Do you feel comfortable with him or her? Does your academic advisor seem to take a personal interest in you? Does the advisor listen actively? Does the advisor provide enough time for you to accomplish what needs to be done? Does he or she either make an effort to get you the information you request or tell you where you can find it yourself?

If your advisor isn't right for you, ask for another advisor. To find one, you might consider asking one of your instructors, perhaps one with whom you have developed a personal rapport or whom you respect. Get his or her agreement, or check with your departmental advising coordinators about other possibilities for advisors. Then make the change officially. *Never* stay in an advising relationship that isn't working for you.

EXERCISE 10.3 Preparing to Meet with Your Advisor

Think ahead to your next appointment with your advisor. What questions do you have in each of the following areas? Record those questions here. (You may be able to answer some of these questions yourself by consulting your catalog.)

1. Your major and potential career:

   _____

   _____

2. Alternate majors and potential careers:

   _____

   _____

3. Classes you need next term:

   _____

   _____

   _____

4. Proper sequencing of classes you need to take:

   _____

   _____

   _____

5. Difficulty level of classes you may be taking next term:

   _____

   _____

   _____

6. Good balance in the combination of class work loads and types of classes you have chosen:

   _____

   _____

   _____

7. Electives you might be interested in:

_____

_____

_____

8. Schedule problems:

_____

_____

_____

9. Teaching styles of specific instructors:

_____

_____

_____

10. General campus information:

_____

_____

_____

11. Information about scholarships, internships, cooperative education, or other opportunities:

_____

_____

_____

12. Other questions or issues including change of major:

_____

_____

_____

Throughout the rest of this term, use this worksheet to record other questions for your advisor as you think of them. The night before your appointment, review the list for any additions or deletions. To make good use of your appointment time and not forget anything, take this list and your catalog with you. If you're considering transferring, also bring the catalog from the school to which you may want to transfer.

■YOUR COLLEGE CATALOG

College is complex and expensive, and the college catalog is a sort of user's manual for your institution. Learn what's in your catalog—it should be a valuable resource throughout your college years.

Much of the information once found only in college catalogs is also available on-line. Campus computer bulletin boards and Internet home pages are especially useful for information that is in constant flux or that has changed recently. In addition to lists of classes and prerequisites, office hours, and student services, you can often search listings of job opportunities, scholarships, schedules, and departmental telephone numbers and e-mail addresses.

A If you haven't already received your catalog, check with your advisor or counselor. If your advisor does not have a copy for you, contact the admissions office, the registration office, the departmental office of your academic major, or your campus bookstore. Make sure you have the catalog that is dated the year you matriculated, or entered a program of study, at your institution, not the year you applied for admission and were accepted.

B Start a file for your catalog and other documents such as your grade reports, advisement forms, fee payment receipts, schedule change forms, and other proof of financial and academic dealings with your institution. Plan to keep all these things until your diploma is in your hands.

C If it is likely that you may transfer to another college to complete an associate or bachelor's degree, also obtain a copy of the catalog for that school. It will be useful when you meet with your advisor to plan your courses.

What's in the Catalog?

First and foremost, the catalog contains valuable information about regulations, requirements, procedures, and opportunities for your development as a student. Although the catalog doesn't contain *everything* students need to know, it does provide an excellent summary of critical information available in greater detail elsewhere on your campus. The style of catalogs varies, but most provide you with the following information.

PUBLICATION DATE AND GENERAL INFORMATION

Colleges and universities are constantly changing admissions standards, degree requirements, academic calendars, and so on. But the catalog in use at the time of your matriculation will generally stand as your individual "contract" with the institution.

It is important for you to know which catalog was in effect when you matriculated (enrolled for the first time) rather than when you applied for admission, because you are subject to the rules and regulations that were in effect at that time.

EXERCISE 10.5 Finding Some Key Dates

Look through your college catalog. Find and record the following important dates:

Publication date of the catalog: _____

	This Term	Next Term
First day of classes	_____	_____
Last day to add a class	_____	_____
Last day (if any) to drop a class without penalty	_____	_____
Midpoint in the term	_____	_____

	This Term	Next Term
Last day of classes	_____	_____
Final exam period (first day)	_____	_____
Final exam period (last day)	_____	_____
Official last day of term	_____	_____
Holidays (no classes held):		
_____	_____	_____
_____	_____	_____
_____	_____	_____
_____	_____	_____
_____	_____	_____

Add these dates to your calendar. If your campus has a Campus Wide Information System or a home page on the Internet, see how many of the items are available on-line.

NOTE: If not in your catalog, this information should be available in the master schedule of classes for the current term.

The introductory information in the catalog usually stresses an institution's unique characteristics, mission, and educational philosophy, which may help determine whether or not you will find a good "fit" at the institution.

Most college catalogs include a current academic calendar, which states the beginning and ending dates of the academic terms as well as dates of holidays and other events within each term. If you are not doing well in a particular class, you may want to drop the course rather than receive a failing grade, but you must do so before the deadline for withdrawal.

GENERAL ACADEMIC REGULATIONS

General academic regulations in your catalog include requirements, procedures, and policies that are applicable to all students regardless of individual majors or student classifications. Fully understanding and complying with these rules will help you progress through your academic years without running into roadblocks.

To be fully and accurately informed, don't rely on secondhand, "grapevine" information. Become familiar with these rules directly from the catalog. If you don't understand something in the catalog, seek clarification from an official source, such as your academic advisor or counselor.

The financial section may have good news for you: detailed information on financial aid, scholarships, loans, and work opportunities. Study this section for sources of financial help.

ACADEMIC PROGRAMS

By far the lengthiest part of most catalogs is the section on academic programs. This summarizes the various degrees offered, the majors within each department, and the requirements for studying in each discipline.

The academic program section also describes the individual courses offered at your institution. Basic information usually includes course number, course title, units of credit, prerequisites for taking the course, and a brief statement of the course content.

Remember, the catalog is only a *summary* of information. Individual department offices frequently offer more detailed information in the form of course descriptions, curriculum checklists, departmental advisement guidelines, and so on. Your academic advisor or counselor may also have such supplemental information.

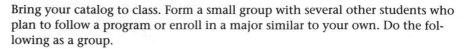

EXERCISE 10.6 **Scoping Out the Catalog**

Bring your catalog to class. Form a small group with several other students who plan to follow a program or enroll in a major similar to your own. Do the following as a group.

1. From information in the catalog, answer the following questions about the program or major:

   a. What are the core requirements of the program?

   b. What prerequisites (if any) are there for the program?

   c. Is there a sequence that must be followed when taking specific courses? (For example, are there some courses that must be taken in order but are taught only in certain terms?)

   d. What courses will each person in the group need or plan to take next term?

   If your campus has a Campus Wide Information System or a home page on the Internet, also look for this information.

2. Find at least one specific piece of information that might be useful or surprising to other members of the class. Prepare to report on that information.

■PLANNING FOR YOUR CAREER

Majors = Careers? Not Always

For some students, choosing a major is a simple decision, but most students who enter college straight out of high school (and even some who've worked a while) don't know which major to select or which career they may be best suited for.

Before you actively begin planning your major or career, consider several truths about majors and their effect on careers. Obviously, if you want to be a nurse, you must major in nursing. Engineers major in engineering. Pharmacists major in pharmacy. There's no other way to be certified as a nurse, engineer, or pharmacist. However, most career fields don't require a specific major, and people with specific majors don't have to use them in usual ways. For example, if you major in nursing, history, engineering, or English, you might still choose to become a bank manager, sales representative, career counselor, production manager, or any number of other things.

In most cases a college major alone is not enough to land you a job. There is tremendous competition for good jobs, and you need experience and competencies related to your chosen field. Internships, part-time jobs, and co-curricular activities provide opportunities to gain experience and develop these competencies.

The most common question college students ask is, "What can I do with my major?" Career planning helps you focus on a more important question: "What do I *want* to do?"

As you attempt to determine what you want to do, the choice of an academic major will take on new meaning. You'll no longer be so concerned with what the prescribed route of certain majors allows you to do. Instead you'll use your career goals as a basis for academic decisions about your major, your minor, elective courses, internships, and co-curricular activities. Consider these goals when you select part-time and summer jobs. Don't confine yourself to a short list of jobs directly related to your major; think more broadly about your goals.

EXERCISE 10.7 Some Opening Questions

Write a brief answer to each of the following questions. Try to answer each question even though you may feel uncertain about it.

1. In general, what kind of work do you want to do after finishing your education?

   _____

   _____

2. What career fields or industries offer opportunities for this kind of work?

   _____

   _____

3. What role will college play in preparing you for this work?

   _____

   _____

4. What specific things might you do to enhance your chances of getting a job when you graduate?

   _____

   _____

   _____

5. Do your career goals seem compatible with your other life goals and values?

   _____

   _____

6. Is it likely that you will need to transfer to another college in order to get the education you need for your career?

   _____

   _____

Biology . . . evolution . . . history . . . literature . . . ? Start your search for your major with some wide-ranging thought about your major interests.

© Rogers/Monkmeyer Press Photo

Factors in Your Career Planning

Some people have a very definite self-image when they enter college, but most of us are still in the process of defining (or redefining) ourselves when we enter college and long after. There are several useful ways to look at ourselves in relation to possible careers:

- **Interests.** Interests develop from your experiences and beliefs and can continue to develop and change throughout life. For example, you may be interested in writing for the college newspaper because you wrote for your high school paper, or because you'd like to try something new. Involvement in different courses may lead you to drop old interests and cultivate new ones. It's not unusual for a student to enter Psych 101 with a great interest in psychology and realize halfway through the course that psychology is not what he or she imagined or wants to pursue.

- **Skills.** Skills are measured by past performance and are almost always improvable with practice.

- **Aptitudes.** These are inherent strengths, often part of your biological heritage or the result of early training. Aptitudes are the foundation for skills. We all have aptitudes we can build on. Build on *your* strengths.

- **Personality.** The personality you've developed over the years makes you *you*, and can't be ignored when you make career decisions. The quiet, orderly, calm, detail-oriented person probably will and should make a different work choice than the aggressive, outgoing, argumentative person.

- **Life Goals and Work Values.** Each of us defines success and satisfaction in our own way. The process is complex and very personal. Two factors influence our conclusions about success and happiness: (1) knowing that we are achieving the life goals we've set for ourselves and (2) finding that we value what we're receiving from our work.

Dr. John Holland, a psychologist at Johns Hopkins University, has developed a number of tools and concepts that can help you organize these various dimensions of yourself so that you can identify potential career choices. For example, Exercise 10.8 is based on his work.

EXERCISE 10.8 What Are Your Life Goals?

The following list includes life goals some people set for themselves. This list can help you begin to think about the kinds of goals you may want to set. Place a check mark next to the goals you would like to achieve in your life. Next, review the goals you have checked and circle the five you want most. Finally, review your list of five goals and rank them by priority (1 for most important, 5 for least important).

_____ the love and admiration of friends

_____ good health

_____ lifetime financial security

_____ a lovely home

_____ international fame

_____ freedom within my work setting

_____ a good love relationship

_____ a satisfying religious faith

_____ recognition as the most attractive person in the world

_____ an understanding of the meaning of life

_____ success in my profession

_____ a personal contribution to the elimination of poverty and sickness

_____ a chance to direct the destiny of a nation

_____ freedom to do what I want

_____ a satisfying and fulfilling marriage

_____ a happy family relationship

_____ complete self-confidence

_____ other: _____

NOTE: Adapted from Human Potential Seminar by James D. McHolland, Evanston, Ill., 1975. Used by permission of the author.

Holland separates people into six general categories based on differences in their interests, skills, values, and personality characteristics—in short, their preferred approaches to life:*

R ● **Realistic.** These people describe themselves as concrete, down-to-earth, and practical—as doers. They exhibit competitive/assertive behavior and show interest in activities that require motor coordination, skill, and physical strength. They prefer situations involving "action solutions" rather than tasks involving verbal or interpersonal skills, and they like to take a concrete approach to problem solving rather than rely on abstract theory. They tend to be interested in scientific or mechanical areas rather than cultural and aesthetic fields.

I ● **Investigative.** These people describe themselves as analytical, rational, and logical—as problem solvers. They value intellectual stimulation and intellectual achievement and prefer to think rather than to act, to organize and understand rather than to persuade. They usually

*Adapted from John L. Holland, *Self-Directed Search Manual* (Psychological Assessment Resources: 1985). Copyright © 1985 by PAR, Inc. Reprinted with permission.

have a strong interest in physical, biological, or social sciences. They are less apt to be "people-oriented."

A • **Artistic.** These people describe themselves as creative, innovative, and independent. They value self-expression and relations with others through artistic expression and are also emotionally expressive. They dislike structure, preferring tasks involving personal or physical skills. They resemble investigative people but are more interested in the cultural-aesthetic than the scientific.

S • **Social.** These people describe themselves as kind, caring, helpful, and understanding of others. They value helping and making a contribution. They satisfy their needs in one-to-one or small group interaction using strong verbal skills to teach, counsel, or advise. They are drawn to close interpersonal relationships and are less apt to engage in intellectual or extensive physical activity.

E • **Enterprising.** These people describe themselves as assertive, risk-taking, and persuasive. They value prestige, power, and status and are more inclined than other types to pursue it. They use verbal skills to supervise, lead, direct, and persuade rather than to support or guide. They are interested in people and in achieving organizational goals.

C • **Conventional.** These people describe themselves as neat, orderly, detail-oriented, and persistent. They value order, structure, prestige, and status and possess a high degree of self-control. They are not opposed to rules and regulations. They are skilled in organizing, planning, and scheduling and are interested in data and people.

Exercise 10.9 provides a means of seeing (roughly) how you yourself relate to Holland's categories.

EXERCISE 10.9 Personality Mosaic

Circle the numbers of the statements that clearly feel like something you might say or do or think—something that feels like you. When you have finished, circle the same number on the answer grid on page 196.

1. It's important for me to have a strong, agile body.

2. I need to understand things thoroughly.

3. Music, color, beauty of any kind can really affect my moods.

4. People enrich my life and give it meaning.

5. I have confidence in myself that I can make things happen.

6. I appreciate clear directions so I know exactly what I can do.

7. I can usually carry/build/fix things myself.

8. I can get absorbed for hours in thinking something out.

9. I appreciate beautiful surroundings; color and design mean a lot to me.

10. I love company.

11. I enjoy competing.

12. I need to get my surroundings in order before I start a project.

13. I enjoy making things with my hands.

14. It's satisfying to explore new ideas.

15. I always seem to be looking for new ways to express my creativity.

16. I value being able to share personal concerns with people.

NOTE: From Betty Neville Michelozzi, *Coming Alive from Nine to Five,* 4th ed. Mountain View, Calif.: Mayfield Publishing Co., © 1980, 1984, 1988, 1992. Used by permission of the publisher.

17. Being a key person in a group is very satisfying to me.

18. I take pride in being careful about all the details of my work.

19. I don't mind getting my hands dirty.

20. I see education as a lifelong process of developing and sharpening my mind.

21. I love to dress in unusual ways, to try new colors and styles.

22. I can often sense when a person needs to talk to someone.

23. I enjoy getting people organized and on the move.

24. A good routine helps me get the job done.

25. I like to buy sensible things that I can make or work on myself.

26. Sometimes I can sit for hours and work on puzzles or read or just think about life.

27. I have a great imagination.

28. It makes me feel good to take care of people.

29. I like to have people rely on me to get the job done.

30. I'm satisfied knowing that I've done an assignment carefully and completely.

31. I'd rather be on my own doing practical, hands-on activities.

32. I'm eager to read about any subject that arouses my curiosity.

33. I love to try creative new ideas.

34. If I have a problem with someone, I prefer to talk it out and resolve it.

35. To be successful, it's important to aim high.

36. I prefer being in a position where I don't have to take responsibility for decisions.

37. I don't enjoy spending a lot of time discussing things. What's right is right.

38. I need to analyze a problem pretty thoroughly before I act on it.

39. I like to rearrange my surroundings to make them unique and different.

40. When I feel down, I find a friend to talk to.

41. After I suggest a plan, I prefer to let others take care of the details.

42. I'm usually content where I am.

43. It's invigorating to do things outdoors.

44. I keep asking "why."

45. I like my work to be an expression of my moods and feelings.

46. I like to find ways to help people care more for each other.

47. It's exciting to take part in important decisions.

48. I'm always glad to have someone else take charge.

49. I like my surroundings to be plain and practical.

50. I need to stay with a problem until I figure out an answer.

51. The beauty of nature touches something deep inside me.

52. Close relationships are important to me.

53. Promotion and advancement are important to me.

54. Efficiency, for me, means doing a set amount carefully each day.

55. A strong system of law and order is important to prevent chaos.

56. Thought-provoking books always broaden my perspective.

57. I look forward to seeing art shows, plays, and good films.

58. I haven't seen you for so long. I'd love to know what you're doing.

59. It's exciting to be able to influence people.

60. Good, hard physical work never hurt anyone.

61. When I say I'll do it, I follow through on every detail.

62. I'd like to learn all there is to know about subjects that interest me.

63. I don't want to be like everyone else. I like to do things differently.

64. Tell me how I can help you.

65. I'm willing to take some risks to get ahead.

66. I like exact directions and clear rules when I start something new.

67. The first thing I look for in a car is a well-built engine.

68. Those people are intellectually stimulating.

69. When I'm creating, I tend to let everything else go.

70. I feel concerned that so many people in our society need help.

71. It's fun to get ideas across to people.

72. I hate it when they keep changing the system just when I get it down.

73. I usually know how to take care of things in an emergency.

74. Just reading about new discoveries is exciting.

75. I like to create happenings.

76. I often go out of my way to pay attention to people who seem lonely and friendless.

77. I love to bargain.

78. I don't like to do things unless I'm sure they're approved.

79. Sports are important in building strong bodies.

80. I've always been curious about the way nature works.

81. It's fun to be in a mood to try to do something unusual.

82. I believe that people are basically good.

83. If I don't make it the first time, I usually bounce back with energy and enthusiasm.

84. I appreciate knowing exactly what people expect of me.

85. I like to take things apart to see if I can fix them.

86. Don't get excited. We can think it out and plan the right move logically.

87. It would be hard to imagine my life without beauty around me.

88. People often seem to tell me their problems.

89. I can usually connect with people who get me in touch with a network of resources.

90. I don't need much to be happy.

Now circle the same numbers below that you circled above.

R	I	A	S	E	C
1	2	3	4	5	6
7	8	9	10	11	12
13	14	15	16	17	18
19	20	21	22	23	24
25	26	27	28	29	30
31	32	33	34	35	36
37	38	39	40	41	42
43	44	45	46	47	48
49	50	51	52	53	54
55	56	57	58	59	60
61	62	63	64	65	66
67	68	69	70	71	72
73	74	75	76	77	78
79	80	81	82	83	84
85	86	87	88	89	90

Now add up the number of circles in each column.

R _____ **I** _____ **A** _____ **S** _____ **E** _____ **C** _____

Which are your three highest scores?

1st _____ **2nd** _____ **3rd** _____

Now go back and reread the descriptions of these three types and see how accurately they describe you.

Holland's system organizes career fields into the same six categories. Career fields are grouped according to what a particular career field requires of a person (skills and personality characteristics most commonly associated with success in those fields) and what rewards particular career fields provide for people (interests and values most commonly associated with satisfaction). As you read the following examples, see how your career interests match the category as described by Holland.

R ● **Realistic.** Agricultural engineer, barber, dairy farmer, electrical contractor, ferryboat captain, gem cutter, heavy equipment operator, industrial arts teacher, jeweler, navy officer, health and safety specialist, radio repairer, sheet metal worker, tailor, fitness director, package engineer, electronics technician, computer graphics technician, coach, PE teacher

I ● **Investigative.** Urban planner, chemical engineer, bacteriologist, cattle-breeding technician, ecologist, flight engineer, genealogist, hand-writing analyst, laboratory technician, marine scientist, nuclear medical technologist, obstetrician, quality control technician, sanitation scientist, TV repairer, balloon pilot, computer programmer, robotics engineer, environmentalist, physician, college professor

A ● **Artistic.** Architect, film editor/director, actor, cartoonist, interior decorator, fashion model, furrier, graphic communications specialist, jewelry designer, journalist, medical illustrator, editor, orchestra leader, public relations specialist, sculptor, telecommunications coordinator, media specialist, librarian, reporter

S ● **Social.** Nurse, teacher, caterer, social worker, genetic counselor, home economist, job analyst, marriage counselor, parole officer, rehabilitation counselor, school superintendent, theater manager, production expediter, geriatric specialist, insurance claims specialist, minister, travel agent, guidance counselor, convention planner, career specialist

E ● **Enterprising.** Banker, city manager, employment interviewer, FBI agent, health administrator, industrial relations director, judge, labor arbitrator, personnel assistant, TV announcer, salary and wage administrator, insurance salesperson, sales engineer, lawyer, sales representative, marketing specialist, promoter

C ● **Conventional.** Accountant, statistician, census enumerator, data processor, hospital administrator, instrument assembler, insurance administrator, legal secretary, library assistant, office manager, reservation agent, information consultant, underwriter, auditor, personnel specialist, database manager, abstractor/indexer

At first glance, Holland's model may seem to be a simple method for matching people to career fields, but it was never meant to oversimplify the process. Your career choices ultimately will involve a complex assessment of the factors that are most important to you. To display the relationship between career fields and the potential conflicts people face as they consider them, Holland's model is commonly presented in a hexagonal shape (see Figure 10.1). The closer the types, the closer the relationships among the career fields; the farther apart the types, the more conflict between the career fields.

EXERCISE 10.10 **The Holland Hexagon**

A Go back to Exercise 10.9 and look at your three categories. Based on the list of careers listed above, how well do the three categories match your career interests?

_____

_____

_____

Figure 10.1 Holland's Hexagonal Model of Career Fields

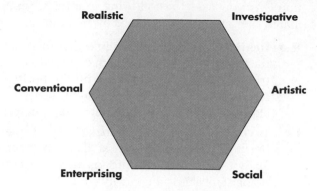

B Now look at the Holland hexagon. See where your first, second, and third choices in Exercise 10.9 are located on the hexagon. Are they close together or far apart? If far apart, do you feel they reflect a conflict in your goals or interests? Write a brief statement about how the conflict has affected you so far.

_____

_____

_____

_____

C Look back at your responses to Exercises 10.8 and 10.9. Discuss your responses and your writing in parts A and B of this exercise with a classmate.

Holland's model can help you address the problem of career choice in two ways. First, you can begin to identify many career fields that are consistent with what you know about yourself. Once you've identified potential fields, you can use the career library at your college to get more information about those fields, such as:

- Daily activities for specific jobs
- Interests and abilities required
- Preparation required for entry
- Working conditions
- Salary and benefits
- Employment outlook

Second, you can begin to identify the harmony or conflicts in your career choices. This will help you analyze the reasons for your career decisions and be more confident as you make choices.

College students often view the choice of a career as a monumental and irreversible decision. Some feel haunted by the choice as they decide on a college major. Others panic about it as they approach graduation and begin to look for a job. They falsely assume that "the decision" will make all the difference in their lives. In its broadest sense a career is the sum of the decisions you make over a lifetime. There is no "right occupation" just waiting to be discovered. Rather, there are many career choices you may find fulfilling and satisfying. The question to consider is, "What is the *best* choice for me *now*?"

Do you already have some career experience? (If you are a returning student who's chosen college as a path to a new career, the following exercise may be especially helpful in sorting out your options.)

1. What interests have you developed from life and work that might be part of your future career planning?

   _____

   _____

   _____

2. What skills do you bring from life and work that might be assets in other careers?

   _____

   _____

   _____

3. What things do you most enjoy about your present or most recent work?

   _____

   _____

   _____

4. What things do you least enjoy about your present or most recent work?

   _____

   _____

   _____

5. Go through your college catalog and list any majors that interest you. At this point, don't worry too much about whether the subject seems unfamiliar or too difficult. List the majors below, along with the reasons they appeal to you. As much as possible, try to link the reasons to your comments in the first four items of this exercise.

   Major: _____   Reasons: _____

   _____

   Major: _____   Reasons: _____

   _____

   Major: _____   Reasons: _____

   _____

   Major: _____   Reasons: _____

   _____

6. Discuss your responses in class, with your academic advisor, and/or with a career counselor. Rethink your choices in light of these discussions.

Internet

Activity 10.1
Internet Career Resources

The Internet offers a variety of resources for choosing a career. These resources include the Oakland University's "Definitive Guide to Internet Career Resources" (http://phoenix.placement.oakland.edu/career/internet.htm#c), an extensive listing of career sites; "The Catapult on Job Web" (http://www.jobweb.org/catapult/catapult.htm), a major guide with links to Career and Job Related Sites; and "The Riley Guide to Employment Opportunities and Job Resources on the Internet" (http://www.jobtrak.com/jobguide/).

Describe the resources available at each site.

_____

_____

_____

Which site is better for gathering information about a future job? Which is better for finding a job immediately?

_____

_____

_____

■TIME FOR ACTION

In selecting a major, ask yourself these questions: Am I interested in learning about the field? Do I have the skills necessary for success? Am I gaining skills and information that will be helpful in my career choices? Then, begin to learn about other academic opportunities, such as internships, independent study, study abroad, and exchange programs.

Throughout this section, you have done exercises aimed at gathering information about yourself and about the world of work and clarifying the most important issues involved in your choice of career and academic major. Here are a few other activities that may help:

- **Career exploration.** Once you've selected possible career fields, talk with people working in those fields and try to spend a day observing them at work. Read what people in this field read. Visit local professional association meetings.

- **Choice of major.** Talk with faculty members about the skills and areas of expertise you'll develop in studying the disciplines they're teaching. Ask if they're aware of careers or jobs in which the skills and knowledge they teach can be used.

- **Connection between major and career.** Ask employers if they look for graduates with certain majors or academic backgrounds for their entry-level positions.

- **Skill development.** Get involved in work experiences or campus activities that will allow you to develop skills and areas of expertise useful to your career plans. Find a summer job in that area, or volunteer as an intern. Keep a record of skills you have demonstrated.

Career planning isn't a quick and easy way to find out what you want to do with your life, but it can point you to potentially satisfying jobs. Career planning can help you find your place in the world of work.

EXERCISE 10.12 Starting a Resume

Before you finish college, you'll need a resume, whether it's for a parttime job, an internship or co-op position, or something to give to a teacher who agrees to write a letter of recommendation for you. Following the model below, write a resume of your accomplishments to date. Then write a second resume that projects what you would like your resume to contain five years from now.

SUSAN R. FIELDS
1143 Kensington Avenue
St. Louis, Missouri 42314-0344
999-456-0723
e-mail: Susan _Fields@aol.com

Education	**University of Florida,** Gainesville, Florida Candidate for B.A., Journalism and Mass Communications, May 2003 Cognate in marketing. Kettler Scholarship for excellence in high school journalism. Alpha Lambda Delta freshman honor society. Exempted first-year English and History by AP exam.
Experience	**Summer 1999. Newspaper internship at the *St. Louis Press Dispatch.*** • Worked on copy desk editing local news stories. • Accompanied reporters on local assignments. • Wrote short announcements. • Learned PageMaker pagination program. • Learned graphics and word processing programs.
Activities	**Class President,** Kensington High School, St. Louis, Missouri. Led student senate of 24 in making decisions about activities, fund raisers, student-teacher relations, and special events such as homecoming weekend and spring week.
Interests	Stamp collecting, track and field, reading biographies of famous Americans, playing acoustic guitar.
Special Skills	Adept at computer programs, including World Wide Web research, spreadsheets, and databases, in addition to skills listed above. Basic carpentry. Door-to-door sales.

SUGGESTIONS FOR FURTHER READING

Bolles, Richard N. *What Color Is Your Parachute? A Practical Manual for Job Hunters and Career Changers.* Berkeley, Calif.: Ten Speed Press, 1994.

Carney, Clarke G., and Cinda Field Wells. *Discover the Career Within You,* 3rd ed. Pacific Grove, Calif.: Brooks/Cole, 1991.

Carter, Carol. *Majoring in the Rest of Your Life.* New York: Noonday Press, 1990.

Dictionary of Occupational Titles (DOT). Washington, D.C.: Bureau of Labor Statistics.

Directory of Directories. Detroit: Gale Research. Published annually.

Encyclopedia of Associations. Detroit: Gale Research. Published annually.

Felderstein, Ken. *Never Buy a Hat If Your Feet Are Cold: Taking Charge of Your Career and Your Life.* El Segundo, Calif.: Serif, 1990.

Harbin, Carey E. *Your Transfer Planner: Strategic Goals and Guerrilla Tactics.* Belmont, Calif.: Wadsworth, 1995.

Holland, John. *The Self-Directed Search Professional Manual.* Gainesville, Fla.: Psychological Assessment Resources, 1985.

Jackson, Tom. *The Perfect Resume.* New York: Doubleday, 1990.

Lock, Robert D. *Taking Charge of Your Career Direction.* Pacific Grove, Calif.: Brooks/Cole, 1992.

Occupational Outlook Handbook. Washington, D.C.: U.S. Government Publication Staff. Published annually.

Salzman, Marian, and Nancy Marx Better. *Wanted: Liberal Arts Graduates.* New York: Doubleday, 1987.

Smith, Devon Coltrell, ed. *Great Careers: The Fourth of July Guide to Careers, Internships, and Volunteer Opportunities in the Non-Profit Sector.* Garrett Park, Md.: Garrett Park Press, 1990.

Stair, Lila B. *Careers in Business: Selecting and Planning Your Career Path.* Homewood, Ill.: Irwin, 1986.

Whitaker, Urban G. *Career Success Workbook: Five Essential Steps to Career and Job Satisfaction.* San Francisco: The San Francisco Learning Center, 1992.

Your college catalog.

Your student handbook.

Your current schedule of classes.

RESOURCES

Thinking about what you want for a career may feel overwhelming, or you may have a clear idea even now, or you may fall somewhere in between. Career interest information, academic program information, and major and course descriptions can sometimes seem abstract. One thing that can help you find the best fit for your talents and strengths is to talk to people who are taking the courses, following the majors, and pursuing the careers that you are interested in. Use this resource page to list people whom you could interview for information about courses, majors, and careers. Be creative. Over the years, this list could grow into a major networking tool.

STUDENTS WHO COULD BE RESOURCES FOR MAJORS AND COURSES

Name:	Major:	Course(s):	Phone number:

PEOPLE WHO COULD BE RESOURCES FOR CAREER AREAS

Don't forget your advisor, professors, relatives, family, friends, and people you met volunteering or through the resource list exercise from Chapter 9.

Name:	Career/Job title:	Phone number:

JOURNAL

NAME _____

DATE _____

Academic advising and career planning are closely linked in terms of the preparations you should be making for the balance of your college years and beyond.

What steps have you already considered or taken that relate to these topics?

....

....

....

....

....

....

....

....

....

Now that you've read this chapter, what steps are you thinking about taking?

....

....

....

....

....

....

....

What steps can you take at this stage in your college career to help reach your goals?

....

....

....

....

....

....

....

....

....

....

CHAPTER

Relationships and Campus Involvement

Tom Carskadon
Mississippi State University

Nancy McCarley
Mississippi State University

N o way am I going to give up living for four or five years just because college is work. I need people. I need fun. I need to get involved in something besides books!

This chapter will help you turn the following keys to success:

1. Find and get to know one individual on campus who cares about your survival.

7. Join at least one study group.

8. See your instructors outside class.

15. Make at least one or two close friends among your peers.

17. Get involved in campus activities.

Chapter Goals *This chapter has been designed to help you*

- *be realistic in seeking a date or a mate.*

- *learn how men and women differ in their approach to relationships.*

- *understand how most relationships progress through a number of stages.*

- *make sensible decisions about getting serious and becoming intimate with a partner.*

- *watch for the warning signs in relationships.*

- *balance marriage and college so that neither suffers.*

- *establish a new kind of meaningful relationship with your parents.*

- *choose supportive friends and roommates.*

- *get involved in campus activities so you'll meet more people.*

The Beatles. The Beach Boys. The Stones. The Supremes. Thirty years ago, we loved to play those groups and many more on our college radio station's Top 40 show. As amateur disc jockeys, we were no competition for Wolfman Jack, but it didn't matter; the music was so good, it carried every show. A generation later, the groups have changed, but one thing hasn't: Almost all the songs are still about love. Good love, bad love, lost love, yearning for love—how many hit songs are there about college algebra?

Once in a while, we teach a class that is so good or so bad that students spontaneously write about it in their journals. Most of the time, though, they write about relationships: with dates, lovers, or lifelong partners; with friends and enemies; with parents and family; with roommates and classmates; and with new people and new groups.

Relationships are more than just aspects of your social life—they also strongly influence your survival and success in college. Distracted by bad relationships, you will find it difficult to concentrate on your studies. Supported by good relationships, you will be better able to get through the rough times, succeed to your full potential, remain in college—and enjoy it.

■ DATING AND MATING

Loving an Idealized Image

Carl Gustav Jung, the Swiss psychiatrist who first described the psychological types you read about in Chapter 4, "Learning Styles," also identified a key aspect of love: the idealized image we have of the perfect partner, which we project onto potential partners we meet. Instead of seeing the person who is really there, we may fall in love with the image we have put there—and become disappointed when the real person turns out to be quite different.

The first task of any romantic relationship, then, is to see that the person you are in love with really exists. Specifically, you need to see beyond attraction to the person who is really there. Face it: Sex drives can be very powerful. Anything that can make your knees go weak and your mouth go dry at a single glance can affect your perceptions as well as your body. Are you in love, or are you in lust? People in lust often sincerely believe they are in love, and more than a few will say almost anything to get what they want. But would you still want that person if sex were out of the question? Would that person still want you? An answer of "No" bodes poorly for a relationship.

Folklore says, "Love is blind." Believe it. Check out your perceptions with trusted friends; if they see a lot of problems that you do not, listen to them. Another good reality check is to look at a person's friends. Exceptional people rarely surround themselves with jerks and losers; if the person of your dreams tends to collect friends from your nightmares, watch out!

You should think carefully and repeatedly about what kind of person you really want in a relationship. If a prospective partner does not have the qualities you desire, don't pursue the relationship. Also, pay attention to where you are looking. You won't catch mountain trout if you fish in a sewer.

Sexual Orientation

Although many people build intimate relationships with someone of the opposite sex, some people are attracted to, fall in love with, and make long-term commitments to a person of the same sex. Your sexuality, and who you choose to form intimate relationships with, is an important part of who you are. Understanding this part of yourself develops throughout your life. An important component of understanding your own sexuality is listening closely to your own feelings, beliefs, and values. Your sexuality is your own; it isn't dictated by your family, by society, or by what the media present as normal.

Although listening to your feelings is very important, there are many resources available if you are struggling with questions about your own sexuality. Talk about your feelings with someone you trust. Read some of the many books on the subject of sexuality and sexual orientation (some are listed in the "Suggestions for Further Reading" at the end of the chapter). Wherever you are in terms of your sexuality, it is important to remember that relationships—as well as communication, trust, respect, and love—are crucial to all people.

Developing a Relationship

Usually, relationships develop in stages. Early in a relationship, you may be wildly "in love." You may find yourself preoccupied—if not obsessed—with the other person, with feelings of intense longing when you are apart. When you are together, you may feel thrilled, blissful, yet also insecure and demanding. You are likely to idealize the other person, yet you may overreact to faults or disappointments. If the relationship sours, your misery is likely

The relationships you make in college can last throughout your life. The key to successful long-term relationships of all kinds is letting yourself see the real person you are involved with—not just falling in love with an unreal ideal.

© Joseph Nettis/Stock Boston

to be intense, and the only apparent relief from your pain lies in the hands of the very person who rejected you. Social psychologist Elaine Walster calls this the stage of *passionate love.*

Most experts see the first stage as being unsustainable—and that may be a blessing! A successful relationship will move on to a calmer, more stable stage. At this next stage, your picture of your partner is much more realistic. You feel comfortable and secure with each other. Your mutual love and respect stem from predictably satisfying companionship. Walster calls this more comfortable, long-lasting stage *companionate love.*

Communication is always a key. If a relationship is to last, it is vital to talk about it as you go along. What are you enjoying, and why? What is disappointing you, and what would make it better? Is there anything you need to know? If you set aside a regular time and place to talk, communication will be more comfortable. Do this every week or two as the relationship first becomes serious. Never let more than a month or two go by without one of these talks—even if all you have to say is that things are going great!

Most relationships change significantly when they turn into long-distance relationships. Many students arrive at college carrying on a relationship with someone back home or at another school. If you are in your late teens or early twenties, such relationships have meager odds of lasting—as do all relationships at that age. College is an exciting scene with many social opportunities. If you restrict yourself to a single, absent partner, you may miss out on a lot; and cheating or resentment can happen.

Our advice for long-distance relationships: Keep seeing each other as long as you want to, but with the freedom to pursue other relationships, too. If the best person for you turns out to be the person you are separated from, then this will become evident, and you can reevaluate the situation in a couple of years. Meanwhile, keep your options open.

Occasionally, a potential relationship will present unusual possibilities—and perils. A prime example is relationships with teachers. Entering into a romantic relationship with one of your teachers can swiftly lead to major problems. Instructors and teaching assistants are hired to have a professional relationship with you that includes certain authority. It is tempting fate to enter into a personal, romantic relationship with someone who has power or authority over you—as you may learn when the relationship goes bad. For this reason, it is best to avoid such entanglements. (See Chapter 13, "Healthy Decisions," if an instructor isn't leaving *you* alone.)

Becoming Intimate

Sexual intimacy inevitably adds a new and powerful dimension to a relationship. Several ideas are key with regard to sexual relationships:

- **Don't hurry into sexual intimacy.**
- **If sexual activity would violate your morals or values, don't do it—and don't expect others to violate theirs.** It is reasonable to explain your values so that your partner will understand your decision; but you do not owe anyone a justification, nor should you put up with attempts to argue you into submission.
- **If you have to ply your partner with alcohol or other drugs to get the ball rolling, you aren't engaging in sex—you are committing rape.** Read Chapter 13 for more information about alcohol and other drugs.
- **A pregnancy will curtail your youth and social life.** Pregnancy can be a consequence for students, even when they take some precautions. If you are sexually active for five years of college, and you use condoms for birth control all five years, data based on real-life use indicate that you have around a 20 to 50 percent chance of becoming pregnant while at college (depending on how carefully and consistently you use the condoms).

Here also are some warning signs that should concern you:

- **Having sex when you don't really want to or enjoy it.** If desire and pleasure are missing, you are doing the wrong thing.
- **Guilt or anxiety afterward.** This is a sign of a wrong decision—or at least a premature one.
- **Having sex because your partner expects or demands it.**
- **Having sex with people to attract or keep them.** This is generally short-sighted and unwise. It will almost surely lower your self-esteem. If sex is what is keeping someone with you, that someone is likely to go looking elsewhere soon.
- **Becoming physically intimate when what you really want is emotional intimacy.**

When passions run high, physical intimacy can surely feel like emotional intimacy, but sex is an unsatisfying substitute for love or friendship. Genuine emotional intimacy is knowing, trusting, loving, and respecting each other at the deepest levels, day in and day out, independent of sex. Establishing emotional intimacy takes time—and, in many ways, more real courage. If you build the emotional intimacy first, not only the relationship but also the sex will be better.

An interesting question is whether sex actually adds to your overall happiness. Believe it or not, a thorough review of the literature on happiness finds no evidence that becoming sexually active increases your general happiness. If you are expecting sex to make you happy, or to make your partner happy, the fact is that it probably won't for long. Sex relieves horniness, but it doesn't make happiness. Loving relationships, on the other hand, are powerfully related to happiness.

One option from the past is being used more today. If you want sexual activity, but you don't want all the medical risks of sex, consider the practice of "outercourse": mutual and loving stimulation between partners that allows sexual release but involves no exchange of bodily fluids. This will definitely require direct and effective communication, but it is an option that can be satisfying and fun in its own way.

Getting Serious

You may have a relationship you feel is really working. Should you make it exclusive? This is an important question to think about. Don't do it just because being only with each other has become a habit. Ask yourself, Why do you want this relationship to be exclusive? For security? To prevent jealousy? To build depth and trust? As a prelude to permanent commitment? An exclusive relationship is a big commitment. Before you make the decision to see only each other, make sure it is the best thing both for each of you and for the relationship. You may find that you treat each other best and appreciate each other most when you have other opportunities. Connections with others can help you decide what you most want in a relationship and who you can build that kind of relationship with.

While dating more than one person can help you clarify what you want, multiple, simultaneous sexual relationships can be dangerous. Besides the health risks involved, we have never seen a good, working relationship where the partners had sex with others as well. Sexual jealousy is very powerful, and it arouses insecurities, anger, and hurt.

Being exclusive can provide the chance to explore a relationship in depth and even get a taste of what marriage might be like. But if you are seriously considering marriage, consider this: studies show that the younger you are, the lower your odds of a successful marriage are. Also, you may be surprised to learn that "trial marriage" or "living together" does not decrease your risk of later divorce.

Above all, beware of what can be called "The Fundamental Marriage Error": marrying before both you and your partner know who you are and what you want to do in life. Many 18- to 20-year-olds change their outlook and life goals drastically later on. The person who seems just right for you now may be terribly wrong for you within five or ten years. Although people may change at any age, many big changes can happen in your teens and twenties. We suggest that you wait to make a permanent commitment until you feel very centered and secure by yourself. The best long-term relationships are made up of two people who are whole people in themselves. You can only bring to a relationship what you have on your own.

Whatever you do, don't marry someone while you are in the first, or passionate, stage of love. In that stage, your brains are often out to lunch, and

Think about it. An exclusive relationship is a big commitment. Are you really ready to make such a commitment?

© Frank Siteman/Stock Boston

as we mentioned earlier, the person you are "in love" with probably doesn't exist. Here is some more good advice: If you want to marry, the person to marry is someone you could call your best friend—the one who knows you inside and out, the one you don't have to play games with (the one who'd know right away if you tried to), the one who prizes your company without physical rewards, the one who over a period of years has come to know, love, and respect who you are and what you want to be. This is what a good marriage becomes, so if you can start with this, you have it made.

Seeing Warning Signs in Relationships

Folklore says you can put a frog in a pan of water and heat it on a stove; do it gradually enough, and the frog won't hop out—he'll stay until he's dinner. We've never tried it, but we have seen good people destroyed as they remained in steadily worsening relationships so long that they forgot what normal, healthy, happy ones were like. Don't be that frog! The key is to be alert to warning signs and act on them. If you encounter the following in a relationship, get out.

- **Never tolerate violence or threats in a relationship.** Drunkenness or rage is not an excuse. We recommend against giving second chances after any significant episode of threat or violence, but if you forgive the first incident and abuse reoccurs, end the relationship immediately and permanently, *no matter what*. If you need counseling or legal help, get it, but get out of the relationship.

Relationships and Campus Involvement

- **Anyone who drinks heavily or takes drugs on a regular basis is not someone with whom you should invest in a relationship.** If your partner is into addictive or dangerous drugs (such as heroin, cocaine, or LSD) or is an alcoholic, forget him or her. Addicts and users are often dangerous and seldom cured; don't let yourself believe that with your love and support, they will change. If your partner has big plans to change you, the same rules apply. Get out of the relationship!

- **Beware of pressure to split from your friends or family.** This takes you away from people who can recognize a bad situation and help you see and deal with the truth.

- **If your partner does not respect the sexual decisions you have made and pressures you to change them, find someone who will love you as you are.** Unwelcome sexual pressure is not part of a healthy relationship.

- **Cheating in a serious, exclusive relationship will surely destroy it.** Someone who will cheat on you now will do more of it later.

- **If being in a relationship is making you feel bad about yourself instead of good, this is not a relationship to continue.** Healthy relationships enhance your self-esteem; they do not diminish it.

- **If you are increasingly disappointed in your partner, and find yourself respecting that person less and less, the relationship is bad for both of you.**

- **Just passing time until someone better comes along is unfair to both you and your partner.** In fact, most of the best prospects won't approach someone already in another relationship.

- **If a relationship has become boring and seems to be inhibiting your personal growth, evaluate it carefully.** If it's just a temporary lull, then things will be better again soon; but if these feelings persist, it is time to move on.

Breaking Up

Change can be scary to think about and painful to create, but that doesn't make it less necessary. When you break up, you lose not only what you had, but also everything you *thought* you had, including a lot of hopes and dreams. No wonder it hurts. But remember that you are also opening up a world of new possibilities. You may not see them right away, but sooner or later you will.

If it is time to break up, break up cleanly and calmly. Don't do it impulsively or in anger. Explain your feelings and talk it out once. If you don't get a mature reaction, take the high road; don't join someone else in the mud. If a relationship does not work the first time, it probably will not work a second time, either. If you do decide to reunite after a trial separation, however, be sure enough time has passed for you to evaluate the situation effectively; and if things fail a second time, you really do need to forget it.

What about being "just friends"? You may want to remain friends with your partner, especially if you have shared and invested a lot. You can't really be friends, however, until you have both healed from the hurt and neither of you wants the old relationship back. That usually takes at least a year or two. Don't rush it.

Beware of intermittent reinforcement! Often, the hardest relationships to end are those that alternate unpredictably between bliss and misery. People will repeatedly let themselves be treated like dirt if every now and then they are treated like royalty. Unfortunately, some people are quite skillful at manipulating their partners with intermittent reinforcement. Good relationships are good most of the time and seldom, if ever, poor.

If you are having trouble getting out of a relationship or dealing with its end, get help. Expect some pain, anger, and depression, but if they are intense, get help. Your college counseling center has assisted many students through similar difficulties, and particular techniques can alleviate these problems. It is also a good time to get moral support from friends and family. There are good books on the subject, including our favorite, *How to Survive the Loss of a Love* (see "Suggestions for Further Reading").

Learning Axioms of Relationships

After nearly a quarter century of helping students deal with relationships, we have come up with these basic principles:

1. **If it is the right relationship, it will work; if it doesn't work, it isn't the right relationship.** If it doesn't work, whatever the reason, get out of it.

2. **Every bad relationship has warning signs.** Learn to put aside your desires or dreams long enough to be sensitive to the warning signs; then believe them and act.

3. **No relationship is better than a bad relationship.** Not having a special someone can be a downer, but that pales in comparison to the grief a bad relationship will bring you.

4. **Don't settle for less than you deserve.** Sometimes the finest people have to wait the longest, because there are fewer people as good as they. Be patient.

5. **Get it right the first time.** Divorce is hell, and all those dating games will feel even sillier when you are 30 or 40 or 50. Don't marry too young. Don't marry in a hurry. Don't marry if you have doubts. If you do marry the wrong person, there's nothing noble about a lifetime of emotional suffering for you and your family. Try your best, but if it is hopeless, get out and rebuild your life.

6. **You'll have the best relationship when you don't need one.** First establish your own independence, confidence, achievement, and happiness. After that, potential relationships will abound—people are attracted to people who are happy and secure—and you can take your pick of the very best. It is much better to want someone than to need someone.

■ MARRIED LIFE IN COLLEGE

Both marriage and college are challenges. With so many demands, it is critically important that you and your partner share the burdens equally; you can't expect a harried partner to spoil or pamper you. Academic and financial pressures are likely to put extra strain on any relationship, so you are going to have to work extra hard at attending to each other's needs.

Activity 11.1
Relationships and the Web

A Join a Mailing List

Discussion of the Internet often includes stories of happy couples who met on the Internet, as well as stories of people who have created fake identities. From one extreme to the other, the Internet provides numerous opportunities for social interchange.

Using the LISZT index of mailing lists (http://www.liszt.com/), locate a mailing list of interest to you.

Name of mailing list   _____

Content   _____

Address for joining   _____

Join the mailing list. What kind of mail do you receive from the list? Is it helpful to you? What have you learned from it?

_____

_____

_____

_____

_____

_____

_____

_____

B Visit a Chat Group

Using the YAHOO index of chat groups (http://www.yahoo.com/Computers_and_Internet/Internet/World_Wide_Web/Chat/) locate a chat group of interest to you.

Interest area   _____

Name of chat group   _____

Address   _____

Log on and see what is being discussed. Is this a chat group you would like to join? What would you gain from being part of it?

_____

_____

_____

_____

_____

_____

_____

Internet

Activity 11.1
(continued)

C Newsgroups

Scan the list of newsgroups available from your Internet provider.

- With Netscape Navigator 3.0, click on Window / Netscape News / Options / Show All Newsgroups
- With Internet Explorer 3.0, clock on Mail / Read News / News / Newsgroups

Locate a newsgroup of interest to you.

Area of interest _____

Name _____

Scan the recent postings _____

What major topics seem to be discussed?

_____

_____

_____

_____

_____

_____

_____

_____

D Connect with a Long-Distance Friend

Using the College/University e-mail address FAQ (Frequently Asked Questions) posting (http://www.qucis.queensu.ca/FAQs/email/college.html), locate the e-mail address of a friend or relative on another campus.

Name _____

College _____

e-mail address _____

Exchange e-mail.

If you are in college but your spouse is not, it is important to bring your partner into your college life. Directly or indirectly, your partner is probably helping you get through college. Share what you are learning in your courses. See if your partner can take a course, too—maybe just to audit for the fun of it. Take your partner to cultural events—lectures, plays, concerts—on your campus. If your campus has social organizations for students' spouses, try them out.

Relationships with spouses and children can suffer when you are in college because you are tempted to take time you would normally spend with

If you are married or have children, take steps to involve your loved ones in your college life.

Dollarhide/Monkmeyer Press Photo

your loved ones and put it into your studies instead. You obviously will not profit if you gain your degree but lose your family. It's very important to schedule time for your partner and family just as you schedule your classes, and keep to the schedule just as carefully.

EXERCISE 11.1 Balancing Relationships and College

A For personal writing and group discussion: If you are in a relationship, what are the greatest concerns you have about balancing your educational responsibilities with your responsibilities to your parents? What can you do to improve the situation? Is there someone on campus you can seek for counseling? If you need counseling but aren't sure where to turn, ask your instructor to help you find that person.

B If you are married and have children, write a letter to your spouse and another to your children, explaining why you must often devote time to your studies instead of to them. Don't deliver the letters; read them first and keep revising them until they sound realistic and convincing. Attempt to strike a sensible balance between your commitments to family and to your future academic and professional growth. If there are other married students in your class, share letters and get reactions. Then decide whether it's prudent to actually share these thoughts with spouses and children.

■YOU AND YOUR PARENTS

If you are on your own for the first time as an independent adult, your relationship with your parents is going to change. Thomas Wolfe said it in the title of his famous novel: *You Can't Go Home Again.* Home will never be as you left it, and you will not be who you were before. So how can you have good relationships with your parents during this period of major changes?

A first step in establishing a good relationship with your parents is to be aware of their perceptions. The most common perceptions are as follows:

1. **Younger students feel they are immortal.** You're not, of course, but you may act that way, taking risks that make older people shudder. You'll probably shudder, too, when you look back on some of your stunts. Sometimes your parents have reason to worry.

2. **Parents think their daughter is still a young innocent.** Some things parents wonder about, they don't really want to know. And yes, the old double standard (differing expectations for men than women, particularly regarding sex) is alive and well.

3. **Parents know you're 20 but picture you as 10.** Somehow, the parental clock always lags behind reality. Maybe it's because they loved you so much as children, they can't erase that image. Humor them a bit, and enlighten them gently.

4. **Parents mean well.** It's generally true. Most love their children, even if it doesn't come out right; very few are really indifferent or hateful, even if they seem that way at times.

5. **Not every family works.** If your family is like "The Brady Bunch," you are blessed. If it is even halfway normal, you will succeed. But a few families are truly dysfunctional. If love, respect, enthusiasm, and encouragement just are not in the cards, look around you: Other people will give you these things, and you can create the family you need. With your emotional needs satisfied, your reactions to your real family will be much less painful.

6. **The old have been young, but the young haven't been old.** Parental memories of youth may be hazy and distorted, but at least they have been there. A younger student has yet to experience the adult perspective.

To paraphrase Mark Twain, when you are beginning college, you may think your parents rather foolish; but when you graduate, you'll be surprised how much they've learned in four years! Your parents probably do have experience, wisdom, and love. Why not take advantage of it? Try setting aside regular times to update them on how college and your life in general are going. Actually ask for and consider their advice. You don't have to take it. If they know these conversations are coming, there may be less nagging in between.

Finally, realize that your parents are not here forever. Don't get hung up on inconsequential quarrels: "Don't let the sun set on your anger." Mend fences whenever you can. Don't let a kind word go unspoken, or love go unexpressed.

EXERCISE 11.2 Gripes

A Student Gripes. In our surveys, these are the most frequent student gripes about parents. Check off the ones that hit "closest to home" for you.

_____ Why are parents so overbearing and controlling, telling you everything from what to major in to whom to date?

_____ Why do parents treat you like a child? Why are they so overprotective?

_____ Why do parents worry so much?

_____ Why do parents complain so much about money?

_____ Why are parents so hard to talk to?

_____ Parents say they want to know what's going on in my life, but if I told them everything, they'd go ballistic and I'd never hear the end of it!

Reflect on the gripes you checked. Why do you think your parents are like that? How do your thoughts affect your relations with them?

B Parent Gripes. Looking at things from the other side, students report the following as the most common gripes their parents have about them. Check off those that ring true for your parents.

_____ Why don't you call and visit more?

_____ Why don't you tell us more about what is going on?

_____ When you are home, why do you ignore us and spend all your time with your friends?

_____ (If dating seriously) Why do you spend so much time with your boyfriend or girlfriend?

_____ Why do you need so much money?

_____ Why aren't your grades better, and why don't you appreciate the importance of school?

_____ Why don't you listen to us about getting into the right major and courses? You'll never get a good job if you don't.

_____ What have you done to yourself? Where did you get that (haircut, tattoo, style of clothes, and so on)?

_____ Why don't you listen to us and do what we tell you? You need a better attitude!

How do such thoughts affect your parents? What do you think they are really trying to tell you?

EXERCISE 11.3 Five over 30

Select five adults over 30 whom you respect. Ask each the following questions.

- What were the best decisions you made when you were 18 to 22?
- What were the biggest mistakes you made in those years?
- What advice would you give someone who is 18?

Are there common themes in what they say? How good is their advice? Bring a summary of what you were told to class, and be prepared to share it.

_____

_____

_____

_____

■FRIENDS

You are who you run with—or soon will be. Studies of students across the country clearly show that the people who influence you the most are your friends. It is important to choose them carefully.

If you want a friend, be a friend. Learn to be an attentive listener. Give your opinion when people ask for it. Keep your comments polite and positive. Never violate a confidence. Give an encouraging word and a helping hand whenever you can. You'll be amazed how many people will respect your opinions and seek your friendship.

Your friends are usually people whose attitudes, goals, and experiences are similar to your own. But in your personal life, just as in the classroom, you have the most to learn from people who are different from you. To truly enrich your college experience, try this. Make a conscious effort to make at least one good friend who is someone:

- of the opposite sex
- of another race
- of another nationality
- of a different sexual orientation
- with a physical handicap
- on an athletic scholarship
- of a much different age
- from a much different religion
- with very different politics

These friendships may take more time and effort, but you will have more than just nine new friends; you will have learned to know, appreciate, and get along with a much wider variety of people than you probably have before. This will serve you well in your later career as well as in your personal life.

■ROOMMATES

Adjusting to a roommate on or off campus can be very difficult at the start of college. Roommates range from the ridiculous to the sublime. You may make a lifetime friend—or an exasperating acquaintance you wish you'd never known. If nothing else, it is good training for later adjustments, such as marriage.

Many students choose roommates they already know and like; but that is no guarantee that your personal habits will be compatible. A roommate doesn't have to be a best friend, just someone with whom you can share your living space comfortably. Your best friend may not make the best roommate at all, and in fact more than a few students have lost friends by rooming together.

EXERCISE 11.4 Common Roommate Gripes

Housing authorities report that the most common areas of conflict between roommates are those listed below. Check those that are true for you.

_____ One roommate needs quiet to study; the other needs music or other stimulation.

_____ One roommate is neat; the other is messy.

_____ One roommate smokes; the other resents breathing or smelling smoke.

_____ One roommate feels free to bring in lots of guests; the other finds them obnoxious.

_____ One roommate brings in romantic bedmates and wants privacy—or goes at it right in front of the other; the other is uncomfortable with this and feels banished from the room that he or she paid for.

_____ One roommate likes it warm; the other likes it cool.

_____ One roommate considers the room a place to have fun; the other considers it a place to get studying done.

_____ One roommate likes to borrow the other's things; the other isn't comfortable with that.

_____ One roommate is a "morning person"; the other is a "night owl."

_____ One roommate wants silence while sleeping; the other feels free to make noise.

_____ One roommate wants to follow all the residence hall rules; the other wants to break them.

If you are rooming with someone, review your checks and write about what you and your roommate(s) can do to improve the situation. If you live alone, which of these gripes would be reason enough for you to not want to share your home with another? How might you overcome such situations if they arose?

_____

_____

_____

_____

If you are rooming with a stranger now, you can do things to get along better. Now or at the next outset, establish your mutual rights and responsibilities in writing. Many colleges provide "contract" forms that you and your roommate can use. If things go wrong later, you will have something to point to.

If you have problems, talk them out promptly. Too often, small, solvable problems become big, unsolvable ones. Dropping subtle hints is not dealing with problems. Talk about the problem directly—politely but plainly. If problems persist, or if you don't know how to talk them out, ask your residence hall counselor for help; he or she is trained to do this.

Normally, you can tolerate (and learn from) a less than ideal situation; but if things get seriously bad, insist on a change—your residence counselor will have ways of dealing with it. If you must change roomates, for your next roommate situation, try to find someone you already know you are compatible with on the issues listed in Exercise 11.4.

EXERCISE 11.5 Roommate Roulette

Pick five persons of the same sex, whom you could imagine sharing a room with, and interview them using the list of common roommate conflicts in Exercise 11.4. See how many points of commonality and difference you would have. Try to determine whether an "ideal" roommate really exists.

For each of the differences that could become conflicts on the list, write down the best compromise solutions you can. Bring your solutions to class and be prepared to have your classmates—some of whom are probably facing these very problems—judge how well they might work.

■ CAMPUS INVOLVEMENT

Many organizations and classes make it easy to form relationships. Your classes are filled with people who have something in common. Many studies prove that studying in groups with them can help you succeed, earn higher grades, and meet people. Be sure that when you form a study group, you pick people whose goals and seriousness match your own. (See Chapter 4, "Learning Styles.")

Almost every college has a wide variety of organizations you may join. Usually, there are organized ways for you to check them out—activity fairs, printed guides, open houses, Web pages, and so on. Organizations allow you to find friends with similar interests and try things you might never again have a chance to try. New students who become significantly involved with at least one organization are more likely to survive their first year and remain in college.

"To Greek or not to Greek?" may be a question on your campus. Fraternities and sororities can be a rich source of friends and support. Some students love them; others find them either philosophically distasteful or else too demanding of time and finances and too constricting of members' freedom. Fraternities and sororities are powerful social influences, so you'll probably want to take a good look at the upper-class students in them. If what you see is what you want to be, consider joining; but if it isn't, steer clear.

Greek organizations are not all alike, nor are their members. You are certainly not inferior if you do not join a fraternity or sorority. Nor are you hot stuff if you do.

They may be noisy, chaotic, and spartan, with neither privacy nor peace, but you're all in that social adventure together, and a residence hall is probably the easiest of all places to make new friends. Don't hesitate to visit new people. Take advantage of residence hall programs and activities, too.

Another good place to make friends is on the job. Working together on a common task, you get to know people quickly and well. Try to avoid starting romantic relationships on the job, though. Dating someone who works over you or under you creates problems in a hurry, and even if both of you are on the same level, you may feel awkward or miserable if the relationship ends but the two of you must still work together.

Always give a job your best because future employers may ask your past employers about you. Also, you probably will want to use them as a reference. A special kind of job available at many schools is the co-op placement. Find out whether your school has a cooperative education program at the career center. If so, be sure to check it out. These programs place you in temporary but paid positions with organizations that hire graduates in your major. Not only will you get excellent firsthand experience working in your field, but also you will form relationships and make contacts that may help a lot when you are looking for a permanent position after graduation.

EXERCISE 11.6 Connecting with Campus Organizations

Get a list of your campus organizations from your campus student center. Choose six that you might enjoy participating in. Find out more about each: Attend a meeting, talk to an officer, and/or obtain and read detailed information. Choose two you would like to get involved with this term. Bring your list to class, and be prepared to discuss what you found and your reasons for the selections you made.

■A PARTING THOUGHT

You are here for your college education; but relationships are an integral part of it and can consume up to two-thirds of your waking hours. Whether you're a traditional-age new student or a returning student with family responsibilities, be sure to approach your relationships with the same effort and planning as you would approach your course work. "Take life as it happens, but try to make it happen the way you want to take it." Long after you have forgotten whole courses you took, you will remember relationships that began or continued in college.

SUGGESTIONS FOR FURTHER READING

Bass, Ellen, and Kate Kaufman. *Free Your Mind: The Book for Gay, Lesbian, and Bisexual Youth—And Their Allies*. New York: HarperCollins, 1996.

Berzon, Betty. *Permanent Partners: Building Gay and Lesbian Relationships That Last*. New York: Plume/Penguin Books, 1990.

Clark, Don. *Loving Someone Gay*. Celestial Arts, 1987.

Cosgrove, Melba, Harold Bloomfield, and Peter McWilliams. *How to Survive the Loss of a Love*. New York: Bantam Books, 1976.

Gaines, Stanley O. *Culture, Ethnicity, and Personal Relationship Processes*. New York: Routledge, 1997.

Gray, John. *Men Are from Mars, Women Are from Venus: A Practical Guide for Improving Communication and Getting What You Want in Your Relationships*. New York: Harper-Collins, 1992.

Hendricks, Gay, and Kathlyn Hendricks. *Conscious Loving: The Journey to Co-Commitment—A Way to Be Fully Together Without Giving Up Yourself*. New York: Bantam Books, 1990.

Kummerow, Jean, and Sandra Hirsh. *LifeTypes*. New York: Warner Books, 1989.

Myers, David G. *The Pursuit of Happiness: Who Is Happy and Why*. New York: William Morrow & Co., 1992.

RESOURCES

Relationships are important throughout life, and the support you get from them can keep you going with confidence and strength, especially during times of transition—moving to a new place, starting college, changing jobs, changing life situations. During transition times you can feel all alone, with no one to really support you. You probably have more resources than you realize. Use this resource page to create a map of the relationships in your life. (See the example. Add photos if you want, or transfer your map to a larger sheet of paper and make a collage of the important people in your life.) When you are feeling down, or stressed, or alone, take a minute to look at this page and see the connections you have with other people. Give someone a call, write a letter, drop by to visit, or if you only have a moment remember the good feelings and times your relationships bring you.

Example:

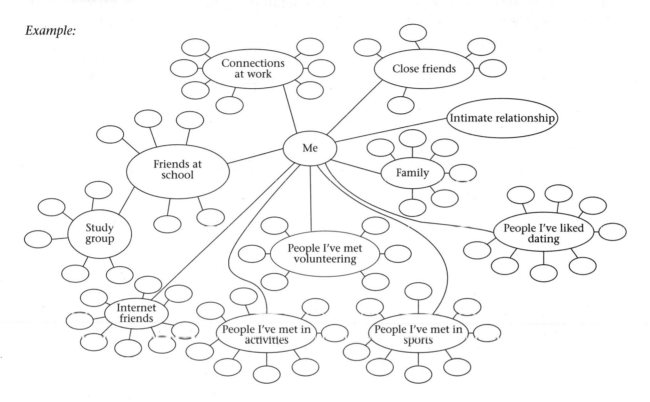

Create your map here:

JOURNAL

NAME _____

DATE _____

This chapter has covered a number of types of student relationships: friends, dating and intimate partners, marriage, parents, roommates, study groups, campus organizations, and jobs. Choose one of your relationships that needs help. Write your thoughts and feelings about the relationship, what you need from it, what you are willing to do to improve it, and what you hope the other person will be willing to do to make it better.

....

....

....

....

....

....

....

....

....

....

....

....

....

....

....

....

....

....

....

Your thoughts will probably be filled with emotion and written in free form, which is a good way to begin clarifying what is most important to you. Now, look back at what you've written, and use it to draft a letter that communicates in a more clear and logical way your needs and expectations about the relationship. You may want to revise your letter a few times to make sure that it says what you want it to say in a way that will support what you want to happen in the relationship. (For example, if you want to be treated with more care and compassion in the relationship, try to ask for that in a caring and compassionate way.) After you've finished your letter, wait a few days, then reread it, and decide whether or not you want to send or give it to the other person. (Sometimes, this process by itself can clarify your feelings about the situation.)

CHAPTER

Diversity on Campus

Joan A. Rasool
Westfield State College

I know "diversity" is in *these days*, but I'm not much into talking about it. I'm not even sure what it means. We had "diversity celebration days" in high school, but nobody took them very seriously. They seemed to separate us, not bring us together. I'm open to meeting other people but I don't want to force anything. Live and let live.

This chapter will help you turn the following keys to success:

15. Make at least one or two close friends among your peers.

17. Get involved in campus activities.

Chapter Goals *This chapter has been designed to help you*

- *appreciate cultural and ethnic differences among your college friends.*

- *understand that virtually everyone has an interesting story to tell about his or her ethnic background.*

- *value the customs and traditions of others as an expression of "unity in diversity."*

- *consider the concerns of gay, lesbian, and bisexual students.*

- *assess the level of diversity on your campus.*

- *realize that prejudice and discrimination of any kind are not to be tolerated.*

▮CULTURAL AND ETHNIC DIVERSITY

Ask almost any person in this country about his or her racial or ethnic background and you have the start of an interesting story:

> *My father is mostly Arab and part Kurdish. He always said that his strength and determination came from his Kurdish background. My mother's background is Scottish and English. She told me her mother's side of the family came over on the* Mayflower. *My parents met when my dad was a graduate student and my mother was an undergraduate. She was studying economics and he agreed to tutor her. I came to this country when I was 4 years old and I'm still figuring out what it means to be an Arab American.*
>
> —*Baidah*

> *My racial background is African American. The other thing I would add is that I see my background as black and working class. Those two things go together for me; they are a part of my roots. How I grew up was kind of varied. On one hand I was born in California and on the other hand I was raised in Texas during segregation. Part of me grew up in a strongly segregated part of the South, and another part of me, as an adolescent, grew up in integrated California.*
>
> —*Terrell*

> *I'm American. I don't feel like I have a strong attachment to any particular group. My family is Italian, Polish, Irish, and French. On St. Patrick's Day, I say I'm Irish. If I go to an Italian restaurant, I pretend I'm Italian! I call one grandmother "Bapshee," and that's about how bilingual I am. Maybe I'm not anything.*
>
> —*Eric*

> *I'm Filipino American, and like most Filipinos I am also Catholic. Family values are stressed in my home. Outsiders might say that my culture is very patriarchal, but I certainly grew up watching my parents share power equally. My mother was a very strong woman, and as I remember, the final decisions were always hers. I am the youngest of six children and am very opinionated so no decision is ever easy in my household. In addition to family, education is heavily stressed. Attaining a college degree is a must—no, not a must, it just should happen—like breathing.*
>
> —*Cristina*

Figure 12.1 A Diversity Attitude Scale

Where do you and your friends rate on this scale?

CELEBRATION:
"We need each other."

AFFIRMATION:
"I've got something to learn from you."

CIVILITY:
"I respect your rights."

TOLERANCE:
"You have a right to be here."

INTOLERANCE:
"I'll work to keep you out."

If you are like most students, you see college as the beginning of an exciting new stage in your life, a time when you can learn a lot about yourself and the world as well as prepare for the future. How can you be sure that you will feel comfortable here, that you can be yourself, and that you will have the opportunity to meet new people and have new experiences? What is your responsibility to help create a campus environment in which all students can pursue their goals? (See Figure 12.1.)

This chapter should increase your appreciation of your own and others' backgrounds. It will also show you how campus culture influences students' academic and personal lives and help you develop strategies for making the campus a more welcoming place for everyone.

EXERCISE 12.1   Sharing Your Background

In the beginning of this chapter, Baidah, Eric, Cristina, and Terrell start to tell "their stories." Now it's your turn. Write a two-part essay. In the first part, describe the racial or ethnic groups to which you belong. Can you belong to more than one? Absolutely. Think of your own background. Be sure to include some of the beliefs, values, and norms in your cultural background. In what ways do you celebrate your background? What if you are like Eric and don't feel a strong attachment to any group? Write what you know about your family history and speculate on why your ethnic identity isn't very strong.

In the second part of your essay, discuss a time when you realized that your racial or ethnic background was not the same as someone else's. For example, young children imagine that their experiences are mirrored in the lives of others. If they are Jewish, everyone else must be too! If their family eats okra for breakfast, then all families do the same. Yet at some point they begin to realize that there are differences. When did you realize that you were African American or Hispanic American or European American or Korean American or biracial or whatever?

Share your essays with other members of the class. In what ways are your stories similar? In what ways are your stories different?

Most colleges make an effort to help students feel welcome, respected, and supported in every way that the students themselves feel is important.

Photo courtesy of Earlham College

Photo by Angela Mann

■ CULTURAL PLURALISM: REPLACING THE MELTING POT WITH VEGETABLE STEW

For years, students were taught that the immigration of different people to the United States created a "melting pot"—as diverse groups migrated to this land, their culture, religion, and customs mixed into this American pot to create a new society. The reality of what happened, however, is more complex. Instead of "melting" into the "pot," most immigrants were asked to become more like what was already here—an Anglo-European soup. For example, in order to get ahead, immigrants had to change their names to make them sound more Anglo-American; they had to make sure their children gave up their native language and learned English; and they had to do business the American way. Some groups could accomplish this more easily (for example, the Irish, French, and Germans), although not without experiencing some discrimination. Today, members of these groups may be more likely to see themselves as Eric does—as "just American." It is important to note, however, that many European Americans have retained strong ethnic ties. Equally important is the recognition that other non-European groups (for example, Africans, Japanese, and Chinese) found both laws and racial barriers impeding their integration into the culture at large.

As a result, many sociologists and educators have concluded that American society is less like a melting pot and more like vegetable stew. While each group has its own unique characteristics and flavor, all the groups together create a common broth. The dominant culture has begun to acknowledge and affirm the diversity of cultures within its borders. After years of stressing commonalities, we are now focusing on our differences.

Cultural pluralism has replaced the melting pot theory. Under cultural pluralism, each group is free to celebrate and practice its customs and traditions, and in return each group is expected to participate in the general mainstream culture and abide by its laws. "Unity in diversity" is the new rallying cry.

Whoever you are, in some ways you are part of the mainstream culture. In other ways, however, you probably feel that you are part of a smaller group, a microculture within society.

EXERCISE 12.2 Creating Common Ground

Examine the items in the following chart. For each item, decide whether you would describe your preferences, habits, and customs as reflecting the mainstream or macroculture or a specific ethnic or microculture. Enter specific examples of your own preferences in the appropriate column (two examples are given). For a given item, you may enter examples under both Macroculture and Microculture, or you may leave one or the other blank. In filling out the chart, you may want to look back at the essay you wrote in Exercise 12.1.

Category	Macroculture	Microculture
Language	_____	_____
Food	hamburgers	sushi (Japanese)
Music (for your peer group)	_____	_____
Style of dress (for your peer group)	_____	_____
Religion	_____	_____
Holidays celebrated	_____	_____
Heroes/role models	_____	_____
Key values	_____	cooperation (Native Amer.)
Lifestyle	_____	_____
Personal goals	_____	_____

Compare answers in a small group. Do most people in the group agree on what should be considered an example of the macroculture and what is an example of a microculture? Is there anyone who identifies completely with the macroculture? Is there anyone who feels completely outside it? What do you and others in your class regard as significant differences among you? In what areas do you share common ground?

Cultural pluralism doesn't mean groups must remain isolated. In fact, as you learn more about another ethnic group's heritage, there may be customs and traditions in which you would like to participate. Particular values stressed in one culture may better suit you. For example, you may prefer the punctuality emphasized in European American cultures or the more "relaxed" time schedule of Arab Americans. You may value the sense of duty and family obligation among Hispanic Americans or admire the sense of individual control and independence offered in the Anglo culture. Or your preferences may be directed toward language, music, food, dress, dance, architecture, or religion. The possibilities are endless.

■UNDERSTANDING THE PERSPECTIVES OF OTHERS

Remember the children's story of the Three Little Pigs? The big bad wolf "huffs and puffs" and blows down the houses of the first two little pigs. He finally meets his downfall when he attempts to climb down the third little pig's brick chimney only to find himself landing in a pot of boiling water. All this is refuted in the recent publication of *The True Story of the 3 Little Pigs! by A. Wolf:*

> *Everybody knows the story of the Three Little Pigs. Or at least they think they do. But I'll let you in on a little secret. Nobody knows the real story, because nobody has ever heard my side of the story. . . . I don't know how this whole Big Bad Wolf thing got started, but it's all wrong. . . . The real story is about a sneeze and a cup of sugar.*

The "real story," it turns out, is that Mr. A. Wolf had a cold the day he went to his neighbor's house to borrow a cup of sugar. Unfortunately, he sneezed so hard that the house fell down killing his good neighbor—the pig. He was then *forced* to eat him because he couldn't let a good meal go to waste!

All these years and no one thought to ask the wolf for his side of the story! And yet that is just the point. If we are going to accept and affirm the differences of other groups, then each group needs to be ready to listen to the other. This is not to say that "the other group" is the villain, but that groups tend to look at one another's perspective or side of the story as misguided, wrong, or backward.

EXERCISE 12.3 Hearing All Sides of a Story

This exercise involves forming caucus groups. A caucus group is defined as any group in which you feel you automatically belong. For example, you might form caucus groups under the following headings: commuters, learning-disabled students, Catholics, biracial students, gay and lesbian students, African American women, men, nontraditional students, and so on. First generate a list of possible caucus groups, and then decide if there are enough potential members in the class to form a group of three or more members.

Join a caucus group. Meet in your group to discuss the following questions: How does your group experience campus life? What are the major academic, residential, or social concerns of your group? How well does your college meet the needs of your group?

As a caucus group, report on your discussion while other class members just listen. Afterward, the listeners may comment or ask questions on what has been said, but they should refrain from challenging the *perceptions* of the group they are listening to.

■EXPANDING OUR VIEW OF DIVERSITY

In recent years, the concept of diversity has expanded to include sexual orientation. If our goal is to make all students feel welcome, then colleges and universities must consider the needs and concerns of gay, lesbian, and bisexual students.

Gary, a mass communications major in his junior year, decided to "come out" during this year's annual National Coming Out Day. He said:

> *I am tired of pretending I am someone I'm not. I need the community of other gay people to help me deal with the homophobia on campus, and I want to celebrate a part of me that I have come to accept and love. Believe me, my life would be a lot easier if I could accept the "normal" heterosexual lifestyle that society keeps shoving down my throat. What do I want from life? I want what most people want—the chance to go to school, have friends, get a job, and find someone to love.*

In order to create a welcoming environment for gay and lesbian students, it is important to unlearn stereotypical ideas. For example, it is *not* possible to tell someone's sexual orientation just by looking at him or her. Both gay and straight people lose when society rigidly categorizes people based on a particular style of dress or haircut, or personal interest such as ballet or sports. Second, being gay or lesbian is not solely a choice. Each year, scientists find further evidence that suggests that sexual orientation may be influenced by genetic factors. Perhaps homosexuality is a combination of genetic material and environmental factors. Last, most child molesters are *not* homosexuals; most child molesters are white male heterosexuals.

■THE DIVERSITY OF CAMPUS CULTURE

How diverse is your campus? Are you aware of the diversity that does exist on your campus? In what ways does your school encourage all students to feel welcome? How easy is it for students to express their culture and to learn about their backgrounds or the backgrounds of others?

EXERCISE 12.4   **Getting the Diversity Facts on Your Campus**

Consider campus diversity in a broader context—among the student body, faculty, administrators, and staff; in the curriculum; in social and residential settings; and at the institutional level (that is, the overall policies and procedures followed by the college).

Internet

Activity 12.1
Questions About Homosexuality

Academic and professional associations are often sources of authoritative information, especially on controversial topics.

The American Psychological Association "Answers to Your Questions About Sexual Orientation and Homosexuality" page provides answers to the following questions. First, write your responses, and then look up the answers provided by the APA.

Is sexual orientation a choice?

_____

_____

_____

Is homosexuality a mental illness or an emotional problem?

_____

_____

_____

Can lesbians and gay men be good parents?

_____

_____

_____

Can therapy change sexual orientation?

_____

_____

_____

Now, compare your answers with the APA's answers, provided at
http://www.apa.org/pubinfo/orient.html.

In a group with three or four other students in your class, investigate one of the areas in the following list. Use the questions under each heading to help guide your research. Your instructor may be able to offer suggestions on where to locate relevant materials or appropriate people to interview. Each group should report to the class their general findings in the various areas. Groups should focus on two questions: (1) How easy is it for students to express their culture and to learn about their backgrounds or the backgrounds of others on this campus? and (2) In what ways does our school try to make all students feel welcome?

Diversity is about more than racial or ethnic and religious background. It also encompasses gay, lesbian, bisexual, and transgendered individuals, who live in a world that is not always tolerant or accepting, much less affirming. All students grow when they learn to find pride in their own communities and to also accept the diverse groups around them.

© Jonathan Nourok/PhotoEdit

A Diversity in Numbers

1. In what ways are your student body, faculty, administrators, and staff diverse? What percentage of students, faculty, administrators, and staff come from different ethnic/racial groups?

2. What religious, linguistic, socioeconomic, gender, and geographic differences are there among students?

B Diversity in the Curriculum

1. What are you learning about the contributions and concerns of people of color in any of your classes? Are you learning about different perspectives as a central focus of your courses, or are the views or contributions of "others" highlighted in special chapters or special sections of chapters? Give examples.

2. What courses or workshops are available if you want to increase your racial awareness and understanding?

3. Are courses offered that include the contributions and perspectives of gays and lesbians?

C Diversity in Social and Residential Settings

1. Who or what groups are reflected in the artwork, sculptures, and names of buildings on your campus?

2. Whose food preferences are served on a regular basis at the college dining facilities?

3. If your school has campus residences, does residential life staff schedule ongoing discussions on issues of sexual orientation, diversity, and tolerance? Who is in charge of these programs?

4. Do students from different ethnic groups have organizations and hold social events? Give some examples. How does school governance support a variety of diverse activities being brought to campus?

5. Do gay and lesbian students have organizations and hold social events? Give some examples. Are there gay and lesbian support groups on campus? Who is in charge of these groups?

6. Where does cross-racial interaction exist on your campus? Is the atmosphere one of peaceful coexistence and/or resegregation? Where do students find opportunities to work, study, and socialize across racial/ethnic lines?

D Institutional Commitment to Diversity

1. How does the mission statement of your school address cultural pluralism? (Your college mission statement may be printed in the college catalog.)

2. What policies and procedures does your school have with regard to the recruitment and retention of students of color? (Contact your admissions office for information.)

3. What policies and procedures does your school have with regard to the recruitment and hiring of faculty and staff of color? (Contact your affirmative action/equal opportunity office for information.)

4. Does your school administration feel responsible for educating students about diversity, or does it assume that students and faculty of color will do this?

5. Does your school administration feel responsible for educating students about tolerance, or does it assume that gay and lesbian organizations will do this?

■ DISCRIMINATION AND PREJUDICE ON COLLEGE CAMPUSES

Unfortunately, incidences of discrimination and acts of prejudice are rising on college campuses. Although some schools may not be experiencing overt racial conflict, tension may still exist; many students report having little contact with students from different racial or ethnic groups. Moreover, a recent national survey, "Taking America's Pulse," conducted for the National Conference of Christians and Jews, indicates that blacks, whites, Hispanics, and Asians hold many negative stereotypes about one another. The good news is that "nine out of 10 Americans nationwide claim they are willing to work with each of the races—even those they felt they had the least in common with—to advance race relations."[*]

In addition to being morally and personally repugnant, you should know that *discrimination is illegal.* Most colleges and universities have established policies against all forms of racism, anti-Semitism, and ethnic and cultural intolerance. These policies prohibit racist actions or omissions including verbal harassment or abuse that might deny "anyone his/her rights to equity, dignity, culture or religion." Anyone found in violation of such policies faces "corrective action including appropriate disciplinary action."

EXERCISE 12.5 Checking Your Understanding

How clear is your understanding of discrimination and prejudice? Check your knowledge by circling T (true) or F (false) for each of the following:

T   F   1. Positive stereotypes aren't harmful.

T   F   2. Prejudice is personal preference usually based on inaccurate or insufficient information.

[*]"Survey Finds Minorities Resent Whites and Each Other," *Jet,* 28 March 1994.

Internet

Activity 12.2
Diversity in the Population and on Campus

To the best of your ability, indicate the percentage of each group listed both in the total U.S. population and in the U.S. undergraduate student population.

	General population	Undergraduate population
American Indian	_____	_____
Asian	_____	_____
Black	_____	_____
White	_____	_____
Hispanic	_____	_____

You can check your estimates

for population at: http://chronicle.merit.edu/.almanac/.almdem2.html

for students at: http://chronicle.merit.edu/.almanac/.almstu5.html

How far off were you in estimating the general population statistics?

_____

_____

_____

What conclusions can you draw about your perception of society?

_____

_____

_____

How far off were you in estimating the student population statistics?

_____

_____

_____

What conclusions can you draw about your perception of the student population?

_____

_____

_____

Locate statistics for your own institution on your institution's home page.

	Your campus
American Indian	_____
Asian	_____
Black	_____
White	_____
Hispanic	_____

The "New Majority"

Why are institutions of higher learning so concerned about diversity on their campuses? One reason has to do with population figures. In 1990, 48 million Americans (about one-fifth of the total population) were identified as "minorities." By the year 2020 they will make one-third of the population, and by the last quarter of the twenty-first century they will be the majority.*

The total U.S. population in 1990 was about 250 million according to the Bureau of the Census.† Here are some of the groups currently considered minorities in the United States, although in some areas of the country they are actually in the majority.

AFRICAN AMERICANS

African Americans make up about 12 percent (30 million) of the U.S. population. They come from diverse cultures and countries in Africa, the Caribbean, and Central and South America. Excluded from the mainstream white culture despite the end of slavery, they developed a system of historically black colleges and universities dating from the mid-nineteenth century. As of 1980, these schools still awarded nearly 70 percent of all bachelor's degrees received by African Americans.

ALASKAN NATIVE/AMERICAN INDIANS

About 2 million Americans identify themselves as (non-Hispanic) Eskimo, Aleut, and American Indian, from more than 300 tribes. Their heritage includes more than 120 separate languages.

ASIAN AMERICANS

Since discriminatory immigration laws ended in 1965, Asians have become one of our fastest-growing groups, expected to reach 10 million (4 percent of the U.S. population) by the year 2000. The largest of the many groups are Chinese, Japanese, Korean, Asian Indian, Filipino, and Vietnamese.

MEXICAN AMERICANS

Hispanics made up 12 percent of the U.S. population in 1990. The fastest-growing Hispanic group is Mexican Americans (almost 13 million). Mexican Americans have deep roots in the American Southwest from past centuries when that region belonged to Mexico and Spain. More than half of Mexican Americans live in Texas and California.

PUERTO RICANS AND CUBAN AMERICANS

Around 1990, Puerto Ricans living on the U.S. mainland numbered 2.3 million, and those living in Puerto Rico 3.3 million. All are U.S. citizens. There are more than a million Cuban Americans, mainly in Florida.

*Quality Education for Minorities Project, *Education That Works* (Cambridge: Massachusetts Institute of Technology, 1990).

†This and other figures below come from the U.S. Bureau of the Census.

T	F	3. The American Psychiatric Association lists homosexuality as a mental disorder.
T	F	4. Racism combines prejudice with power.
T	F	5. The problem of racism was solved years ago.
T	F	6. Racism hurts everyone.

(See page 238 for the answers.)

A healthy diversity on campus depends on a general willingness to let social groups form in whatever patterns are helpful and constructive. It also depends on groups and individuals welcoming communication and exchange.

Photo by Hilary Smith

EXERCISE 12.6 Combating Discrimination and Prejudice on Campus

What experiences have you had dealing with discrimination or prejudice on campus? Write briefly about the incident. Describe what happened and how you felt about it. Did you or anyone you know do anything about it? Did any administrator or faculty member do anything about it? Describe what was done. Do you think this was an effective way to deal with the incident? Explain.

If you have not experienced any problems like this, find out how your college would deal with acts of discrimination and prejudice. You may want to contact the college affirmative action/equal opportunity office for information. Find out what steps students would need to take if they wished to follow up on an incident.

Share your answers and information with other class members.

You don't have to wait for your school to take the lead in making your campus a more welcoming place. Everyone can work to create a community where diverse groups feel celebrated by "advocating for pluralism." For example, Cristina can stop laughing at her friends' racial jokes; Baidah can ask her English instructor to include some works by writers of color. Eric and Terrell can attend the gay, lesbian, and allies support group on campus with Gary.

EXERCISE 12.7 Constructive Steps: Advocating for Pluralism

As a class come up with a list of steps that students could take at your school to "advocate for pluralism."

EXERCISE 12.8 / Is Hate Speech Permitted on Your Campus?

In a small group, evaluate your campus policy on "hate speech." Develop an argument for or against complete freedom of expression on Internet newsgroups accessible on campus computers. What values and what ideas about the nature of college or society does your argument reflect?

SUGGESTIONS FOR FURTHER READING

Bell, D. *Faces at the Bottom of the Well: The Permanence of Racism.* New York: Basic Books, 1992.

Bennett, C. *Comprehensive Multicultural Education,* 2nd ed. Boston: Allyn & Bacon, 1990.

Boswell, J. *Same Sex Unions in Pre-Modern Europe.* New York: Villard, 1994.

Carrion, A. M. *Puerto Rico: A Political and Cultural History.* New York: Norton, 1983.

De Lauretis, T. *The Practice of Love: Lesbian Sexuality and Perverse Desire.* Bloomington, Ind.: Indiana University Press, 1994.

DeVita, P. R., and J. D. Armstrong. *Distant Mirrors: American as a Foreign Culture.* Belmont, Calif.: Wadsworth, 1993.

Divoky, D. "The Model Minority Goes to School." *Phi Delta Kappan* (November 1988): 219–22.

Fisk, E. B. "The Undergraduate Hispanic Experience." *Change* (May/June 1988): 29–33.

Giovanni, N. "Campus Racism 101." *Essence* (August 1991): 71–72.

Halpern, J. M., and L. Nguyen-Hong-Nhiem, eds. *The Far East Comes Near: Autobiographical Accounts of Southeast Asian Students in America.* Amherst: University of Massachusetts Press, 1989.

Mathews, J. *Escalante: The Best Teacher in America.* New York: Holt, Rinehart & Winston, 1988.

Paley, V. G. *White Teacher.* Cambridge, Mass.: Harvard University Press, 1989.

Smith, S. G. *Gender Thinking.* Philadelphia: Temple University Press, 1992.

Stalvey, L. M. *The Education of a WASP.* Madison: University of Wisconsin Press, 1989.

Tatum, B. D. "Teaching About Race, Learning About Racism: The Application of Racial Identity Development in the Classroom." *Harvard Educational Review* 62, no. 1 (1992): 1–24.

Wiley, E. "Institutional Concern About Implications of Black Male Crisis Questioned by Scholar." *Black Issues in Higher Education 7,* no. 9 (1990): 1, 8–9.

Zinn, H. *A People's History of the United States.* New York: Harper & Row, 1980.

ANSWERS (to Exercise 12.5):
1. *False.* Stereotypes, even if positive, assume that all members of a group are the same.
2. *True.* Racism reflects attitudes and actions rooted in ignorance.
3. *False.* The American Psychiatric Association removed homosexuality from its list of disorders in 1973.
4. *True.* Racism occurs when individuals use their prejudice to deny others their civil rights.
5. *False.* Check current newspapers, periodicals, and television reports for the latest incidents of racism.
6. *True.* Everyone benefits when all individuals are allowed to reach their full potential. A victim of racism might just be the person who could find a cure for AIDS.

RESOURCES

How many connections with diverse communities do you already have in your life? Look back at the relationships map that you made for the Resources in Chapter 11. Think about the different kinds of diversity and different communities discussed in this chapter.

Copy part or all of your relationship map below. Using different color markers, highlight all the people (including yourself) by gender, racial/ethnic background, sexual orientation, religious background, and so on. Make a key at the bottom of the map to show which color represents which group. (Keep in mind that most people will fall into several groups.)

After you acknowledge the diverse communities that you already have in your life, the next step is to educate yourself about communities you don't know as much about. For example, you may know a great deal about the contributions of Native Americans in U.S. history but know little about the role Asian Americans have played. You may know a lot about African American artists but little about classical music. Consider some specific activities that would further your knowledge and understanding. (For example, you could plan to attend a lecture that challenges your present thinking, interview a fellow student about his or her experiences on campus, switch the dial on your radio, or make a meal!)

List at least three activities that you plan to do this semester to expand your understanding of and appreciation for diversity.

JOURNAL

NAME _____

DATE _____

Reflect on your thoughts and feelings about your racial and ethnic background and about diversity issues on campus.

Comment on something that came up in one of the class discussions concerning diversity.

....
....
....
....
....
....
....
....
....
....
....
....

Which ideas or areas still present problems for you? What can you do about them?

....
....
....
....
....
....
....
....
....
....
....
....
....

CHAPTER

Healthy Decisions: Stress, Sexuality, and Drugs

Kevin W. King
Counseling Psychologist

Lisa Ann Mohn
University of South Carolina

N. Peter Johnson
University of South Carolina

Preston E. Johnson

*B*irth control, AIDS, drinking, drugs ... I know they're important issues to think about, but it's not as though I don't have enough to deal with already. Besides, I don't really do anything dangerous. Sometimes I just need something to help me make it through the week or give me a little relief! After I'm out of college maybe I'll worry about my health—right now I just want to make it through!

This chapter will help you turn the following keys to success:

2. **Learn what helping resources your campus offers and where they are located.**

18. **Take your health seriously.**

Chapter Goals *This chapter has been designed to help you*

- *understand the relationship between healthy habits for academic and personal success and unwise decisions about sex, alcohol, and drugs.*

- *plan your personal health plan.*

- *learn how to deal with stress before it gets the best of you.*

- *decide when and if you're ready to enter into a sexual relationship.*

- *understand advantages and disadvantages of various types of birth control.*

- *know what to do if you or your partner is infected with a sexually transmitted disease; know how to avoid such diseases.*

- *understand that the HIV virus, which causes AIDS, is not restricted to any single group of people.*

- *realize that sexual assault happens on campuses and learn whom to contact if you are a victim.*

This chapter is about dealing with stress, sexual decisions, and alcohol and other drugs. The best starting point is to be in good shape physically and mentally by eating, sleeping, and exercising reasonably.

■STRESS

At manageable levels, stress is a natural sign of vitality. The primary way to manage stress is to modify it with something that enhances our feeling of control in the situation. Relaxation is very important in counteracting stress. It's impossible to be tense and relaxed at the same time, and relaxation is a skill that we can learn just like any other skill.

The body has two basic responses to stress: to stand and fight against the cause of stress or to try to avoid it by running away. Because many sources of stress in college are unavoidable (heavy work loads, exams, and personal changes), you need to recognize your sources of stress and learn how to live with them.

Identifying Your Stress

There are two prevailing theories about the origins of stress: the life events theory and the overload of personal hassles theory. The life events theory attributes health risks and life span reduction to an accumulation of effects from events that have occurred in the previous twelve months of a person's life.

 **Start Healthy**

GET ENOUGH REST

Aim for 8 hours of sleep each night. Listen to your body, and rest more when you need to.

GET ENOUGH EXERCISE

1. **Mode.** Pick something you enjoy and will stick with. You can cross-train doing different exercises as long as they cumulatively meet the next three criteria. Find exercise partners to help you keep going.

2. **Frequency.** Exercise at least three times weekly. You will see even greater improvements if you build gradually to four to six times weekly. Give yourself at least one day a week free of exercise so your body can recover.

3. **Duration.** Exercise for at least 20–30 minutes at a time. Even when you begin, maintain exercise for at least 20 minutes.

4. **Intensity.** Monitor the intensity of your workout. In order to get aerobic benefits, your heart must be beating at a target rate. To determine this rate, subtract your age from 220 and multiply by .60. Then subtract your age again from 220 and multiply this time by .75. These two answers are the high and low limits of what your heart rate (pulse) should be during exercise.

EAT FOR HEALTH

1. **Eat a balanced diet each day.**

2. **Watch your caffeine content.**

Item	Caffeine (milligrams)
1 cup brewed coffee	85
1 cup instant coffee	60
1 cup tea	30–50
12-ounce cola drinks	35–65
Many aspirin compounds	30–60
Various cold preparations	30
1 cup cocoa	2–10
1 cup decaffeinated coffee	3

3. **Eat when you are hungry.** Don't eat for comfort or distraction. Use food to fuel your body with energy. If you are looking for emotional support or cheering up, try connecting with a good friend or exercising, rather than turning to the cookies or chips.

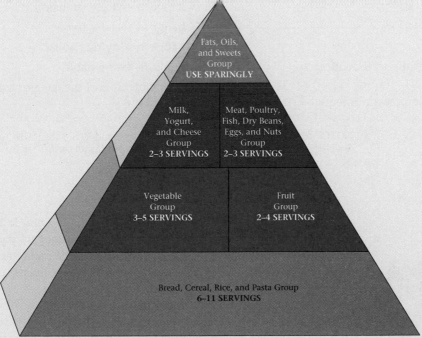

Food Guide Pyramid
A Guide to Daily Food Choices

The College Readjustment Rating Scale

The College Readjustment Rating Scale is an adaptation of Holmes and Rahe's Life Events Scale. It has been modified for college-age adults and should be considered as a rough indication of stress levels and possible health consequences.

In the College Readjustment Rating Scale each event, such as one's first term in college, is assigned a value that represents the amount of readjustment a person has to make in life as a result of change. In some studies people with serious illnesses have been found to have high scores on similar scales. Persons with scores of 300 and higher have a high health risk. Persons scoring between 150 and 300 points have about a 50-50 chance of serious health change within two years. Subjects scoring 150 and below have a 1 in 3 chance of serious health change.

To determine your stress score, circle the number of points corresponding to the events you have experienced in the past six months or are likely to experience in the next six months. Then add the circled numbers.

Event	Points	Event	Points
Death of spouse	100	Sexual difficulties	45
Female unwed pregnancy	92	Serious argument with significant other	40
Death of parent	80	Academic probation	39
Male partner in unwed pregnancy	77	Change in major	37
Divorce	73	New love interest	36
Death of a close family member	70	Increased workload in college	31
Death of a close friend	65	Outstanding personal achievement	29
Divorce between parents	63	First term in college	28
Jail term	61	Serious conflict with instructor	27
Major personal injury or illness	60	Lower grades than expected	25
Flunk out of college	58	Change in colleges (transfer)	24
Marriage	55	Change in social activities	22
Fired from job	50	Change in sleeping habits	21
Loss of financial support for college (scholarship)	48	Change in eating habits	19
Failing grade in important or required course	47	Minor violations of the law (for example, traffic ticket)	15

NOTE: Adapted with permission from T. H. Holmes and R. H. Rahe, "The Social Readjustment Scale," in Carol L. Otis and Roger Goldingay, *Campus Health Guide* (New York: CEEB, 1989).

If you find that your score on the preceding exercise is 150 or higher, it would be good preventive health care to think about why you experienced each of the scored events. In addition, you might consider what skills you need to learn either to repair the damage that these events caused or to prevent their recurrence.

The other major theory about the sources of stress attributes our general level of stress to an overload of personal hassles and a deficit of uplifts or reliefs. This theory encourages us to evaluate our immediate problems but, while doing so, to focus on what's good about our lives and to strive to notice positive events instead of taking them for granted. We are all going to experience reversals, whether it's because we don't get along with our roommate, can't register for the course or time slot we want, can't find a parking space, and so on. What we can control is our *reaction* to these hassles. If we can adopt the attitude that we will do what we can do, seek help when appropriate, and not sweat the small stuff, we won't be as negatively affected by disappointments and hassles.

EXERCISE 13.2 Personal Reflection on Stress

Record your thoughts: What seem to be the main sources of stress in your life right now? Can you point to any incidents in the past week that were particularly stressful? How do you tend to respond to stress?

A Stress Relief Smorgasbord

Everyone finds different activities relaxing. To provide yourself with a sense of relief, you need to do those things that help you to let go of stress or invigorate your mind and body. However, many of the traditional things that people do with the intention of relieving stress—such as drinking alcohol, taking drugs, sleeping, or eating—don't relieve stress and may actually increase it! There are many other ways of handling stress that truly work, such as the following:

Get Physical

1. Relax your neck and shoulders.
2. Take a stretch.
3. Get a massage.
4. Exercise.

Get Mental

1. Count to ten.
2. Control your negative thoughts by yelling "stop!" in your mind.
3. Fantasize a minivacation.
4. Congratulate yourself.
5. Ignore a problem that can't be solved right now.

Get Spiritual

1. Meditate.
2. Pray.
3. Remember why you are in a particular situation.

Use Mind and Body Together

1. Take a break and take a walk.
2. Get or give a hug (or a smile, a compliment, or a kind word).
3. Try progressive relaxation as described in the box on page 247.

Lynn Howlett Photography/photo courtesy of Willamette University

4. Laugh.
5. Find a pet.

Develop New Skills

1. Learn something that will help reduce your stress.
2. Practice a hobby that gives you a sense of accomplishment and pleasure.

Seek Help

1. Get counseling.
2. Use your network of supportive people.

You may also want to consider the values that your current physical, emotional, and spiritual circumstances reflect. Are those values similar to or different from those of your family and friends? Are you acting in accordance with your values? Is this a source of stress? Remember, whatever you do to cope with stress, you will be coping either productively or counterproductively—it's your choice.

■SEXUAL DECISIONS

Not all first-year students are sexually active, so if you're in this category you need not feel alone. However, college seems to be a time when recent high school graduates begin at least to think more seriously about sex. Re-

A Progressive Relaxation Process

Settle back and get comfortable. Take a few moments to allow yourself to listen to your thoughts and to your body. If your thoughts get in the way of relaxing, imagine a blackboard in your mind and visualize yourself writing down all of your thoughts on the blackboard. By doing this you can put those thoughts aside for a while and know that you will be able to retrieve them later.

Now that you are more ready to relax, begin by closing your eyes. Allow your breathing to become a little slower and a little deeper. As you continue breathing slowly and deeply, let your mind drift back into a tranquil, safe place that you have been in before. Try to recall everything that you could see, hear, and feel back there. Let those pleasant memories wash away any tension or discomfort.

To help yourself relax even further, take a brief journey through your body, allowing all of your muscles to become as comfortable and as relaxed as possible.

Let's begin that journey down at your feet. Begin by focusing on your feet up to your ankles, wiggling your feet or toes to help them to relax, then allowing that growing wave of relaxation to continue up into the muscles of the calves. As muscles relax, they stretch out and allow more blood to flow into them; therefore they gradually feel warmer and heavier. Continue the process on up into the muscles of the thighs; gradually your legs should feel more and more comfortable, more and more relaxed.

Then concentrate on all of the muscles up and down your spine, and feel the relaxation moving into your abdomen; as you do so you might also feel a pleasant sense of warmth moving out to every part of your body. Next focus on the muscles of the chest. Each time that you exhale, your chest muscles will relax just a little more. Let the feeling flow up into the muscles of the shoulders, washing away any tightness or tension, allowing the shoulder muscles to become loose and limp. And now the relaxation can seep out into the muscles of the arms and hands; gradually your arms and hands become heavy, limp, and warm.

Now move on to the muscles of the neck—front, sides, and back—imagining perhaps that your neck muscles are as floppy as a handful of rubber bands. And now relax the muscles of the face, letting the jaw, cheeks, and sides of the face hang loose and limp. Now relax the eyes and the nose, and now the forehead and the scalp. Let any wrinkles just melt away. And now, by taking a long, slow, deep breath, cleanse yourself of any remaining tension.

gardless of the reasons it can be quite helpful to explore your sexual values and to consider whether sex is right for you at this time.

Which of the following apply in your life?

Encouragers	Discouragers
Hormones	Family values/expectations
Peer pressure	Religious values
Alcohol/other drugs	Sexually transmitted diseases
Curiosity	Fear of pregnancy
The media	Concern for reputation
An intimate relationship	Feeling of unreadiness
Sexual pleasure	Fear of being hurt or "used"

For your protection against such pressures, try to clarify your own values and then act in accordance with them. Those who do this usually wind up happier with their decisions.

Personal Reflection on Sexuality

A Ask yourself the following questions to prepare for part B: Have you taken time to sort out your own values about sexual activity? If you aren't willing to commit to a particular plan of action at this time, what keeps you from doing so? If you are sexually active, do your values take into account your own and your partner's health? If that's not a priority for you, what would it take to get you to a point where safer sex took priority over unsafe sex?

B Write down some of your thoughts and intentions about sexuality. This should be for you alone to read. The act of writing may help you organize your thoughts. Committing your values to paper may also help you live by them when faced with tough decisions.

Birth Control

What is the best method of preventing an unwanted pregnancy? Any method of birth control that you are prepared to use correctly and consistently, each time you have intercourse. When choosing a method of contraception, consider all aspects of the method before you decide. Table 13.1 compares the major features of some common methods. Note the table's emphasis on whether each method protects against STDs. Because of their importance in preventing disease, more information about condoms is included later in this chapter.

Always discuss birth control with your partner so that you both feel comfortable with the option you have selected. For more information about a particular method, consult a pharmacist, a medical practitioner at your student health center, a local family planning clinic or Planned Parenthood affiliate, the local health department, or your private physician. Get information and resolve to protect yourself and your partner each and every time you choose to have sexual intercourse.

Sexually Transmitted Diseases (STDs)

In recent years, an epidemic number of students have become infected with sexually transmitted diseases. If you choose to be sexually active, particularly with more than one partner, exposure to an STD is a very real possibility. The consequences of the most common STDs reach far beyond the embarrassment you might feel if diagnosed with such a problem.

This section will discuss the STDs you need to be most aware of. Approximately 5–10 percent of visits to college health services nationally are for the diagnosis and treatment of STDs. For more information about any of these diseases, or others, contact your student health center, your local health department, or the National STD Hotline (1-800-227-8922).

CHLAMYDIA. Over 4 million new cases of chlamydia are diagnosed each year in the United States. Chlamydia is particularly threatening to women because a large proportion of women who are infected do not show symptoms, allowing the disease to progress to pelvic inflammatory disease (PID), now thought to be the leading cause of infertility in women. When chlamydia does produce symptoms in women, the symptoms may include mild abdominal pain, change in vaginal discharge, and pain and burning with urination.

Table 13.1 Methods of Contraception

ABSTINENCE (100%)*

What It Is
Choosing not to have intercourse.

Advantages
Only method that provides total protection against pregnancy and STDs.

Disadvantages
Does not allow for the benefits people look for from sexual intercourse.

Comments
Not an acceptable practice for many people.

NORPLANT (99.9%)

What It Is
Six matchstick-sized silicone rubber capsules, inserted into a woman's arm, that continually release a very low dose of progesterone.

Advantages
Highly effective. Works for up to five years. Allows for sexual spontaneity. Low dose of hormones make this medically safer than other hormonal methods.

Disadvantages
Removal may be difficult. Very expensive to obtain initially.

Comments
Users may have typical side effects of hormonal methods, causing them to discontinue during the first year. This makes it somewhat risky due to the high initial cost.

DEPO-PROVERA (99.7%)

What It Is
A progestin-only method, administered to women by injection, every three months.

Advantages
Highly effective. Allows for sexual spontaneity. Relatively low yearly cost.

Disadvantages
A variety of side effects typical of progestin-type contraceptives may be present and persist up to six to eight months after termination.

Comments
Method is easy and spontaneous, but users must remember to get their shots.

STERILIZATION (99.5%)

What It Is
Tubal ligation in women; vasectomy in men.

Advantages
Provides nearly permanent protection from future pregnancies.

Disadvantages
Not considered reversible and therefore not a good option for anyone wanting children at a later date.

Comments
While this is a common method for people over age 30, most college students would not choose it.

ORAL CONTRACEPTIVES (97–99%)

What They Are
Birth control pills.

Advantages
Highly effective. Allows for sexual spontaneity. Most women have lighter and shorter periods.

Disadvantages
Many minor side effects (nausea, weight gain), which cause a significant percentage of users to discontinue. Provides no protection against STDs.

Comments
Available by prescription only, after a gynecological exam.

INTRAUTERINE DEVICE (IUD) (98–99%)

What It Is
Device inserted into the uterus by a physician.

Advantages
Once inserted, may be left in for one to eight years, depending upon the type. Less expensive than other long-term methods.

Disadvantages
Increased risk of certain complications such as pelvic inflammatory disease and menstrual problems. Possible increased risk of contracting HIV, if exposed. No protection against STDs.

Comments
Women who have not had a child may have a difficult time finding a doctor willing to prescribe it.

CONDOM (88–98%)

What It Is
Rubber sheath that fits over the penis.

Advantages
Only birth control method that also provides good protection against STDs, including HIV. Actively involves male partner.

Disadvantages
Less spontaneous than some other methods because it must be put on right before intercourse. Belief of some men that it cuts down on pleasurable sensations.

Comments
Experts believe that most condom failure is due to misuse of condoms rather than breakage. Using condoms in conjunction with additional spermicide can increase effectiveness to near 100 percent.

DIAPHRAGM (80–95%)

What It Is
Dome-shaped rubber cap that is inserted into the vagina and covers the cervix.

Advantages
Safe method of birth control with virtually no side effects. May be inserted up to 2 hours prior to intercourse, making it somewhat spontaneous. May provide some protection against STDs.

Table 13.1 (continued)

Disadvantages
Wide variance of effectiveness based on consistent use, the fit of the diaphragm, and frequency of intercourse. Multiple acts of intercourse require use of additional spermicide.

Comments
Must be prescribed by a physician. Must always be used with a spermicidal jelly and left in for 6–8 hours after intercourse.

FEMALE CONDOM (80–95%)

What It Is
A polyurethane sheath that completely lines the vagina acting as a complete barrier. Two rings hold it in place, one inside and one outside the vagina.

Advantages
Highly safe medically. Does not require any spermicide. Theoretically provides excellent protection against STDs—almost perfectly leakproof and better than the male condom in this regard.

Disadvantages
Lower effectiveness rate than many other methods. Visible outer ring can be aesthetically displeasing.

Comments
While the research is not yet conclusive, this method seems to offer good STD protection that is controllable by the woman.

CONTRACEPTIVE SPONGE (80–90%)

What It Is
Small polyurethane sponge containing the spermicide Nonoxynol-9.

Advantages
Easy to obtain (over the counter) and use. Once inserted, effective for 24 hours with no additional spermicide needed.

Disadvantages
Frequent difficulty with removal. For women who have had a child, effectiveness is less than indicated here.

Comments
Must be left in for 6–8 hours after intercourse.

CERVICAL CAP (80–90%)

What It Is
Cup-shaped device that fits over the cervix.

Advantages
Similar to diaphragm, but may be worn longer—up to 48 hours.

Disadvantages
Not widely available due to lack of practitioners trained in fitting them.

Comments
Longer wearing time increases risk of vaginal infections.

SPERMICIDAL FOAMS, CREAMS, AND JELLIES (80–90%)

What They Are
Sperm-killing chemicals inserted into the vagina.

Advantages
Easy to purchase and use. Provide some protection against STDs, including HIV.

Disadvantages
Lower effectiveness than many methods. Can be messy. May increase likelihood of birth defects should pregnancy occur.

Comments
As with condoms, it is suspected that failure is due to misuse. However, spermicides seem to work better in combination with other methods (such as condoms).

NATURAL FAMILY PLANNING (80%)

What It Is
Periodic abstinence based on when ovulation is predicted.

Advantages
Requires no devices or chemicals.

Disadvantages
Requires a period of abstinence each month, when ovulation is expected. Also, requires diligent record-keeping. Provides no protection against STDs.

Comments
For maximum effectiveness, consult a trained practitioner for guidance in using this method.

COITUS INTERRUPTUS (80%)

What It Is
Withdrawal.

Advantages
Requires no devices or chemicals. Can be used at any time, at no cost.

Disadvantages
Relies heavily on the man having enough control and knowing when ejaculation will occur to remove his penis from the vagina in time. Also may diminish pleasure for the couple.

Comments
Ejaculation must be far enough away from partner's genitals so that no semen can enter the vagina. Provides no protection against STDs.

*Percentages in parentheses refer to approximate effectiveness rates based on one year of using the method. Where two numbers are given, the lower percentage refers to the *typical* effectiveness, while the higher number refers to the *possible* effectiveness if used correctly and consistently.

In men symptoms are typically pain and burning with urination, and sometimes a discharge from the penis. Occasionally the symptoms will be too mild to notice. Men who go without treatment may also become infertile, although this happens much more rarely than it does in women. In both sexes symptoms usually appear one to three weeks after exposure. Even if symptoms are not apparent, an individual infected with chlamydia is still contagious and may transmit the disease to subsequent sexual partners. If detected, chlamydia is completely treatable with antibiotics.

GONORRHEA. Gonorrhea is a bacterial infection that produces symptoms similar to chlamydia. Approximately 2 million new cases are discovered nationwide each year. As with chlamydia, men will usually show symptoms, but women often do not. Gonorrhea is treatable with antibiotics, but in recent years new, more resistant strains of gonorrhea have made this process more difficult. Untreated gonorrhea, like chlamydia, can lead to more severe infections in men and women.

HERPES. Before AIDS came along, herpes was considered the worst STD one could get, because there is no cure. There are approximately 200,000 new cases nationwide per year, but an estimated 30 million people are infected with genital herpes, many of them asymptomatic (showing no symptoms). The characteristic blisters one gets on the genitals are very similar to the cold sores and fever blisters people get on their mouths, and in fact they are both caused by varieties of the herpes virus. (The strains of the virus are even interchangeable above and below the waist if transmitted through oral sex.)

Symptoms appear on the genitals two days to two weeks after exposure in the form of small blisters or lesions that erupt into painful sores. The first outbreak is usually the most severe, and about 50 percent of those infected will never have another outbreak. The other 50 percent are likely to have outbreaks several times a year, particularly when they are under stress or their immune system is being taxed.

Although there is no cure, the prescription drug Zovirax seems to reduce the length and severity of herpes outbreaks. People are most contagious after or right before lesions erupt, so it is important to abstain from any sexual contact at this time. It is difficult to determine exactly how contagious a person is at other times, but asymptomatic people can transmit the disease because the virus continues to live in the body.

HUMAN PAPILLOMAVIRUS (HPV). HPV is the leading STD affecting the health of college students. There has been a 600 percent increase of HPV in this population in the past twenty years, and some recent studies show that as many as 40–50 percent of sexually active college students may be infected.

HPV is the cause of venereal warts, which affect both men and women on their outer genitals and in the rectum of those who practice anal receptive intercourse, and it may even grow inside a man's urethra or a woman's vagina. A typical incubation period for venereal warts is one to three months, though symptoms may not appear for several months or years after exposure. Genital warts may be small, flat, pink growths, or they may be larger, with a cauliflowerlike appearance. In either case they are usually not painful.

Because HPV is a virus, there is no cure, but there are treatments for removing the warts. As with herpes the virus remains in the body and may cause recurrences and be transmitted to a partner over an indefinite period of time.

Living with AIDS

Most people only die once. I've already died twice. The first time was in the fall of 1981 when I surrendered to the fact that I was an alcoholic and pill-head. The second time was on a warm, sunny day in late April 1987, when my doctor said, "With these symptoms, I have to conclude that it's the AIDS virus."

Being dead can have its advantages. Sometimes I say to myself, "You're dead, you can do whatever you want. What are they going to do, shoot you?" You get to eat what you like. In fact, like the scene from Sleeper, the doctors encourage you to eat steaks and ice cream. People don't castigate you when you sleep in. Planning for the future means drawing up a will. You don't save for retirement, you should live that long. I have a friend who went $27,000 into debt and then kicked the bucket. Now, he got the joke.

Generally, though, being dead isn't much fun. Old friends often treat you like the proverbial hot potato, or like a time bomb. They pass you around, hoping you don't go off around them. Not that I blame them: We've all gone to too many funerals.

So you find yourself gravitating to the other HIVs. Then the game becomes more like musical chairs. Who's the next one out? When your friends start the fast slide, they are instantly old men, the shadow-dead. Hair turns into fragile wisps, bodies gaunt down, eyes disappear into the recesses of emaciated faces. Then everyone knows, not much longer for this one.

Some are deserted by their families. More often, families kill with a kind of kindness. Well-intentioned,

misguided, they nurse you through the last months, but they really want you to go out on their terms. I have a friend who was an invalid for his last six months while his ... family screened out all gay callers and "converted" him to Christ and prayer and away from the gay life.

Another unpleasant thing about being dead is that people objectify you, treat you like a thing rather than a person. This is, of course, what we do to dead things. Bad enough that the doctors and hospital medical staff treat you like a faulty piece of equipment to keep running and keep clean (although I've had indigent friends who were denied even that slim dignity in the final countdown). You begin to wonder how to justify all this expense and bother. Soon you hear subtle messages like, "Do you realize how much your decision to stay alive is costing us?"

Then there is all the shame that goes with being too sick to meet obligations, with losing your looks, with becoming helpless. Shame is an awesome thing. My mother, who has otherwise been remarkable, cannot tell her friends that her son has this virus and is probably dying. She simply cannot do it.

Then there are all the lies. I lost a job because they found out why I was sick. I lost a job because I couldn't risk telling them I was sick. Better to leave with a question mark than with that trailing after you. Outside of the gay community I tell only a select few. I'll be [damned] if I'll surrender my personal power....

Gradually the gritty process of closing out a life begins. Can't make it into the office at nine? Go on

The major long-term health concern associated with HPV affects women. Certain strains of HPV don't cause the visible warts but invade the cervix and incorporate themselves into the DNA of the cells there. The subsequent cervical cell changes produce dysplasia, a precancerous condition that can lead to cervical cancer. Most experts believe HPV is responsible for the large majority of cases of cervical cancer in our country today. The incubation period for these changes can take many years. Fortunately, if women are screened regularly with Pap smears, precancerous changes can be detected and treated before they lead to cervical cancer.

HEPATITIS B. Most of the 300,000 new cases of hepatitis B nationwide each year occur in adolescents and young adults. Hepatitis B is transmitted through unprotected sex and through contact with infected blood, and it is

© Paul Conklin/Photo Edit

The Names Project Quilt has toured many American campuses and cities. It is both an urgent appeal for everyone to face the reality of AIDS and a moving celebration of the lives of thousands of people—male, female, gay, straight—cut short by HIV.

disability. Can't keep your apartment up? Move in with Mom and Dad. Learn to like daytime television. Let's not even talk about a sex life. You end up disempowered, nudged to the edge of things by the busy, ignored, untouched, living in limbo....

Memorize this equation: silence = death. The mountains of medicine labor to bring forth a mouse.

When you get an undeserved death sentence, you have the right to be angry. It is only the most belligerent and unpleasant among the sick who can hope to hope.

SOURCE: Adapted and reproduced, with permission, from the *Student Union* (a publication by students at Carnegie-Mellon University), 6, no. 3 (1990).

100 times more infectious than HIV. This means you have a much greater risk of contracting it if you are exposed.

Many people who are infected with hepatitis B show no symptoms. For others, symptoms may include those similar to a stomach virus, in addition to yellowing of the skin and eyes. Occasionally people become very ill and are disabled for weeks or months. Most people will recover completely, but some remain carriers for life, able to transmit the virus to others. A small percentage of infected people go on to get chronic liver disease, which puts them at risk for cirrhosis and liver cancer.

There is no cure for hepatitis B, and no treatment other than rest and a healthy diet. What makes this STD unusual is that there is a vaccine available to prevent it. The series of three shots is recommended by the Centers for Disease Control and the American Academy of Pediatrics for all young adults. The major drawback to the vaccine is that it's very costly—up to $150 for the three shots.

HIV/AIDS. HIV/AIDS is very difficult to discuss briefly. Be aware that AIDS and the virus that causes it—HIV—continue to increase. During 1994, in the thirteenth year of the epidemic, the number of cases of AIDS had grown to almost 400,000, more than twice the number there were in 1990! The Centers for Disease Control estimate that at least 1–1½ million people are infected with HIV. The routes of transmission for HIV are through blood, semen, vaginal fluids, and breast milk, or by being born to an HIV-infected mother.

While men who have sex with men and intravenous drug users still comprise the majority of AIDS cases to date, other groups have rapidly increasing rates of infection, including women, teens, heterosexuals, Hispanics, and African-Americans (who continue to be disproportionately represented among those with AIDS). Although we're discussing "risk groups" here, keep in mind that it's not who you are but what you do that puts you at risk for contracting HIV.

AIDS had not been a major problem on most college campuses as of the early 1990s. However, as more and more people become infected with HIV, college students are more likely to be exposed and to contract the virus. Because of the long incubation period suspected for AIDS, students may become infected with the virus while they are in college but not become sick until several years afterward.

Since other STDs are occurring at such a high rate, many students obviously are engaging in the behaviors that put them at risk for HIV. In addition, having other STDs may actually predispose people to contract HIV more readily if they are exposed to the virus. Each person must try to evaluate his or her own risk of becoming infected and take precautions.

As with other STDs, abstinence, monogamy, and condoms (in that order) are the best ways to prevent the sexual spread of AIDS. Get as much information as you can through your student health service, your local health department, or the National AIDS Hotline (1-800-342-AIDS).

Preventing STDs

Sexually transmitted disease is very serious and very scary. However, good methods of protection are available, and you can choose what's right for you. The worst thing you can do is nothing. If you let concerns about sexual risks overwhelm you, they will. People who do not make conscious choices in advance are often caught making a decision that doesn't suit their values and may compromise their health.

Abstinence doesn't have to mean a lack of intimacy, or even of sexual pleasure, for that matter. Abstinence (with a partner) encompasses a wide variety of behaviors from holding hands to more sexually intimate behaviors short of intercourse. These carry a lower risk of spreading disease, having an unwanted pregnancy, or possibly regretting sex than do vaginal or anal intercourse. Even if you've had intercourse in the past, you can return to a "secondary virginity" if you choose.

MONOGAMY. Another very safe behavior, in terms of disease prevention, is having sex exclusively with one partner who is uninfected. Unless you're both virgins, ask your health center about getting tested for all STDs before becoming sexually involved with a monogamous partner. Your chances of

Condoms

When selecting a condom, always consider the following:

1. **Use condoms made of latex rubber.** Latex serves as a barrier to the virus. "Lambskin" or "natural membrane" condoms are not good because of the pores in the material. Look for "latex" on the package.

2. **Use condoms with a spermicide to get more protection.** Spermicides have been shown in laboratory tests to kill viruses. Use the spermicide in the tip and outside of the condom.

3. **Use a lubricant with a condom.** Check the list of ingredients on the back of the lubricant package to make sure the lubricant is water-based. Do not use petroleum-based jelly, cold cream, baby oil, or cooking shortening. These can weaken the condom and cause it to break.

SOURCE: Adapted from *Understanding AIDS: A Message from the Surgeon General*. HHA Publication No. (CDC) HHS-88-8404 (Washington, D.C.: Government Printing Office).

remaining uninfected are better the more limited the number of sexual partners you have during your lifetime and the longer you progress in monogamous relationships disease free.

CONDOMS. In the 1990s the condom needs to be a "given" for those who are sexually active. Other than providing very good pregnancy protection, it can help to prevent the spread of STDs, including HIV/AIDS. The condom's effectiveness against disease holds true for anal, vaginal, and oral intercourse.

Other methods of birth control, particularly those with spermicides containing Nonoxynol-9, may provide some extra protection against STDs during heterosexual contact, but no other method rivals the protection offered by condoms.

Unfortunately, the condom has long had a reputation of being a less spontaneous method and of diminishing pleasurable sensations. It may take some discussion to convince your partner that using condoms is the right thing to do.

■SEXUAL ASSAULT

Sexual assault is any form of nonconsensual sex. It includes but is not limited to rape (forced intercourse). Sexual assault seems to be increasing on campus, or at least, victims are beginning to come forward in greater numbers. As a result more and more schools are developing sexual assault policies and procedures

Anyone is at risk for being raped, but the majority of victims are women. By the time they graduate, an estimated 1 out of 4 college women will be the victim of attempted rape, and 1 out of 6 will be raped. Most of these women will be raped by someone they know, a date or acquaintance, and

Many people find it hard to talk about sex with a potential partner. That's no excuse. Express your needs and concerns. Be sure you understand the other person's feelings and concerns as well.

Photo by Heather Dutton

most will not report the crime. Alcohol is a factor in nearly three-quarters of the incidents. Whether raped by a date or a stranger, the victim can suffer long-term traumatic effects.

First-year students are at particular risk for being raped because they are in a new and unfamiliar environment, may not realize the risks, want to fit in, and may even appear to be easy targets. You can take concrete actions to avoid being raped or being accused of raping someone.

Potential Victim of Sexual Assault

1. Know what you want and do not want sexually, and when the issue comes up, communicate it loudly and clearly to a partner.

2. Go to parties or social gatherings with friends, and leave with them. Sexual assaults happen when people get isolated.

3. Avoid being alone with people you don't know very well, such as accepting a ride home with someone you just met or studying alone in your room with a classmate.

4. Trust your gut. If a situation feels uncomfortable in some way, don't take chances. Get out of it even if it means a few minutes of embarrassment.

5. Be alert to unconscious messages you may be sending. While it in no way justifies someone taking advantage of you, be aware that if you dress in a sexy manner, spend the evening drinking together, and then go back to your companion's room, that person may think you want something you are not necessarily interested in.

6. Be conscious of how much alcohol you drink, if any. It is easier to make decisions and communicate them when you are sober, and also easier to sense a dangerous situation.

Person Potentially Accused of Sexual Assault

1. Realize that it is never okay to force yourself sexually on someone.

2. Don't assume you know what your companion wants. He or she may

want a different degree of intimacy than you do in the same situation. If you're not sure, ask.

3. If you're getting mixed messages, also ask. You have nothing to lose by stopping. If someone really wants you, he or she will let you know. If you don't receive that message, stop.

4. Be aware of the effects of alcohol. It makes it more difficult to understand each other, and it is more likely to instigate violent behavior.

5. Remember that rape is legally, morally, and ethically wrong. If you have the slightest doubt about whether what you're doing is right, it's probably not.

The following people or offices may be available on or near your campus to deal with a sexual assault:

- Campus sexual assault coordinator
- Local rape crisis center
- Campus police department
- Counseling center
- Student health services
- Student affairs professionals
- Women's student services office
- Residence life staff
- Local hospital emergency rooms
- Campus chaplains

Regardless of whether a victim chooses to report the rape to the police, she or he should get a medical exam and seek some type of counseling to begin working through this traumatic event.

■ALCOHOL AND OTHER DRUGS

College students are more prone to heavy alcohol usage than are their non-college peers. Heavy drinking has been increasing on campus even as it declines among young people not in college. College students use fewer drugs, but drink more alcohol. Male college students use more drugs and alcohol than female college students, with one exception: More college women than men are smokers.

EXERCISE 13.4 **Personal Reflection on Alcohol and Other Drugs**

How would you define *drug*? How would you define *drug abuse* or *addiction*? Spend some private time writing about the current extent of your involvement with alcohol or other drugs. No one else will read this, but the activity of writing will help you organize your thoughts. In what ways do you think your involvement with drugs, if any, might affect your performance in college?

Rape Does Happen

I can remember a friend of mine talking about a party that she went to this summer. She was telling me about how she liked this guy and was flirting with him a little bit. She ended up having too much to drink and passed out in a friend's room. In the morning she woke up next to the guy she had been flirting with the night before. She thought that she was OK because she had all her clothes on, but when she was walking home she noticed that her underwear was in her pocket.

Every day I walk to school and in the past couple of weeks I have noticed stencils on the sidewalk—one saying "stop raping" and the other saying "sex – yes = rape." The sight of these are kind of eerie to me. Where are the rape victims on our campus? Do they have no one to turn to and therefore resort to making their concerns and hurts on the sidewalk?

This graffiti makes me think of the statistics that I hear floating around about 1 out of every 3 women getting sexually assaulted by the time they graduate from college. Sometimes I feel lucky because I got my one time over with already and the person did not get very far except for scaring me. But then I tell myself I am not that lucky—this could happen again at any time.

I was standing against a fraternity wall and someone that I knew pretty well came up to me and pushed his body against mine and started putting his hand up my shirt while trying to kiss me. I kept turning my head against the wall so he couldn't kiss me on the lips and I was trying to push him away by pushing on his shoulders. It was scary because he was bigger and stronger than I was. Even though I was pushing as hard as I could, he was stronger. After about a minute, which felt like an eternity, he got really embarrassed and backed off and said, "I'm sorry, I'm sorry, I know I shouldn't do that to you," and then he ran away.

That incident made me feel very uncomfortable and very scared. Uncomfortable because I felt a little guilty—like maybe it was my fault. I asked myself, "Why didn't I scream? What if someone else saw?" I was scared because something like that could happen to me and I was not strong enough to stop it. Also it scared me that this was someone that I knew. I had spent time alone with him in his room in the past and he had never touched me. I was confused about why all of a sudden, in the middle of this party, he would attack me. I became distrusting of him, but also of other men that I am not very close to.

It's very frightening to think about, but too often there comes a time when a woman's resistance to sexual advances is simply chalked up to her need for further seduction, for further convincing. Suddenly the female in question is no longer a feeling individual, she's just a woman, one of the ones who would eventually say "yes" anyway. At this point an act of what might have been sexual desire turns into a desire to control the situation and the woman. It is in these cases, when the someone is denied the right to say NO, that sexual assault occurs.

To understand even faintly what the experience of sexual assault is like, you must consider what it would be like to be robbed of something very personal. There are very few things that we can personally exert control over in this life, and when someone takes the control of your own body away from you, it is devastating. When something that you own is stolen, you will be justifiably upset and insecure. When your body is violated and control over your own person is taken from you, you can never regain the security of knowing that your self (physical, emotional, mental) is your own.

SOURCE: Reproduced, with permission, from Ingrid Bromberg, "Rape Does Happen at CMU," the Student Union (a publication by students at Carnegie-Mellon University), 6, no. 3 (1990).

Alcohol

Alcohol consumption is the number-one cause of problems for college students. Unfortunately, most of us forget or ignore its consequences until forcefully reminded by friends who suffer discipline problems, broken bones, head injuries, automobile crashes, sexual assaults including acquaintance rape, academic failure, near deaths, and death itself. Then in six months we ignore or forget again until still another tragedy strikes.

If you drink, you should know that there are ways to reduce the quantity of alcohol you consume per hour. If you tend to gulp drinks, try alternating noncarbonated, nonalcoholic drinks with mixed drinks to keep the alcohol quantity down. Stay away from college drinking games, such as "quarters," "thumper," and "Indians," in which participants must consume large quantities of alcohol in short periods of time. And never drink on an empty stomach; an empty stomach rapidly absorbs alcohol, especially from carbonated beverages.

You should also know that the passage of time is the only thing that will sober you up after drinking. The enzymes in your liver process alcohol at a rate of about half a regular drink per hour. Cold showers, coffee, and exercise will not help. The joke is that coffee only makes for a more wide-awake drunk, but it really isn't funny.

Just as important is that rate of intoxication depends on age, body weight, gender, and tolerance levels. For example, women and older persons reach higher blood alcohol levels for the same amount of alcohol consumption, even if body weights are the same as those of younger men. Also, because of physiological differences, a woman weighing the same as a man may need only drink 45 percent of what the man drinks to reach the same level of intoxication.

If you play sports, be aware that moderate drinking results in loss of muscle coordination for at least 12–18 hours after consumption. And since processing alcohol disrupts the liver from its normal process of making fuel for the body, muscles tend to tire faster. For 48 hours or longer you can also expect impaired reaction time, balance, and hand–eye coordination; distorted perception; reduced ability to make smooth, easy movements; decreased strength; increased fatigue; and a host of other problems. Alcohol impairs memory, too; isn't college tough enough as it is?

Drinking and driving is a special problem for college students. For example, the highest automobile crash rates are for persons ages 18–24. This age group also ranks highest in binge drinking and per capita alcohol consumption. Almost 250,000 college students are arrested for driving under the influence (DUI) each year, and 75 percent of first-time DUI offenders will later be diagnosed as alcoholic. The likelihood of alcoholism for second-time DUI offenders is 90 percent. Driving a motor vehicle under the influence of alcohol also costs in many ways: jail time, legal fees (at least $500), and thousands of dollars in increased insurance costs. The estimated lifetime cost in 1991 for DUI offenses is $10,000, even if no repeat occurrences take place.

Alcoholism should be a special concern for you if alcohol problems have occurred in your immediate family. If a parent, sibling, aunt, uncle, or grandparent has a problem, your likelihood increases.

Marijuana

Approximately 20 percent of college students use marijuana, and about 5 percent of all college students develop serious habits. That's a disturbing number to those familiar with the effects of heavy use on many people and with recent changes in the drug itself.

The ingredient most responsible for the "high" is delta-9-tetrahydrocannabinol, or THC, which is absorbed through the lungs and into the bloodstream immediately. Strains of marijuana available today contain higher levels of THC than ever before. For example, sinsemilla reportedly is as much as 15 times stronger than the marijuana of the 1960s and 1970s.

Once in the bloodstream, THC is absorbed by, stored in, and gradually released by fat cells. A single puff of marijuana has a half-life in the body of between three and seven days, depending on the potency and the smoker. Recent research shows that the measurable pharmacologic effects of marijuana can last for one full day, and the behavioral effects may last much longer. After a period of chronic, heavy use, it can take as long as a month for THC to clear your system.

One acquaintance of ours lost a job because marijuana showed up on a drug test even though he was not a user. Rather, for the previous year he had been regularly exposed to the second-hand smoke of a roommate and family members. He had stored up so much THC in his fat cells that it was as if he were smoking marijuana himself.

If you think marijuana isn't really that bad for you, perhaps you should consider the following list of potential adverse effects from chronic use.

- Chronically slowed reaction times
- Decreased tracking capability by the eyes
- Impaired hand–eye coordination
- Altered perception of time (for example, "slow motion" sensations)
- Impairment of depth perception
- Impairment of recent memory
- Increased suggestibility, suspiciousness, and fearfulness
- Apathy, loss of drive, unwillingness or inability to complete tasks, low frustration tolerance, unrealistic thinking, increased shyness, total involvement in the present at the expense of future goals
- Increased number of lung infections
- Increased likelihood of cancer (marijuana contains *ten times* more cancer-causing agents than found in cigarettes)
- Breast enlargement in males

Cocaine

Cocaine is a powerful chemical extracted from the leaves of the coca plant. People in the Andes Mountains use coca mixed with a little lime to avoid hunger pangs and to make work at high altitudes go easier. In concentrated form cocaine is a powerful stimulant; it overstimulates the pleasure centers of the brain. The user literally loses touch with even basic biological needs during a cocaine "high." Laboratory animals have been observed to self-administer cocaine until they die of thirst or starvation, ignoring their needs for food, water, and sex. Cocaine is one of the most addictive drugs known.

The street drug cocaine hydrochloride (what most people call cocaine) is sniffed into the nose. "Crack" is smokable cocaine from which the hydrochloride has been removed. Once the drug is in the bloodstream, both forms produce the same symptoms, although the way the drug is delivered (smoked or snorted) causes differences in the immediate severity. Snorting cocaine causes runny noses, and in the long term it can "burn" a hole through the septum of the nose. Smoking crack causes respiratory problems and has destructive effects on the lungs and breathing tubes. Incidentally these same problems occur with methamphetamine, or "ice," its smokable form.

Cocaine produces an intense experience by enhancing certain chemical processes in the brain. For the cocaine user thoughts seem to come more quickly, each of the five senses seems heightened, physical energy seems unlimited, attitude becomes one of unwavering self-assurance, and fatigue and hunger disappear. It is easy to see why some students are attracted to this potent drug.

However, what goes up must come down—and in this case, rather quickly. A cocaine high starts in a few minutes, peaks in 15–20 minutes, and goes away in less than an hour. A crack high peaks within seconds and lasts about a minute. It is this speed of delivery that causes rapid addiction for many people. During the crash the user may feel tired and unmotivated. Mood may swing rapidly to depression and agitation, and the user may feel paranoid and restless and be unable to sleep.

Cocaine in any form can lead to a staggering number of physical, mental and emotional problems, both short- and long-term. If you or any of your acquaintances are using cocaine, think seriously now about talking to someone who can help you decide what you are prepared to do to face the seriousness of this problem.

Tobacco

Although tobacco is the number-one killer drug, relatively few college students smoke. Because more women than men now smoke, the rate of cancer in women has surpassed that in men. The easiest time to break an addiction is before it starts. After that it takes courage and willpower, but in the long run, it's worth it.

The best defense against alcohol and drug abuse is information, and there's plenty of it available. You can start by contacting the alcohol and drug program on your campus. Hospitals are another excellent source of information. You can also call the National Clearinghouse on Alcohol and Drug Information at 1-800-729-6686. For cocaine information call 1-800-COCAINE.

EXERCISE 13.5 Divide and Conquer

A Identify one problem or potential problem for yourself related to the topics of this chapter. Use the goal-setting process in Chapter 1 to start working on the problem. Or,

B Choose a topic that interests you most from this chapter and form a group with a few classmates who share a similar interest.

As a group, discuss your general reactions to what the chapter had to say about your shared area of interest.

Also, as a group, learn about the campus, local, and other resources that are available to people who need help in dealing with a particular problem. Report your findings to the class. Or,

C As a group or individually (as your instructor requires), research and prepare a written or oral presentation for the class on a topic related to the chapter.

Internet

Activity 13.1
Sex and Drug Information On-line

The Internet has many resources for learning about issues involving sexuality and drugs. Some of the best have been assembled by university health departments. Read the following pages:

Duke University Healthy Devil On-Line Guide to Health Concerns
http://h-devil-www.mc.duke.edu/h-devil/

State University of New York at Buffalo Counseling Center Self-Help Home Page
http://ub-counseling.buffalo.edu/

What information did you learn from them that you can put to use now?

_____

_____

_____

_____

_____

_____

_____

SUGGESTIONS FOR FURTHER READING

Benson, H., and M. Z. Klipper. *The Relaxation Response.* New York: Morrow, 1976.

Clum, George A. *Coping with Panic: A Drug-Free Approach to Dealing with Anxiety Attacks.* Pacific Grove, Calif.: Brooks/Cole, 1990.

Cooper, Kenneth H. *The Aerobic Program for Total Well-Being.* New York: Evans, 1982.

Hatcher, Robert, et al. *Sexual Etiquette 101.* Decatur, Ga.: Bridging the Gap Communications, 1993.

Otis, Carol, and R. Goldingay. *Campus Health Guide.* New York: College Entrance Examination Board, 1989.

Parrot, Andrea. *Coping with Date Rape and Acquaintance Rape.* New York: Rosen, 1988.

Pennebaker, James W. *Opening Up: The Healing Power of Confiding in Others.* New York: William Morrow, 1990.

Smith, Jonathan C. *Stress Scripting: A Guide to Stress Management.* New York: Praeger, 1991.

Strauss, R. H., ed. *Drugs and Performance in Sports.* Philadelphia: Saunders, 1987.

Travis, John W., and Regina Sara Ryan. *Wellness Workbook.* Berkeley, Calif.: Ten Speed Press, 1988.

Vorst, J. *Necessary Losses.* New York: Fawcett, 1986.

———. *Facts About Drugs and Alcohol.* New York: Bantam Books, 1986.

RESOURCES

List the resources that will help you make healthy decisions about how you can handle stress, sexuality, and alcohol or other drugs.

RESOURCES TO HELP HANDLE STRESS
For each of the following, list at least one specific activity that you can use to relieve stress.

Get Physical

Get Mental

Get Spiritual

Use Mind and Body Together

Develop New Skills

Seek Help

RESOURCES FOR HEALTHY DECISIONS ABOUT SEXUALITY
Fill in the names, addresses, and phone numbers for any of the following resources that you might use to gather information for decisions about your sexuality.

Doctor

Student Health Center

Planned Parenthood

Local AIDS Foundation or Project

Local Gay/Lesbian Resource Center

Rape Crisis Center

Counseling Center

Spiritual Advisor/Pastor/Rabbi

RESOURCES FOR HEALTHY DECISIONS ABOUT ALCOHOL AND OTHER DRUGS
Fill in the names, addresses, and phone numbers for any of the following resources that you might use to gather information for decisions about alcohol and drug use. (Some people from the list above can also help with information in this area.)

Alcoholics Anonymous

Narcotics Anonymous

Alcohol and Drug Treatment Clinics

JOURNAL

NAME _____

DATE _____

Write about the effect the issues in this chapter may have on your present and future success in college.

....

....

....

....

....

....

....

....

....

....

....

....

Which of these issues poses the largest threat to doing well in college? Why?

....

....

....

....

....

....

....

What initial steps should one take to make positive changes happen?

....

....

....

....

....

....

....

CHAPTER

Managing Money

Ray Edwards
Gunnison Country Partners, Inc.

*M*oney's no problem for me.
Either I have it or I don't.
If I have it, I spend it. Once it's
gone, I stop. By the way, can you
lend me fifty bucks until I get paid
next week?

This chapter will help you turn the following keys to success:

2. Learn what helping resources your campus offers and where they are located.

5. If you're attending classes full time, try not to work more than 20 hours a week.

21. Try to have realistic expectations.

Chapter Goals *This chapter has been designed to help you*

- *realize that managing money is an achievable goal for any college student.*
- *learn a money management process that is easy to use.*
- *set priorities among those expenses that are flexible rather than fixed.*
- *set a realistic budget for yourself and learn to stick to it.*
- *understand the different types of financial aid you may be eligible for.*
- *approach loans with caution.*
- *avoid the perils of credit card debt.*

I f you are putting yourself through school, you probably have more expenses and less income than you had in the past. If your parents are helping you pay for college, you are probably responsible for making and spending more money now than you ever were before.

This chapter will help you take control of your money so that you can worry less about it and focus more on your education. The first part is about managing what you have. The second part is about making up the difference if your budget doesn't balance.

■SOME BASIC MISCONCEPTIONS

There are several common misconceptions about the management of money.

- **Misconception 1:** Financial management is a magical process known only by a few wizards. (The truth is, there's nothing mysterious about it. Financial management is a skill that you can learn.)
- **Misconception 2:** In order to *manage* money, you need a lot more of it. Otherwise what is there to manage? (Actually it is probably more important to manage your money well when you don't have much than it is when you have money to burn.)
- **Misconception 3:** If you have enough money, you don't need to worry about how you spend it. (If you are handling most of your own finances for the first time now—paying for your room and board, buying expensive books, and so on—you may feel that you have more money than you need. Nevertheless, you need to keep track of where that money is going.)
- **Misconception 4:** You can keep track of your personal finances just by balancing your checkbook. (Balancing your checkbook is certainly important, but it has little value in relation to planning for your financial needs.)

Fortunately, money management represents nothing more than the application of common sense, planning, and self-discipline—applying some simple techniques in an organized, logical way.

■ THE MONEY-MANAGING PROCESS

Money management boils down to three primary activities: analysis, planning, and budgeting.

Analysis

Analyze your finances by identifying and comparing your expenses with your resources. Unless you know what your costs are and how much you have available, you are not going to be in control of anything. Think in terms of your academic year (August or September through May or June).

EXPENSES

Start by making a list of all the expenses you can think of, under two main categories of costs: educational and noneducational. *Educational expenses* are those you incur because you are a student, including tuition, fees, books, supplies, lab equipment, and so on. *Noneducational expenses* include all your other costs: housing, food, transportation, and miscellaneous and personal needs.

Be especially careful as you identify noneducational expenses because these costs are often hard to estimate. For example, it is easy to determine how much your tuition and fees are going to be (you need only consult your institution's published schedule of costs), but it is not so easy to estimate utility bills or food and transportation costs. Be as methodical as you can. If you are careless, you may end up being "nickeled and dimed to debt."

Table 14.1 shows most of the types of costs you will face. If you have other expenses, add them to the list.

EXERCISE 14.1 Listing Your Expenses

Note: If you're doing the exercises in this chapter on paper, be sure to use a pencil so that you can revise your numbers as you go. Better yet, use a computer word processing or spreadsheet program. Creating your own budget is a great way to learn how to use a simple computer spreadsheet.

1. Spend a few minutes writing down all the types of expenses you can think of that will apply to you during this term or academic year. Then compare your list with the list in Table 14.1.

2. Using Table 14.1 as a rough model, list your expenses. Find the total.

If you have trouble deciding how much to put down for a category such as clothing or personal items, try listing specific items you will need and estimate a cost for each. Use the estimates to help decide on a dollar total for the category.

RESOURCES

Next, identify your resources. Again, list your sources of financial support by category (savings, employment, financial aid, parents, spouse, and so on). Be realistic—neither overly optimistic nor too pessimistic—about your resources. Table 14.2 lists some common types of monetary support. List any additional sources.

Table 14.1 Typical Expenses (academic year)

Educational Expenses

Tuition	$ 800
Fees	1,200
Books	325
Supplies	75
Subtotal educational expenses	$2,400

Noneducational Expenses

Housing	$1,250
Food	1,500
Personal	100
Phone	120
Transportation	750
Clothing	450
Social/entertainment	360
Savings	250
Subtotal noneducational expenses	$4,780
Total educational and noneducational expenses	$7,180

Table 14.2 Typical Resources (academic year)

A. Parents/Spouse	
Cash	$1,000
Credit union loan	1,500
B. Work	
Summer (savings after expenses)	1,000
Part-time during year	1,500
C. Savings	
Parents	0
Your own	150
D. Financial Aid	
Grants	400
Loans	700
Scholarships	0
E. Benefits	
Veterans	0
Other	0
F. Other	
ROTC	900
Relatives	0
Trusts	0
Total	$7,150

EXERCISE 14.2 Listing Your Resources

1. Spend a few minutes writing down all the types of resources you have that will apply to you during this academic year. Then compare your list with the list in Table 14.2.

2. Using Table 14.2 as a model, list your resources. Find the total.

COMPARING EXPENSES WITH RESOURCES

Once you have identified your expenses and resources, compare the totals. Remember that this is a tentative tally, not a final evaluation. This is especially important to note if your costs exceed your resources.

EXERCISE 14.3 Comparing Resources with Expenses

1. Subtract your total expenses from your total resources (or resources from expenses). Do you have more money than you need (a positive balance)? Or do you have less (a negative balance)? Is the difference large enough to worry about?

2. If you have more money than you need, check your expenses to be sure that you are not seriously underestimating anything. Change any numbers that should be changed and compare totals again. If you still have more money than you need, increase the amount you plan to save so that your expense total equals your resources.

To bring your finances in focus, you must now complete the third step of your analysis: setting priorities and revising. To do this, classify your expenses as fixed or flexible. *Fixed expenses* are those over which you have no control; *flexible expenses* are those you can modify (flexible does not usually mean completely avoidable). Tuition, fees, and residence hall costs are generally fixed, since the institution requires you to pay specific amounts. Food may be fixed or flexible, depending on whether you are paying for a residential board plan or cooking on your own.

Table 14.3 shows some typical new-student costs divided into fixed and flexible expenses. The flexible expenses are listed in order of importance.

If the total of your expenses exceeds the total of your costs, you can start revising your flexible costs, such as telephone, clothing, and entertainment. Although cutting wardrobe and entertainment costs may be less than enjoyable, good money management means maintaining control and being realistic.

Table 14.3 Typical Expense Priorities (academic year)

Fixed Expenses

Tuition	$ 800
Fees	1,200
Books	325
Supplies	75
Housing	1,250
Subtotal fixed expenses	$3,650

Flexible Expenses

Food	$1,500
Transportation	700
Clothing	450
Personal	100
Phone	120
Social/entertainment	360
Savings	250
Subtotal flexible expenses	3,530
Total fixed and flexible expenses	$7,180

Table 14.4 Sample Monthly Budget (September)

Resources

Summer savings	$1,000
Parents/spouse	750
Financial aid	500
ROTC	100
Part-time job	166
Total	$2,516

Fixed Expenses

Tuition and fees	$1,000
Books	175
Dorm room	625
Total	$1,800

Flexible Expenses

Food (meal cash card)	$150
Supplies	35
Personal	35
Phone	15
Transportation	10
Social	40
Total	$285

Summary

Total resources	$2,516
Less total expenses	2,085
Less savings	50
Balance	$ 381*

*Carried forward to October.

For college students, many expenses come at the beginning of the semester. Planning and prioritizing can help you to better manage your finances.

Photo by Angela Mann

EXERCISE 14.4 Setting Priorities

Note: Do this exercise if Exercise 14.3 showed that your expenses are significantly higher than your resources.

1. Using Table 14.3 as a model, create a list that separates your costs into fixed versus flexible expenses. Then focus on the flexible costs and see which of them can be reduced. Change your figures to improve the balance of costs and resources. However, be realistic. Don't lower expenses that cannot realistically be lowered.

2. If your expenses are still greater than your resources, continue reading the chapter to see how you might add more to the resource side. Then come back and rework your figures to achieve a balance.

Planning

Having analyzed your costs and resources, you now have a good overall perspective on your financial situation. Next you need to plan how you will manage your money. Focus on timing, identifying *when* you will have to pay for various things and also when your resources will provide income.

For planning, you will need an academic schedule for your school (which probably appears in your college catalog or bulletin) and a calendar, preferably organized on an academic schedule such as August through July. First, review your institution's academic schedule for its overall time frame and specific dates. Determine your school's registration and payment schedules. When is the latest you can pay your housing deposit for living on campus? What is the deadline for tuition and fees? What is the school's refund policy and schedule? Enter these critical dates on your own planning calendar for the entire academic year. Find out if your school accepts credit cards for tuition payments.

Then turn your attention to other important dates that are not institutionally related. For example, if you pay auto insurance semi-annually, when is your next big premium due?

After you have recorded the important dates of your major expenditures, do the same thing for your revenue. This knowledge is essential for planning, since you can't very well plan *how* you're going to pay for things if you don't know *when* you'll have the money. For example, financial aid is typically disbursed in one lump sum at the beginning of each academic term, whereas paychecks come in smaller, more frequent installments.

Do you have any timing problems? Are there going to be points at which your costs exceed your cash? If there are, you must adjust either when you must pay or when your income will arrive. If you will be a bit strapped paying all of your tuition and fees at the start of the term, see if your school has an installment plan that will let you stretch out the payments or if you can reschedule semi-annual payments (such as car insurance premiums) as monthly payments. Many schools also allow payment by credit card, but be careful about "overloading" your cards. This is a major reason students drop out of college.

EXERCISE 14.5 Timing Income and Expenses

Get the academic schedule for your school and any monthly calendar that is convenient.

1. On the academic schedule, find the dates when your school's registration fees, charges for room and board, and other charges are due. Record these amounts on the calendar.

   Look over your expenses to see whether there are any other dates when large payments may be due for things such as automobile insurance, license fees, and required course materials. Record these amounts also on the calendar.

2. Now look at your list of resources and record the dates and amounts on your calendar when portions of your resources will be available.

3. Are there any points in the term when your resources won't cover your expenses? After reading the rest of this chapter, use the goal-setting process in Chapter 1 to solve the problem.

Once you have determined the critical dates of income and expenses, planning becomes very simple. But keep in mind that most significant of all planning destroyers, the dreaded Murphy's law: If something can go wrong, it will—and at the worst moment. For example, you might leave the cap off your car's radiator and accidentally crack the engine block. Or a roommate might suddenly split for Bali, leaving you to pay extra rent.

How can you prepare for and minimize the damage caused by unscheduled calamities? Frankly, you can't do everything, but you can prepare to some extent by being emotionally ready to deal with such things when they happen, by building up an emergency fund (even a small one), and by not departing from your money management plan. These principles not only are important for you now, but also are good habits to follow throughout your life.

Having completed the process of planning your expenditures, you should feel much more in control of your finances. Being totally aware of where you are will alleviate much potential stress.

Budgeting

The last step in developing a sound money management plan is budgeting. Budgeting takes self-discipline. Develop both a monthly budget and an academic year budget.

The budgeting process overlaps with the financial planning you did when you identified the timing of your "big ticket" items and income. The academic year budget transforms what you have on your academic calendar into a scheme that also includes your smaller, less dramatic, ongoing expenses.

The monthly budget is a specific plan for each month's income and outgo—the final details necessary to make your management system work. It eliminates any confusion about what you must do in the near future, within a manageable block of time. It is also your method for maintaining continual control over your finances. Since it coincides with the cycle of your checking account, it also facilitates monthly balancing and scheduling.

To develop your monthly budget, put your expenses and income together on one sheet, as shown in Table 14.4 on page 269. After listing your fixed expenses, your flexible expenses, and your resources, subtract expenses from resources to create a summary for the month. Settle your fixed outlays, and revise the flexible ones as necessary to achieve a reasonable balance. The September budget shown in the chart happens to include the major "start-up" costs for tuition, fees, and so on. Make sure your budget is comprehensive and keeps track of how you spend what you spend.

EXERCISE 14.6 ## A Monthly Budget

Create a sample monthly budget to plan your income and expenses on a monthly basis.

Note that Table 14.4 includes tuition, books, fees, and other expenses that may be paid in one lump sum at the beginning of the term. This means that your budget for the first month may be very different than for later months. For this reason, you may want to use the second or third month of the term for your sample monthly budget.

Once you have done this for a month or two, you will probably have a good idea of how things are going and will not need to go through such a formal process again, except in months when you foresee unusual expenses.

Financial worries can be stress-inducing, but you can minimize this stress by analyzing, planning, and budgeting well. Good money management supports your total health and well-being.

The way you handle your money in college says a lot about how you approach life in general. When you manage your personal finances well, you are facing up to realities that will confront you for the rest of your life. Developing the required seriousness and skill will continue to pay off long after you have finished college.

■ INCREASING RESOURCES

Once you're doing everything to manage your current finances well, you may still need more money. How you acquire more aid has both immediate and long-term implications.

Most college students work at least part-time. Evidence suggests that students who hold part-time jobs generally do better academically than students with more free time.

Photo by Heather Dutton

Over the past twenty years, inflation has eroded the savings of many families. In fact, the United States currently has one of the lowest percentages of per capita savings among industrialized countries. Most American families today are not paying for their children's college education out of savings. Because of this, and because the price of a college education has risen sharply over the same period, most students must now rely mainly on their family's current income and loans to finance college.

Such overreliance on current income and loans has been harmful to parents and their student/dependents in two ways. First, families are forced to make difficult sacrifices. Second, the repayment "legacy" of educational loans usually extends long after the student has finished college.

For their part, colleges and universities have been caught by the same economic forces as families, and college expenses over the past twenty years have risen faster than the overall inflation rate. It simply costs more each year for schools to provide the same level of service. Both public and private colleges have had little choice but to increase fees, and you will likely have to pay more each year you are in college.

The average annual cost of an education (including room and board) at a public four-year university or college in 1996 was around $9,300, with some schools costing close to $17,000. Average annual costs at private colleges were around $20,000, with some schools costing over $27,000.

If you are commuting to a local public institution, the cost (not including any living expenses) may still be as low as a few thousand dollars a year. Of course, even that may be a large sum for you and your family to afford.

If you are going to be able to deal with your college expenses, it is essential that you see them realistically. Only by knowing how much your education is going to cost can you go about planning how to pay for it. If it is clear that you and/or your family cannot handle all of the costs, you should certainly apply for financial aid.

Applying Critical Thinking to the Money Management Process

Write a critical analysis of your current approach to managing money. You will need to consider your expenses, resources, budgeting, priority-setting, planning, and timing of income and expenses. Try to be as objective as you can. How do you assess the logic and appropriateness of your most important financial decisions? Can you identify any alternative strategies you might consider? Discuss these.

Monitoring the Media

For a week or so, keep track of advertisements you see on television, hear on radio, or read in newspapers or magazines that not only hype credit cards, but also suggest you need to own certain material things in order to be successful and happy. Subject these to a critical analysis. How do the positive outcomes depicted square with the impact of credit cards on your life? What essential facts, truths, and realities do these ads fail to portray? How would your life be different if credit cards or some other forms of borrowing money did not exist?

Financial Aid

This chapter will not go into detail about applying for financial aid because it is a complex process that varies from school to school and may change from year to year. What we will do is help you get started thinking about how financial aid works and about what questions you might ask at your school's financial aid office.

Financial aid refers to any type of funding you receive to assist yourself in paying for college. Most financial aid money is given on the basis of need, often according to "demonstrated financial need." *Demonstrated financial need* is eligibility determined by some specific financial scale, most commonly the federal needs analysis system called the "congressional methodology." Other types of financial aid awards may not depend on this type of eligibility.

Financial aid is categorized as either gift or self-help assistance. *Gift assistance* is that which does not have to be repaid. *Self-help assistance* requires you to do something in return, such as work or repay the money. An academic scholarship is gift assistance; a student loan is self-help assistance.

The basis upon which financial aid is awarded varies, but typical criteria are academic merit, financial need, or some combination of the two. The large federal aid programs and most state programs are based on financial need and acceptable progress toward a degree.

Financial aid can be further categorized into two types of gift assistance—grants and scholarships—and two types of self-help assistance—loans and work opportunities.

GRANTS

Grants are gift assistance and so do not have to be repaid. Most institutions offer numerous grants programs, the largest funded by the federal and state governments. Generally, grants are aimed at students with the greatest demonstrated

The Perils of Plastic

Believe it or not, credit card debt by first-year students has contributed significantly to the dropout rate for this group. You may have already received letters from banks and other businesses offering credit cards or other types of charge cards. Their goal is to lend you money so that you will pay high interest rates in return. They may also charge you annual or monthly fees. In 1994, the interest rates for such student accounts were generally over 15 percent. Rates often go as high as 20 percent, which is much higher than the interest you would pay for many student loans.

At the same time, credit cards and other charge cards are sometimes very convenient. Before you decide to use a credit card or which card to choose, consider this advice:

1. Don't accept or keep cards that you don't really need.

2. Choose the right card. Before you accept a card, be able to answer these questions:

   a. Is there an annual or monthly fee or any other charge apart from interest you may have to pay? What are these fees?

   b. What is the interest rate?

   c. Is there a grace period (the time between making a purchase and paying off the charge, before you will be charged interest)? How long is it?

   d. Does the card allow cash advances? What fees and interest rates apply? (Cash advances are generally the most expensive way to borrow money.)

   e. Are there any fringe benefits to the card that would clearly be valuable to you or your family? Some cards offer a lower rate on phone calls, small cash rebates, or credit miles on "frequent flyer" programs. Usually the benefits are not significant unless you are charging large amounts.

3. If you accept a card, sign it right away. Keep a separate record of the card's number and expiration date and the number to call if it is lost or stolen.

4. Destroy carbons or incorrect slips that have not been processed.

5. Save your charge slips so that you can be certain you have been correctly charged.

6. Never lend your card or tell its number to anyone except when necessary for a transaction. (If someone uses your number, you are not responsible for these charges, but you may go through a lot of trouble trying to show the bank which charges were yours and which were fraudulent.)

7. If the card is lost or stolen, you will probably have to pay no more than $50 of any charges made with the stolen card. Report any loss of the card or other problems immediately by phone.

financial need. Students can often receive more than one type of grant simultaneously, but institutions do place limits on the total amount of grant assistance they will award to any one individual, since such funds are limited. Most schools want to spread grants out among as many students as possible.

SCHOLARSHIPS

Scholarships are awarded on the basis of superior academic achievement or merit, although financial need may also be a criterion. Most colleges and universities have scholarships for new students as well as for continuing stu-

Internet

Activity 14.1
Pell Grants

Many students who cannot afford college expenses may be eligible for federal Pell grants. Unlike loans, Pell grants do not have to be repaid.

Eligibility for Pell grants is determined on the basis of your Expected Family Contribution (EFC), the amount you and your family are expected to contribute toward your education. To calculate your EFC, indicate how much you and your family can contribute to the following:

Cost of attendance	You	Your family
Tuition and fees	_____	_____
Room and board	_____	_____
Books	_____	_____
Supplies	_____	_____
Transportation	_____	_____
Loan fees	_____	_____
Dependent care	_____	_____
Costs related to a disability	_____	_____
Miscellaneous expenses	_____	_____
Total	_____	_____

Your financial aid administrator calculates your cost of attendance (COA), and subtracts the amount you and your family are expected to contribute toward that cost (including any other financial aid). If there's anything left over, you're considered to have financial need and are eligible for a federal Pell grant, assuming you meet all other eligibility requirements.

For more information, see
http://www.ed.gov/prog_info/SFA/StudentGuide/1996-7/fpg.html#def.
What did you learn here that can help you finance your college education?

_____

_____

_____

_____

_____

_____

dents. Thousands of scholarships are also available from hundreds of national foundations, organizations, state and federal agencies, businesses, corporations, churches, and civic clubs.

The best way to find scholarship opportunities is to start with your institution and work your way out. Check the availability of scholarships from groups and organizations in your home region. Review information from

A Caution About Loans

Student loans are an extremely valuable component of the total financial aid picture, but it is important to remember that they are exactly what they are called: loans. They must be repaid. Failure to repay a student loan can have very negative consequences, including damaged credit, garnishment of wages, confiscation of income tax refunds, and litigation. Be very careful in assuming loan indebtedness during college, since a sizable monthly loan repayment can become a heavy burden. Take out student loans only to the extent that they are absolutely necessary for you to stay in school. Keep track of exactly how much you have borrowed as you go. Otherwise, the student loan that seems like such a boon now may be a tremendous bane later.

the primary education-related agency or organization in your state. Go to the library or financial aid office at your school to ask for assistance and to review publications listing scholarships. Our best advice is, *ask, ask, ask.*

LOANS

Over the past fifteen years, long-term, low-interest educational *loans* have become the major means for financing college. There are a number of public and private student loan programs, most of which allow extended repayment periods (up to ten years, depending on the amount borrowed) and very reasonable rates (5–10 percent). Though the practice is not recommended unless absolutely necessary, it is possible to receive assistance from more than one loan program at a time.

The large federal student loan programs are based primarily on need. In addition to student loans there is also a federally sponsored loan program for parents that does not require demonstrated need. The interest rate for this program can be as high as 12 percent, and repayment generally begins shortly after the loan is made. This program has become popular among parents whose dependents do not qualify for need-based aid.

WORK OPPORTUNITIES

Part-time work is a valuable type of self-help aid. The College Work–Study Program is a federal student aid program based on need that lets you earn some of the aid for which you may be eligible through employment, generally on campus. In addition, many schools have their own programs through which students earn money or in-kind support such as board. This type of assistance has two advantages. First, you are not indebted after graduation. Second, you may be able to work in areas related to your major, thereby gaining an edge in later job hunting.

Cooperative education (co-op) programs are another great opportunity for students at many institutions. These programs provide employment off campus in public and private agencies, business, and industry. Work may parallel education (part-time course load, part-time work) or alternate with it (full-time study one term, full-time work the next). This type of experience can also be invaluable when you look for that first job after graduation. Many graduates are offered permanent, full-time positions as a result of co-op experience.

Internet

Activity 14.2
Myths About Financial Aid

Which of the following statements about college financing are true?

_____ 1. Large amounts of private-sector aid go unclaimed each year because students don't know where to look.

_____ 2. Some scholarship search services have as high as a 96 percent success rate.

_____ 3. It isn't worth saving money for college, because the more money you have, the less financial aid you will receive.

_____ 4. Financial aid is charity.

_____ 5. Financial aid is only available for the poor.

_____ 6. When you apply for federal student financial aid, your financial information becomes public knowledge.

Check your answers at Finaid's "Myths about Financial Aid" page (www.finaid.org/finaid/overview/myths.html) and Scholarship Scam Alert (www.finaid.org/finaid/scams.html).

How well did you do? What did you learn that you can use?

_____

_____

_____

_____

_____

_____

_____

_____

The Financial Aid Process

Unfortunately, where there is money, there is bureaucracy. Consequently, you are going to have to deal with red tape. This may be frustrating, but remember that the potential payoff can be well worth the aggravation. Be prepared to fill out forms and to stand in lines.

The largest financial aid programs are those based upon need and regulated by state and/or federal agencies. For these most institutions require at least two basic documents: a needs analysis document and an institutional application/information form. Another routine financial aid form is the scholarship application. Such forms vary widely depending on the scholarship sought and the organization awarding it, but they usually gather information about past performance, honors, leadership, and so on.

THE NEEDS ANALYSIS DOCUMENT

The term *needs analysis* is sometimes used to refer to the general process of analyzing a student's financial resources in order to determine whether the student needs any further assistance to attend college. Frequently, however, it refers specifically to the federal system that provides a consistent national standard for deciding who will get federal financial aid. Of course need is relative. How much help a student or family may feel they need in order to send someone to college depends on many subjective opinions and feelings. At best, needs analysis is simply a relative measure comparing a given family's ability to pay for a college education with that of other families.

In order to operate this system, the federal government requires certain basic information for determining your eligibility, which you must provide on a needs analysis document. The two federal forms you are most likely to use are referred to by their acronyms—the "FAF" and the "FAFSA." Before you fill one out, however, check with the financial aid office at your school to determine which form or forms it uses.

THE INSTITUTIONAL APPLICATION/INFORMATION FORM

Many institutions have their own financial aid forms in addition to the needs analysis document. These forms typically ask for different information than is requested in the needs analysis.

APPLYING FOR FINANCIAL AID

When you apply for financial aid, remember to do the following:

1. **Plan ahead.** Find out what is available at your institution, how to go about applying, and when you must apply. You need to determine what information will be required and allow enough time to gather it.

2. **Allow sufficient time for the process to work.** The financial aid application process is often slow. (Summer is the peak season, so allow extra time in the summer.) After you have submitted your initial application, you may be asked to provide additional information to support or clarify it. Be prepared to do this promptly.

3. **Keep copies of everything.** Maintain a file with copies of everything you complete or send, including the date it was completed or sent. This will help you avoid confusion or costly delays due to miscommunication or things getting lost in the mail.

You are responsible for helping to finance your college education. Aside from working to help earn some of what you need, you can contribute in two other ways.

First, stretch your dollars. Be as frugal as possible in areas where you can be flexible, such as personal expenses. Think twice before you spend your money. Is what you're spending it on necessary, or can you live without it?

Second, be serious about your education. By applying yourself to the best of your abilities, managing your time wisely, keeping up in your classes, and not having to repeat courses because of poor grades, you will get the most value for your investment.

Increasing Your Resources

If you need more resources to pay for college, first consult your parents or anyone else who is helping you pay for college. Then visit your school's financial aid office and talk with a financial aid counselor. Then use the goal-setting process in Chapter 1 to line up additional resources.

Many students receive scholarships, grants, and loans to help finance their education. Go to the financial aid office early to begin the application process.

Photo by Heather Dutton

SUGGESTIONS FOR FURTHER READING

Adams, Janelle P., ed. *The A's and B's of Academic Scholarships.* Alexandria, Va.: Octameron Associates. Published yearly.

Chany, Kalman A., and Geoff Martz. *The Student Access Guide to Paying for College.* New York: Villard Books. Published yearly.

College Check Mate: Innovative Tuitions Plans That Make You a Winner. Alexandria, Va.: Octameron Associates. Published yearly.

The College Costs and Financial Aid Book. Princeton, N.J.: College Board Publications. Published yearly.

Dacyczyn, Amy. *The Tightwad Gazette: Promoting Thrift as a Viable Alternative Lifestyle.* New York: Villard Books, 1993.

Directory of Special Programs for Minority Group Members, 4th ed. Garrett Park, Md.: Garrett Park Press, 1986.

Earn and Learn: Cooperative Education Opportunities with the Federal Government. Alexandria, Va.: Octameron Associates. Published yearly.

Financial Aid Fin-Ancer: Expert Answers to College Financing Questions. Alexandria, Va.: Octameron Associates. Published yearly.

Keesler, Oreon. *Financial Aids for Higher Education,* 4th ed. Dubuque, Iowa: Brown, 1991.

Kennedy, Joyce, and Herm Davis. *The College Financial Aid Emergency Kit.* Cardiff, Calif.: Sun Features. Published yearly.

Paying Less for College. Princeton, N.J.: Peterson's. Published yearly.

Schlacter, Gail A. *Directory of Financial Aids for Women.* Santa Barbara, Calif.: Reference Service Press, 1991.

Schlacter, Gail A., and David R. Weber. *Directory of Financial Aids for Minorities.* Santa Barbara, Calif.: Reference Service Press, 1993.

Student Consumer Guide. Washington, D.C.: Government Printing Office. Published yearly.

RESOURCES

One key in managing your finances is finding sources of income. Use this page to list major sources of money that you could tap into to help finance your education.

Go to your campus or academic department's scholarship office. If there isn't a specific office, there may be a person (ask your academic advisor) who knows about scholarships and grants.

Make a list of scholarships that you are eligible to apply for:

....

....

....

....

....

....

....

Make a list of grants that you are eligible to apply for:

....

....

....

....

....

....

....

....

Consider applying for one or more of these (make sure to add the application deadlines to your calendar).

Go to your campus's financial aid office. Get information on work-study programs and loans.

Make a list of work-study jobs and loans that you are eligible to apply for:

....

....

....

....

....

....

....

....

If your finances get out of control, consider using the following resources:
The National Foundation for Consumer Credit (for help with debt management): 1-800-388-2227
Experian (to get a copy of your credit report): 1-800-682-7654

JOURNAL

NAME _____

DATE _____

How well are you controlling your finances at this point?

....

....

....

....

....

....

....

....

What challenges do you face controlling your finances?

....

....

....

....

....

....

....

....

What can you do now to improve your current money management and financial situation in the near future?

....

....

....

....

....

....

....

....

Index